THE OTTOMAN EMPIRE

Halil Inalcik is Professor Emeritus of History at the University of Chicago. Born in Istanbul, he was a Professor of Ottoman History at the University of Ankara from 1952 until 1972. He then joined the University of Chicago where he taught until his retirement in 1986. He is currently Professor of Ottoman History at Bilkent University in Ankara. He is an honorary member of the Asiatic Society and a member of the American Academy of Arts and Sciences.

Also by Halil Inalcik

The Ottoman Empire: Conquest, Organization and Economy

Studies in Ottoman Social and Economic History

The Middle East and the Balkans Under the Ottoman Empire

An Economic and Social History of the Ottoman Empire
1300–1600 (ed)

An Economic and Social History of the Ottoman Empire
1600–1914 (ed)

Journal of Ottoman Studies (ed)

Volume V of a History of Scientific and Cultural History of
Mankind (UNESCO) (ed)

THE OTTOMAN EMPIRE

The Classical Age 1300–1600

Halil Inalcik

PHOENIX

A PHOENIX PAPERBACK

First published in Great Britain
by Weidenfeld & Nicolson in 1973
This paperback edition published in 2000
by Phoenix,
a division of The Orion Publishing Group Ltd,
Orion House, 5 Upper St Martin's Lane,
London WC2H 9EA

An Hachette Livre UK company

10 9 8 7 6

A CIP catalogue record for this book
is available from the British Library.

Printed and bound in Great Britain by
Butler & Tanner Ltd, Frome and London

ISBN 978-1-8421-2442-0

The Orion Publishing Group's policy is to use papers that
are natural, renewable and recyclable products and
made from wood grown in sustainable forests. The logging
and manufacturing processes are expected to conform to
the environmental regulations of the country of origin.

www.orionbooks.co.uk

CONTENTS

LIST OF ILLUSTRATIONS

Between pages 132 and 133

vii

LIST OF MAPS

ACKNOWLEDGEMENTS

Acknowledgement is due to the following for plates in this book: Library of the Topkapï Palace, Istanbul, 4–11, 34–39; Österreichische Nationalbibliothek, Vienna, 12, 13–30, 32, 33, 43–52; Museo Civico Correr, Venice, 31, 40–42; Turkish Ministry of Tourism and Press, 54–57; The Trustees of the National Gallery, London, 1; British Museum and R.B.Fleming and Co. Ltd., 2, 3; Editions Eugène de Boccard, Paris, 53.

PREFACE

While this book is primarily intended as an introduction to the institutions and society of the Ottoman Empire for the general reader, it may also be of some use to the more specialised student. Its publication has unfortunately been delayed for nearly five years as a result of various factors and thus certain sections might bear some elaboration. Furthermore, given the linguistic problems involved in the preparation of such a work, it is unavoidable that the specialist may find some inconsistencies in the transliteration of names and terms.

I would like to express my gratitude to Professor Bernard Lewis who encouraged me in writing this book. Professor Norman Itzkowitz and Dr Colin Imber, moreover, kindly agreed to translate the book into English, which required not only linguistic competence in Turkish, but also considerable expertise in Ottoman studies. I am also indebted to Dr Colin Imber for preparing the glossary.

My thanks are due to Dr Metin And for letting me use the photographs from the albums in the Nationalbibliothek, Vienna, cod. 8626 and cod. 8615, and from those in the Museo Civico Correr, Venice. I am also grateful to Mrs Eva Halasi-Kun for her kind assistance in reading the old German captions in the Nationalbibliothek albums. I am further indebted to Mr Kemal Çığ, director of the Topkapı Palace Museum, Mrs Filiz Çağman and Zeren Akalay for their help and suggestions in making selections from the miniatures in the museum library.

Finally, it would have been impossible for me to write this book without the constant help and encouragement of my wife.

H.I.

xi

Turkish words, regardless of their language of origin, place-names within the boundaries of modern Turkey, and the names of Ottoman Turks have been transcribed according to the official modern Turkish orthography. This presents few difficulties to a reader of English, but the following pronunciations should be noted:

c – pronounced 'j' as in 'John'

ç – pronounced 'ch' as in 'church'

ğ – a soft guttural, something like the 'gh' in 'brougham'

ı – pronounced something like the 'o' in 'atom'

ö – pronounced like the French 'eu', as in 'peu'

ş – pronounced like the 'sh' in 'shell'

ü – pronounced like the French 'u', as in 'lune'

A circumflex indicates a lengthened vowel

The anglicized forms are used for some well-known place-names (e.g. Suez, Cairo) and Turkish words (e.g. vizier, pasha).

In this book, İ has been used to represent the letter ı (dotless i).

Italics: italics are used for foreign and technical terms included in the glossary. They are used *only* when a word is used for the first time.

Part I

AN OUTLINE OF OTTOMAN HISTORY
1300–1600

INTRODUCTION

THE PERIODS OF OTTOMAN HISTORY

At the time of its foundation at the turn of the fourteenth century, the Ottoman state was a small principality on the frontiers of the Islamic world, dedicated to Gazâ, the holy war against infidel Christianity. This insignificant frontier state gradually conquered and absorbed the former Byzantine territories in Anatolia and the Balkans and, with the conquest of the Arab lands in 1517, became the most powerful state in the Islamic world.

By the reign of Süleymân I (1520–66), continued military success, in an area stretching from central Europe to the Indian Ocean, had given the Ottoman Empire the status of a world power; but in the long wars of the seventeenth century the balance turned in favour of Europe. Ottoman power declined, and with the recognition of western superiority in the eighteenth century the empire became politically and economically dependent on Europe. Finally, the continued existence and possible collapse of the empire became a problem of European politics, the 'Eastern Question'. Ottoman political life continued until 1920 under European tutelage.

The structure and institutions of the empire changed with the differing circumstances of these periods. The changes in its internal structure and its political development show how, from being a frontier principality, it became, by the end of the sixteenth century, an empire in the traditions of the ancient near-eastern states, such as the Sassanid and, more especially, the Abbasid Empire. The Ottoman Empire of the late sixteenth century, with its traditions of statecraft and administration, financial policies, land system and military organization, was a most highly developed example of a near-eastern empire. During the period of decline, however, European military and economic superiority made the Ottomans themselves aware that the traditions of the near-eastern state had outlived their usefulness and that they were ill-suited to the new era.

From this time onwards Ottoman history is a record of the decayed forms of ancient imperial institutions; or, more correctly, the history

3

of a near-eastern state's efforts to adapt itself to the European economic, political and cultural challenge. It was only after 1924, and only after a radical revolution, that the Turks finally abandoned this concept of state.

Thus the 1590s mark the main dividing line in Ottoman history. This book describes the first period, stressing how the Ottomans adapted the institutions of the near-eastern state, and how these institutions began to disintegrate in the face of modern Europe.

CHAPTER I

THE ORIGINS OF THE OTTOMAN STATE

In the early fourteenth century violent internal crises were shaking the great empires situated between the Oxus and the Danube – the Ilkhanid Empire in Iran, the Golden Horde in eastern Europe and the Byzantine Empire in the Balkans and western Anatolia. By the end of the same century, the descendants of Osmân, a frontier *gâzî* and founder of the Ottoman dynasty, had established an empire stretching from the Danube to the Euphrates. The ruler of this empire was Bâyezîd I (1389–1402), known as 'Yĭldĭrĭm', the Thunder-bolt. At Nicopolis in 1396 he had routed a crusader army of Europe's proudest knights; he had defied the Mamlûk sultanate, at that time the most powerful Islamic state, and captured its cities on the Euphrates. Finally he challenged the great Timur, the new ruler of central Asia and Iran.

This first period of Ottoman history presents the problem of how Osmân Gâzî's small frontier principality, dedicated to a Holy War against Christian Byzantium, grew to be an empire of such power and extent. One theory maintains that by accepting Islam and uniting with the Muslims the Greek population of the Marmara basin revived the Byzantine Empire as a Muslim state. Scholars familiar with eastern historical sources now recognize this theory as groundless speculation. These historians maintain that the origins of the Ottoman Empire must be sought in the political, cultural and demographic developments of thirteenth- and fourteenth-century Anatolia.[1]

The Mongol invasions of the Muslim near east from the 1220s mark the first stage in these developments. After the Mongol victory at the Battle of Kösedağ in 1243 the Seljuk sultanate of Anatolia became a vassal state of the Ilkhanids of Iran. The immediate result of the Mongol invasions was the westward migration of the Turcomans, powerful nomadic Turkish tribes. These had come first from central Asia to Iran and eastern Anatolia and now, once again, they moved westwards, concentrating on the frontier between Byzantium and the Seljuk sultanate, in the mountainous regions of western Anatolia.

5

In Anatolia in 1277 there was an uprising against the idolatrous Mongols. Muslim Mamlûk forces entered Anatolia to assist the rebels, but the Mongols cruelly suppressed the uprising. Thereafter they kept forces permanently stationed in Anatolia, tightening their grip on the country. Nevertheless there were frequent revolts and Mongol recriminations in the following half century. The frontier region became a place of refuge for troops and political figures fleeing the Mongol government and, at the same time, a place where many destitute villagers and townsmen sought a new life and future. As a result, the population of the frontier districts increased. Seeking an opportunity to settle the rich plains on the Byzantine side of the border, the restless frontier nomads incited men to a gazâ, a Holy War against Byzantium. Warriors gathered around gâzî leaders of various origins, and their raids on Byzantine territory became more and more frequent.

Between 1260 and 1320 these gâzî leaders who organized the warlike Turcomans founded independent principalities in western Anatolia, in the lands which they had wrested from Byzantium. The contemporary Byzantine historian Pachymeres records that the Palaeologi, who had recaptured Constantinople only in 1261, were preoccupied with Balkan affairs to the consequent neglect of the Asiatic frontiers, and thus making way for Turcoman inroads. In the last decade of the thirteenth century the raids of these Turcoman gâzîs in western Anatolia amounted almost to a general invasion. Osmân Gâzî, of all the *beys*, held territory furthest to the north and closest to Byzantium and the Balkans. According to Pachymeres, in about 1302 Osmân Gâzî laid seige to Iznik (Nicaea), the former Byzantine capital. The emperor sent against him a mercenary army of two thousand men, which he ambushed and defeated at Baphaeon in the summer of 1302. His defeat of an imperial army spread his fame. Ottoman and contemporary Byzantine sources described how gâzîs from throughout Anatolia flocked to his standard; as in other frontier principalities they took the name of their leader and became known as *Osmanlis*. The prospect of easy conquest and settlement attracted fresh waves of settlers of various origins from central Anatolia. It was after this victory of 1302 that the Ottoman principality became truly established.

The ideal of gazâ, Holy War, was an important factor in the foundation and development of the Ottoman state. Society in the frontier principalities conformed to a particular cultural pattern, imbued with the ideal of continuous Holy War and continuous expansion of the *Dârülislâm* – the realms of Islam – until they covered the whole world. Gazâ was a religious duty, inspiring every kind of enterprise and sacrifice. In frontier society all social virtues conformed to the ideal of gazâ. The advanced civilization of the hinterland, with its religious orthodoxy, scholastic theology, palace literature composed

6

in an artificial literary language, and *şerîat* law, gave way in the frontier lands to a popular culture, characterised by heretical religious orders, mysticism, epic literature and customary law. In the principalities of Anatolia, Turkish became for the first time the administrative and literary language. Frontier society was both tolerant and complex. A common background brought the Byzantine frontier troops, the *akritai*, into close contact with the muslim gâzîs. Mihal Gâzî, a Greek frontier lord who accepted Islam and cooperated with Osmân's warriors, is a famous example of the process of assimilation.

Holy War was intended not to destroy but to subdue the infidel world, the *dârülharb*. The Ottomans established their empire by uniting Muslim Anatolia and the Christian Balkans under their rule and, although continuous Holy War was the fundamental principle of the state, the empire emerged, at the same time, as protector of the Orthodox Church and millions of Orthodox Christians. Islam guaranteed the lives and property of Christians and Jews, on the conditions of obedience and payment of a poll tax. It allowed them free exercise of their own religions and to live according to their own religious laws. Living in a frontier society and mixing freely with Christians, the Ottomans applied these principles of Islam with the greatest liberality and tolerance. During the early years of the empire the Ottomans pursued a policy of attempting to secure the voluntary submission and confidence of the Christians, before resorting to warfare.

The protective administration of the Islamic state, with its religious laws and guarantees of tolerance, succeeded the terrifying raids of the gâzîs. Furthermore, the protection of the peasantry as a source of tax revenue was a traditional policy of the near-eastern state, and one which encouraged an attitude of tolerance. Income from the poll-tax *haraç*, formed a large portion of Ottoman state revenue, just as it had constituted an important part of the revenue of the early Islamic caliphate.

The Ottoman Empire was thus to become a true 'Frontier Empire', a cosmopolitan state, treating all creeds and races as one, which was to unite the Orthodox Christian Balkans and Muslim Anatolia in a single state.

The gâzî principalities of western Anatolia soon adopted the tradition and institutions of the Seljuk sultanate. Cities such as Kastamonu, Karahisar or Denizli, established in the old Seljuk frontier districts, became centres of Seljuk civilization. Administrators and scholars brought the traditions of Islamic statecraft and civilization from these towns and from the cities of central Anatolia to Milas, Balat, Birgi, Izmir, Manisa and Bursa, which had become the capitals of the gâzî principalities established on former Byzantine territory. Each principality became a small sultanate. For example, Orhan, the son of Osman, struck his first silver coins in Bursa in 1327, and established a *medrese* in Iznik in 1331; in 1340 he created a trading centre in Bursa, with the construction of a bazaar and a *bedestan*, an enclosed market for the sale of valuable goods. The Arab traveller Ibn Battuta[2] visited Bursa in about 1333 and described it as 'a great city with fine bazaars and broad streets.'

This was the general social and cultural background to the foundation of the Ottoman and other frontier principalities. Holy War and colonization were the dynamic elements in the Ottoman conquests; the administrative and cultural forms adopted in the conquered territories derived from the traditions of near-eastern politics and civilization.

CHAPTER II

FROM FRONTIER PRINCIPALITY TO EMPIRE
1354–1402

In the 1350s the Ottoman state was no more than one of many frontier principalities, but events after 1352 so firmly established its superiority over the others that, within thirty years, they had become Ottoman vassals. The crucial event was the Ottomans' gaining a foothold in the Balkans, with prospects of limitless expansion towards the west. The initial crossing from Anatolia into Europe was a difficult task, since the Dardanelles were in Christian hands, and any force which the Ottomans might land in Thrace would be unable to hold out and would be annihilated by the Byzantines. The principality of Karesi, lying on the eastern side of the Dardanelles, resolved the problem for the Ottomans.

A series of events led up to this Ottoman success. A struggle for the throne of Karesi in 1345 gave Orhan an opportunity to annex the principality. The troops from Karesi which had entered Ottoman service began to advocate an expedition across the Dardanelles and, under the command of Orhan's son, Süleymân, the commander of the western frontier, they prepared for the venture. Events were on their side. In 1346, Orhan had made an alliance with John V Cantacuzenus, a claimant to the Byzantine throne, and had married John's daughter, Theodora. This provided the Ottomans with an opportunity to intervene in the domestic problems of Byzantium and to participate in the war in Thrace. When, in 1352, Süleymân went to Adrianople, to the assistance of Cantacuzenus against Serbian and Bulgarian forces, he took possession of Tzympe on the Eastern shore of the Gallipoli isthmus. Despite the insistent requests of Cantacuzenus, he refused to evacuate the fortress and began to reinforce this bridgehead with fresh troops from Anatolia, at the same time laying siege to the fortress of Gallipoli. On the night of 1–2 March 1354, an earthquake destroyed the walls of Gallipoli and other fortresses in the area; Süleymân's forces immediately occupied these strongpoints. He repaired the forts and garrisoned them with troops from Anatolia, firmly establishing the Ottomans on European soil. The event aroused great anxiety in Byzantium and the western Christian world. In

August 1354 the Venetian *bailo* in Constantinople wrote that Constantinople, faced with this danger, was prepared to place itself under the protection of a powerful Christian state; in Europe there were plans for a crusade, intended not to recapture Jerusalem but to save Constantinople from the Ottomans; the project for the union of the Latin and Greek Churches was taken up again with renewed zeal.

Gregory Palamas, the Archbishop of Salonica, whom the Ottomans captured in 1354 after the conquest of Gallipoli, reported his captors as having told him that the continued advance of Islam from east to west was clear proof that God aided them and that Islam was the true religion.[1]

In order to strengthen his European bridgehead, Süleymân transported Muslims, particularly nomads who could easily be re-settled, from Anatolia to Europe. New Turkish villages were established and the frontiers, under the general command of Süleymân, were organized into right, left and centre marches, each under the authority of a gâzî lord. The Ottoman raids continued and the area of Ottoman occupation expanded. However, Süleymân's sudden and tragic death in 1357 and the Phocaeans' capturing Orhan's youngest son, Halîl, forced Orhan to make peace with Byzantium. Events encouraged the Byzantines to attempt to regain Thrace by diplomatic means. Süleymân's conquests were threatened, and the frontier forces were anxious and restless. When Halîl was released in 1359, the gâzîs realized that to delay action was to invite defeat and necessitate the evacuation of Europe. The sultan's son, Murâd, the commander of the Gallipoli march, and his tutor Lala Şâhîn, a dedicated warrior, began an offensive aimed at the eventual capture of Adrianople. In the first year they took the fortresses along the Maritsa valley and those on the road from Constantinople to Adrianople, thus cutting off the supply lines to the city. In 1361 the final sortie by the defending forces failed and Adrianople, the capital of Thrace, surrendered in the same year.

The conquests in Thrace followed the same pattern as those in Anatolia. In the face of continued gâzî raids, the local Greeks took refuge in the citadels. The inhabitants of towns which submitted voluntarily were left unmolested; if the inhabitants resisted they were forced to leave their town to the Turks. The Ottoman government encouraged Turks from Anatolia, sometimes by forcible deportation, to settle the newly conquered lands. Dervishes, too, founded in-numerable *zâviyes* – hospices, which were later to become the nuclei of new Turkish villages. Turkish colonization rapidly followed the conquests in Thrace, creating a firm base for future Ottoman expansion in Europe.

Geographical conditions determined the pattern of Ottoman conquest in the Balkans. They followed the direction of the historic Via Egnatia towards the west, reaching the Albanian coast in 1385, by way of Serres, Monastir and Okhrida. The local lords in Macedonia and Albania accepted Ottoman suzerainty. A second line of advance was against Thessaly, with the port and city of Salonica falling in 1387; a third followed the road from Constantinople to Belgrade and, in 1365, the Maritsa valley came, with little resistance, under Ottoman control.[2] Crossing the Balkan passes, in 1385, they entered the Morava valley by way of Sofia and Nish, and in the following year reduced the kingdom of Serbia to vassalage. The gâzîs on the left flank followed the Tundzha valley, crossing the Balkan range through the Karnobad Pass. In 1372 the Despot of the Dobrudja and the King of Bulgaria became Ottoman vassals. By now the Ottomans controlled the main routes in the Balkan peninsula and, as they had done after the conquest of Gallipoli, they brought nomads from Anatolia, including powerful *yürük* groups, and settled them along the main highways and in the surrounding mountainous regions. The principal Ottoman cities in the Balkans were originally frontier settlements along the main routes of advance. Densely populated Turkish colonies were established in the frontier regions of Thrace, the Maritsa valley and the Tundzha valley. The local lords in the areas bordering on Ottoman territory in the Balkans accepted the sovereignty of the Ottoman sultan, now master of the peninsula.

It is not difficult to account for the ease of Ottoman conquest in the Balkans. The Ottoman invasion coincided with a time of political fragmentation, when many independent kings, despots and lords of small Balkan principalities did not hesitate to seek outside help in the settlement of their own local disputes. In the midst of the anarchy prevailing in the Balkans only the Ottomans pursued a consistent policy, and only they possessed the military strength and centralized authority necessary for its execution. The Ottomans possessed another great advantage in the *Janissary* corps, the first standing army in Europe. The sultan had formed the corps from prisoners of war, after the capture of Adrianople, and it was directly under his command. At the same time, in every Balkan state there was a faction ready to ally itself with the Hungarians or other Latin Christians and a faction ready to cooperate with the Ottomans. In general, the aristocracies, the upper ranks of the priesthood, men of letters and courtiers looked to western Christendom for assistance. The Greek Orthodox populations were fanatically opposed to the domination of the Italians and to all Latin influences; and the Ottomans who supported them in their struggles soon began to regard the Orthodox Christians as vassals. Between 1346 and 1352 the Ottomans had entered Thrace as allies of John Cantacuzenus; again in 1356–66, when the King of Bulgaria was hard pressed by the Byzantines, Hungarians and Wallachians, his Ottoman allies sent him reinforcements.

The Ottomans respected the principles of feudalism. They at first demanded only a small yearly tribute from vassal princes, as a token of their submission to the Islamic state. They later demanded that a vassal prince's son should be held as hostage, that the prince should come to the Palace once a year to swear allegiance, and that he should send auxiliary troops on the sultan's campaigns. Vassal princes were required to treat the sultan's friends and enemies as their own. If the vassal failed in these duties, his lands would again be declared dârülharb open to the merciless raids of the gâzîs.

After the Pope's failure to organize, on the condition of the union of the Orthodox Church with Rome, a crusade to relieve Byzantium, and after the rout of the Serbian princes at Chermanon in 1371, the Balkan princes one by one accepted Ottoman suzerainty. It was after this Ottoman victory that the Byzantine emperor became virtually an Ottoman vassal, with the members of the Palaeologus family seeking the sultan's support to hold the Byzantine throne. The other Balkan rulers followed the Byzantine example.

During the early period no major state opposed the Ottomans either in the Balkans or in Anatolia, nor did they meet any European crusader army, even though the pope had proclaimed a crusade against the Ottomans in his Bull of 25 December 1366. A large crusader fleet or army could effectively have checked Ottoman advances. Their strongest rival at this time was the kingdom of Hungary which sought to use the Ottoman advance in the Balkans to expand Hungarian rule in the lower Danube basin. The main Ottoman weakness was lack of naval power. Christian states controlled the Dardanelles, the crossing point between Rumelia and Anatolia. In 1366 Amadeo VI of Savoy captured Gallipoli and in the following year returned it to the Byzantines, leaving the Ottomans in a dangerous situation. Ottoman forces in Rumelia were cut off from Anatolia until, in October 1376, Adronicus IV agreed to return the fortress of Gallipoli to Murâd I who had secured for him the Byzantine throne.

Ottoman expansion in the Balkans was aided as much by social as by political conditions.[3] Recent research has shown that the decline of central power in the Byzantine Empire and its Balkan successor states was simultaneous with the rise of feudalism. Monasteries and influential persons in the provinces were gaining possession of *pronoia* lands previously under state control, whose tax revenues had been distributed among the army. By obtaining financial and legal concessions from the state, they converted these lands into holdings with life tenure and they were able to increase the taxes and feudal dues extracted from the peasantry.[4]

In the regions under direct Ottoman administration, these lands again came under state control and were either converted into *timars* or distributed, in return for military service, to the *yayas*, Turkish farmers serving with the army. All local imposts not prescribed in the simple tax regulations of the kânûn-i osmânî – the Ottoman code – were abolished. Only the decree of the sultan could establish any income or privilege. Everything had first to be fixed by regulation whose execution was entrusted to a *kâdî*, acting independently of the local authority. The Ottoman regime thus established a centralized administration in place of feudal decentralization, and general regulations in place of the taxes and privileges that had been at the discretion of feudal overlords.[5] For the peasantry, the new regime must have been an improvement on the old. To understand the superiority of the Ottoman to the local Balkan administrations one has only to compare Ottoman laws with the code of the Serbian monarch, Stephan Dušan. For example, Dušan's code required the peasant to work for his lord two days a week; Ottoman regulations required the *reâyâ* to work only three days a year on the *sipâhî*'s land. Protection of the peasantry against the exploitation of local authorities was a basic principle of Ottoman administration. At the same time, the Ottomans officially recognized the Orthodox Church, suppressing, in principle, the Catholic Church throughout their realms. All these factors are important in explaining the ease and speed of Ottoman expansion in the Balkans, and why the peasantry did not join their overlords in resisting the Ottomans.

The Ottomans did not, however, regard themselves as representatives of any specific social creed. They knew that by pursuing a conciliatory policy towards Christians they could more easily extend their realms and increase their sources of revenue. It was also part of their expansionist doctrine to treat with tolerance the indigenous nobility and military class. With the exception of those who openly opposed them, the Ottomans took members of the military class into their own service, and thus, in Bulgaria, Serbia, Albania, Macedonia and Thessaly, they retained the services of thousands of native troops, known by the Slavic name, *voynik*. They enjoyed the usufruct of a fixed portion of state land, were exempt from taxation, and served as combatants in the Ottoman army. The Vlachs, Christian nomads of Serbia, were exempt from certain taxes in return for service as frontier guards and raiders. The Ottomans distributed timars to former pronoia holders who, as cavalrymen, were of a higher social class, but at the same time divested them of their feudal privileges. Many of the soldiers levied from vassal states served in the Ottoman army under the command of their own princes or overlords, without having accepted Islam. Islam, in time, gained more and more converts, but at the end of the fifteenth century there were still timar holders whose families had remained Christian through three or four generations. The Ottomanization of a conquered region was not a sudden and radical transformation but a gradual development.[6]

When, in the mid-fourteenth century, the Ottomans began their career of conquest in the Balkans, they had already established a strong state in Anatolia, stretching from Ankara to the Dardanelles. With the disintegration of Stephan Dušan's Serbian Empire and the kingdom of Bulgaria, no Balkan state could compare with the Ottoman state in size and strength. Ottoman advances in Europe were always paralleled by an expansion of their territory in Asia, an advance on one front following an advance on the other. Throughout their history the Ottomans were careful to avoid having to fight simultaneously on both fronts. During the early period, when they did not control the Dardanelles, this was a matter of life or death.

In the second half of the fourteenth century two powerful states rivalled the Ottomans in Anatolia: the principality of Eretna, with its capital Sivas, the former seat of the Mongol governors, and the principality of Karaman which by then included Konya, the old Seljuk capital. In 1354 the Ottomans took Ankara from Eretna but still faced an alliance between Eretna and Karaman. In 1362 Ankara was lost and again retaken.

During the reign of Murâd I (1362–89), a career in the expanding Ottoman state was an alluring prospect to the gâzîs and settlers from Anatolia. Contemporary near-eastern sources describe the sultan as the lord of all the frontier principalities, and for this reason the Ottomans had no great difficulty in annexing important parts of the principality of Germiyan, with its capital at Kütahya, and Hamidili, further to the south. They always tried, however, to legitimize these acts of aggression, maintaining that they had accepted territory from Germiyan as part of Prince Bâyezîd's dowry and that they had purchased the lands in Hamidili. The annexation of Hamidili seriously threatened the capital of Karaman. When Karamanid forces marched against them, the Ottomans proclaimed that this was an act of treason against the Holy War which they were waging, claiming that this offensive assisted the enemies of the Faith and that, therefore, according to the şerîat, it was a pious duty to remove the Karamanids. The Ottomans frequently used this policy when attacking their Muslim neighbours in the east. They were later to repeat the same charge against the Mamlûks of Egypt, Uzun Hasan and the Safavids of Iran, broadcasting it through fetvâs to the entire Islamic world.

In 1387, Murâd met the Karamanid attack with the forces which his Christian vassals in the Balkans – the Byzantine emperor, the Serbian despot and the other Serbian princes – had contributed and decisively defeated his Muslim rival, whose army was composed mainly of tribal elements. After this victory, the independent rulers in Anatolia – the Karamanids, the Candarids in Kastamonu, and a branch of the Hamid dynasty in Antalya – recognized the Ottoman sultan as their suzerain. Only Kâdî Burhâneddîn, who had replaced the dynasty of Eretna at Sivas, challenged the Ottoman ruler and prevented Ottoman expansion towards Amasya, an important city on the silk-route.

While Anatolian affairs occupied Murâd, Serbia, Bulgaria and Bosnia united against him in the Balkans, and an Ottoman army was defeated at Ploshnik by the Bosnians in 1388; but a lightning campaign in the same year brought Danubian Bulgaria to submission. Next spring Murâd crossed over into Europe with the auxiliary forces contributed by the vassal princes, and on 15 June 1389 defeated the combined Serbian and Bosnian armies in a hard-fought battle on the Plain of Kossovo. This victory firmly established Ottoman rule in the Balkans.

Thus by 1389 the Ottomans had founded an empire of vassal principalities in the Balkans and Anatolia. It should, however, be added that these were to use every opportunity to rebel against Ottoman rule, eventually forcing the Ottomans to remove the dynasties and convert each principality into a directly administered province.

When the word spread that a Serb had assassinated Murâd at the Battle of Kossovo, the dynastic rulers in Anatolia rose in revolt. Between 1389 and 1392 the new sultan, Bâyezîd I (1389–1402), annexed most of the Anatolian principalities, appointing to their administration slaves brought up in his own Palace.

While Bâyezîd was occupied in Anatolia, Ottoman influence in the Balkans declined. The ambitions of Hungary and Wallachia in Danubian Bulgaria and the Dobrudja put the truncated kingdom of Bulgaria in a difficult situation. Mirčea, the Hungarian-protected Prince of Wallachia, had occupied the Dobrudja, and Silistra on the right bank of the lower Danube, while the Hungarians sought to establish themselves in Vidin. Ottoman protection, however, was no way of escape from these dangers. The Ottoman ruler came to the Balkans and in 1393 brought Danubian Bulgaria under direct Ottoman rule, installed the Bulgarian king as a vassal prince in Nicopolis, and expelled Mirčea from Silistra and the Dobrudja. Although in the same difficult position of acting as a buffer state between the Hungarians and the Ottomans, the despotate of Serbia did not suffer the same fate. The despot rendered his homage to the sultan. At the same time, the death of Murâd 1 had encouraged the Palaeologi in Byzantium and the Morea. By promising the union of the two churches they sought to persuade the pope to organize a crusade. In the Morea, Venetian influence had reached its height.

Faced with this situation, Bâyezîd summoned all the vassal princes in the Balkans, including the Palaeologi, to Verria in 1394, to reaffirm their ties of vassalage. On the flight of the Palaeologi, he blockaded Constantinople, occupied Thessaly, and sent raiders into the Morea. Another Ottoman army brought Albania under direct Ottoman rule, expelling the local lords. In 1395 Bâyezîd undertook a campaign as far as Slankamen on the Danube and then, entering Wallachia, defeated Mirčea at Argesh. Advancing to Nicopolis, Bâyezîd arrested and executed King Shishman of Bulgaria, accusing him of having collaborated with the enemy. By removing the local dynasties he went some way towards creating an empire with a centralized government in place of one composed of vassal states. By eliminating the kingdom of Bulgaria the Ottoman state assumed direct responsibility for the defence of the Danube region against Hungary, no longer leaving it to a weak buffer kingdom. Wallachia, too, was reduced to vassal status. The crusade of Nicopolis in 1396 marked the climax of the struggle between the Ottomans and the Hungarians for control of the lower Danube. Venice, too, was concerned in the struggle for the Balkans. In this war, she sought to use her fleet to cut communications between Anatolia and the Balkans at the Dardanelles; for the western knights the campaign was simply a crusading adventure, where the crusader army was utterly defeated.

The victory at Nicopolis not only confirmed Ottoman control of the Balkans but greatly raised Ottoman prestige in the Islamic world. Bâyezîd, at the height of his glory, returned to Anatolia in 1398 and annexed Karaman and the principality of Kâdî Burhâneddîn, creating a centralized empire stretching from the Danube to the Euphrates. In an attempt to capture Constantinople, which would have been the natural centre for this empire, he intensified his blockade of the city. At the same time, in central Aisa and Iran, Timur (1336–1405) had founded a powerful empire and proclaimed himself heir to the sovereign rights of the Ilkhanids over Anatolia. The Ottoman sultan challenged Timur, but at the Battle of Ankara on 28 July 1402 was routed and taken prisoner. During the battle, the local Anatolian cavalrymen went over to the side of their former lords who had taken refuge in Timur's court. Under Timur's protection, these former sovereigns everywhere re-established their old, independent principalities. Bâyezîd's attempt at empire ended in failure. The remaining Ottoman territory was divided among Bâyezîd's sons who accepted Timur's sovereignty. On Timur's death they began an intensive struggle for control of the whole territory.[7]

CHAPTER III

THE INTERREGNUM AND RECOVERY

After the rout at Ankara, the Ottoman state could well have disintegrated completely, but by 1415 the Ottomans were already able to re-establish their former position in Rumelia and Anatolia. With the capture of Constantinople in 1453, they realized Bâyezîd I's imperial ambitions. The central historical problem of the period between 1402 and 1453 is to explain how the Ottoman Empire made this amazing recovery, at a time when civil war, crusader invasions and other crises threatened to destroy it altogether.

Bâyezîd's youngest son, Çelebi Mehmed, established his rule in Anatolia, first in Amasya and then in Bursa, seeking to bring Rumelia and Edirne (Adrianople) under his control. His elder brother, Çelebi Süleymân (1402–11), ruling in Edirne, attempted to extend his rule to Anatolia. Both realized that an Ottoman state limited to Rumelia or Anatolia could not survive. The local states and rulers in the Balkans and Anatolia took a negative part in this struggle, attempting to preserve the *status quo* established in 1402. Just as the independent principalities of Anatolia had been re-established after 1402, so too in Rumelia the rulers of Byzantium, Serbia, Wallachia and Albania regained some of their lands and began to act independently. In 1403, Süleymân Çelebi signed a treaty with the Byzantines, by which he relinquished some territory on the coast, including Salonica. To preserve the equilibrium, during the interregnum the Byzantine emperor always supported the weakest of the Ottoman princes against the strongest. When Çelebi Mûsâ's (1411–13) power in Rumelia became too great, the Byzantines helped Çelebi Mehmed to cross to the Balkans. The Despot of Serbia, too, made an alliance with Mehmed, assisting him in his final victory. However, when he annexed some of the Anatolian principalities and reduced others to vassal status, Byzantium and the Balkan princes began to regard him as a threat. In 1416, Venice, Byzantium and Wallachia adopted such an aggressive policy that the Ottoman state, reunited under Mehmed, again faced the danger of dismemberment and destruction.

While Mehmed's brother, Mustafa, incited by Byzantium and Wallachia, led a revolt against him in Rumelia, on 29 May 1416, the Venetian fleet destroyed an Ottoman naval force at Gallipoli. The Prince of Wallachia, Mirčea, first encouraged Mustafa and later protected Şeyh Bedreddîn who led a dangerous revolt in western Anatolia and the region of the Dobrudja and Deliorman on the Rumelian frontier. Mirčea tried to gain control of this region. Çelebi Mehmed forced Mustafa to seek refuge with the Byzantines, and in the autumn of 1416 suppressed Şeyh Bedreddîn's revolt. He saw the necessity of peace with Byzantium and signed a treaty, according to which the emperor was to keep Mustafa imprisoned, while he for his part promised to maintain the *status quo*. Meanwhile, in Anatolia, Timur's son Shâhrukh threatened anyone who might attempt to reverse the situation which his father had established. Mehmed petitioned Shâhrukh, presenting himself as his loyal vassal and claiming that he attacked the principalities only because they prevented his waging a Holy War. In the Balkans, Mehmed attacked only Mirčea, driving him to the other side of the Danube, making Giurgiu, in 1419, an advanced Ottoman outpost on the left bank of the river. After 1416, realizing that it was still too early to revive the centralized empire of Bâyezîd, Mehmed pursued a policy of conciliation.

The events of this period show that influential Anatolian families, who held the land as *vakif* – pious foundation – or *emlâk* – freehold property – and the tribes which formed the fighting forces, opposed the centralized administration of the Ottomans. Against the Ottomans they supported the former dynasties who guaranteed their own privileges. The local dynasties in the Balkans were in a similar position. The population of the marches, continuing the old traditions of the frontier state, equally opposed centralization, supporting pretenders to the sultanate and playing a vital part in the civil wars. In the fifteenth century, Dobrudja-Deliorman, the most densely populated frontier region, became a hotbed of rebellion.

There were, however, powerful factors working in favour of Ottoman unity and the centralized administration. The most potent factor was the Ottoman *kul* – slave – system. In particular the Janissary corps, whose numbers had risen to six or seven thousand, gave the Ottoman sultan an undisputed superiority over his rivals. In the provinces the Ottomans created a corps of military administrators of slave origin and an army of sipâhîs, who greatly strengthened the central authority which they represented and which guaranteed their own status. The peasantry and merchants, too, benefited more from the centralized Ottoman administration than from the former feudal regimes. A final factor was the immense prestige of the Ottoman sultan in the eyes of the Muslim population; he was the greatest leader of the Holy War, a status which brought with it important moral and material advantages.

Three years of crisis followed the death of Mehmed I in 1421. The Byzantines freed Prince Mustafa, who agreed to cede Gallipoli. All Rumelia recognized him as sultan. The Janissaries and the *ulema* supported Mehmed's seventeen-year-old son, Murâd, who had ascended the throne in Bursa, the Ottoman capital. In 1422 he defeated his uncle, who had marched against him from Rumelia at the head of the frontier lords. Murâd II gathered all his forces, and between 2 June and 6 September 1422 besieged Byzantium, which had supported his rival. Thereupon, all the subject princes in Anatolia rose in revolt, recapturing all Mehmed' I's hard-won conquests. They encouraged Murâd's younger brother, Mustafa, to revolt and surrounded Bursa. Murâd raised the siege of Constantinople, defeated his brother on 20 February 1423 and punished the Anatolian rulers who had incited him. He suppressed the principalities of western Anatolia, except for those of the Candarids and the Karamanids. The young sultan had by now resolved the state's internal problems and restored the situation to what it had been before his father's death; he then turned his attention to the states which threatened his Balkan possessions.

The Hungarians were profiting from Ottoman pressures to extend their influence on the lower Danube, while the Venetians were doing the same in order to gain possession of the Byzantine lands. During the siege of Constantinople the Venetians had opened negotiations with the Byzantines for the control of Salonica and the Morea. In the summer of 1423 the Byzantines ceded Salonica, then under an Ottoman blockade, to Venice. Fearing that they would also cede Constantinople, the Ottomans concluded an agreement with the Byzantines. In return for an annual tribute and the cession of territory taken in 1403, they agreed not to attack Byzantium. At the same time, Murâd II made peace with the Anatolian rulers and gathered all his forces to attack the Venetians in Salonica. The Venetian war continued until the Ottoman conquest of Salonica in 1430.

During the Ottoman civil wars, Hungarian influence had increased in Wallachia and Serbia, and in 1427 conflict over the Serbian succession broke out between Hungary and the Ottomans. George Branković was recognized as Despot of Serbia, with the despotate becoming a buffer state between the Hungarians in Belgrade and the Ottomans in Golubać. The two sides signed a treaty in 1428.

After the conquest of Salonica in 1430, the Ottomans adopted a more aggressive policy in the Balkans. They clearly understood that the territory south of the Danube would be secure only if it were under their direct control, and that they therefore had to counter Hungarian claims to Serbia and Venetian claims to the Morea and Albania.

When the Hungarian treaty expired in 1431, Sigismund's ambassador requested that the sultan recognize the King of Hungary's suzerainty over Bosnia, Serbia, and Danubian Bulgaria. Fružin, a pretender to the Bulgarian throne, had taken refuge with Sigismund. Caught between the rival claims of Hungary and the Ottoman Empire, these buffer states struggled for their very existence. Seeing the increasing influence of Hungary in Serbia and Wallachia, the Ottomans after 1434 pursued a policy of aggression. Sigismund's death in 1437 provided them with their opportunity. In the following year, an Ottoman army under the sultan's personal command crossed the Danube and advanced as far as Sibiu (Hermannstadt), the administrative centre of Transylvania. Following this show of strength against Hungary, the Ottomans occupied the despotate of Serbia, declaring it an Ottoman province in 1439. In 1440 they tried unsuccessfully to dislodge the Hungarians from Belgrade. In 1441 and 1442 John Hunyadi defeated the Rumelian forces that had entered Transylvania, and in the following year a Hungarian army under his command crossed the Danube and advanced as far as the Balkan mountains, creating panic on the Ottoman side. In Anatolia the Karamanids passed to the attack and occupied the former territory of Hamidili. Murâd returned to a peaceful policy, signing a treaty with Hungary at Edirne on 12 June 1444. The king and the Despot of Serbia endorsed the treaty at Szeged. The Ottomans conceded the re-establishment of the despotate of Serbia, while the Hungarians agreed not to cross the Danube and not to press their claim to Bulgaria.

Murâd returned to Anatolia, and at the Treaty of Yenişehir in the summer of 1444 ceded the lands in Hamidili to the Karamanids. In this way he was satisfied that he had guaranteed the state's eastern and western frontiers. The Byzantines, however, were sheltering Orhan, a grandson of Bâyezîd, presenting a threat of civil war which caused grave concern to Murâd. In 1444, while still in good health, he abdicated in favour of his son Mehmed, hoping thus to establish him securely on the throne. The Byzantines and the pope, not wishing to waste this opportunity, encouraged the Hungarian war party. Ladislas, the King of Hungary and Poland, regarded the peace treaty as invalid and prepared for war. Former local dynasts all over Rumelia took up arms against the Ottomans. One of these was George Kastriota, known as Iskender Beg, who sought to recover his father, Ivan Kastriota's legacy in northern Albania.

Many of the panic-stricken people of Edirne fled to Anatolia. Orhan, freed by the Byzantines, went to the Dobrudja, where he attempted to instigate a revolt. The twelve-year-old sultan, Mehmed II, was not in control of events. A power struggle broke out between the grand vizier Çandarlî Halîl and the sultan's tutors, Zaganos and the *beylerbeyi* of Rumelia, Şihâbeddîn. A fire in Edirne destroyed thousands of homes; a combined Hungarian and Wallachian army crossed the Danube and marched through Bulgaria towards the Ottoman capital; a Venetian fleet closed the Dardanelles. In the midst of this crisis the former sultan was summoned to Rumelia. Crossing the straits only with the greatest difficulty, Murâd II met the enemy at Varna on 10 November 1444. The Ottoman victory sealed the fate of the Balkans and the Byzantine Empire. Holding the Byzantines responsible for the crisis, the Ottomans laid plans for a final assault on Byzantium. Şihâbeddîn and Zaganos, two old warriors, strongly advocated the plan, thinking that it would enable the young sultan to hold his throne in security. Çandarlı Halîl, who had risen from the ranks of the ulema, opposed it, fearing that it would lessen his own power and again place the state in serious difficulties.

Ottoman policy towards Byzantium was thus closely linked with the power struggle. Finally, Çandarlı Halîl engineered a Janissary revolt, removed Mehmed II and his advisers from power, and in May 1446 once again brought Murâd II to the throne.

Murâd spent his second sultanate in campaigns to subdue the Balkan vassals who had revolted in the crisis of 1444. In 1446 he campaigned against the Despot of Morea and, in 1448 and 1450, against Iskender Bey. In 1448 he repulsed Hunyadi's invasion after a fierce struggle at Kossovo. When he died on 3 February 1451 the Ottoman Empire had fully recovered from the blow of 1402.

Murâd believed, as his father had done after the crisis of 1416, that the security of his throne depended on the preservation of the *status quo*. Although he annexed some of the principalities in western Anatolia, he remained at peace with the Karamanids and the Candarids and was careful not to provoke Timur's son, Shâhrukh. He had soon realized, however, that his policy of reconciliation endangered Ottoman rule in the Balkans, where he was forced to continue fighting. In the course of these wars, the Ottomans were quick to adopt from their enemies the superior weapons of the west – cannon and muskets – and the tactic of surrounding their camp on all four sides with carts, a manoeuvre which Hunyadi had used successfully. The Ottomans used large cannons in the siege of Constantinople in 1422, and muskets at Varna in 1444. The war with Venice similarly led to the development of the Ottoman navy. In 1442 the Ottomans maintained sixty ships at Gallipoli and a river fleet of eighty to a hundred light vessels on the Danube. The growing strength of the Ottoman navy forced the Venetians to strengthen their own fleet.[1]

Murâd II's reign was a period of important economic development. Trade increased and Ottoman cities such as Bursa and Edirne expanded considerably. In 1432 the traveller Bertrandon de la Brocquière noted that Ottoman annual revenue had risen to 2,500,000 ducats, and that if Murâd II had used all available resources he could easily have invaded Europe.[2]

When Murâd II died the Ottoman Empire was strong enough to allow the young Mehmed II and his advisers, Şihâbeddîn and Zaganos, to realize their schemes of conquest. Mehmed's principal aim was to revive the empire of his ancestor, Bâyezîd, by bringing all the lands in Europe south of the Danube, and all the lands in Asia west of the Euphrates, under direct Ottoman rule; but unlike his great grandfather his first objective was the conquest of Constantinople. He realized that this would assure him of the prestige and authority necessary to create an empire. Although on his accession he maintained Çandarlï in office as grand vizier, the real power had passed to the war party. After a short campaign against the Karamanids, who on Murâd's death had risen in revolt in the summer of 1451, they began preparations for the conquest of Constantinople.

CHAPTER IV

THE DEFINITIVE ESTABLISHMENT OF THE OTTOMAN EMPIRE, 1453–1526

For half a century after Timur's invasion, the Byzantine Empire was able, by manipulating Ottoman pretenders and by the threat of crusades, to hold out against the Ottomans. While Mehmed II was attacking Karaman, Byzantine ambassadors were able to gain a few concessions by threatening to free the pretender Orhan. On 12 December 1452 the first ceremony performed in accordance with the agreement on Church unity was held in the Hagia Sophia, in the emperor's presence; this was as much as anything a demonstration of unity against the Ottomans.

External as well as internal reasons forced Mehmed to conquer the city as soon as possible. To counter their suspicions, Çandarlı had signed treaties with Hungary and Venice. By the time that Venice had sent her fleet in May 1453, time was running short. Before laying siege to the city, the Conqueror gained control of the Bosphorus by building the fortress of Rumeli Hisarı on the European shore, opposite Anadolu Hisarı, the fortress which his grandfather, Bâyezîd, had built. All ships required his permission to pass through the Bosphorus. The siege of Constantinople lasted fifty-four days, from 6 April to 29 May 1453. The defending force numbered some 8,500 men; the regular Ottoman army numbered not less than fifty thousand. The Conqueror battered the city with cannons, larger than any that had yet been seen. The storming of the city walls, the strongest fortifications of the Middle Ages, was a victory for these modern weapons. Ottoman and western sources agree that the Turks entered the city in a general attack through a breach in the walls opened by cannon. A company of Genoese mercenaries formed the defenders' main regular force, and when the Genoese commander, Guistiniani-Longo, was wounded and fled to his ship, the defenders' morale collapsed. The Venetian bailo and the Ottoman pretender, Orhan, took part in the defence of the walls. During the siege, many of the Greek troops in the pay of the emperor returned home, and conflict broke out between the Italians and the local Greeks.

the Ottoman Empire 1300–1600.

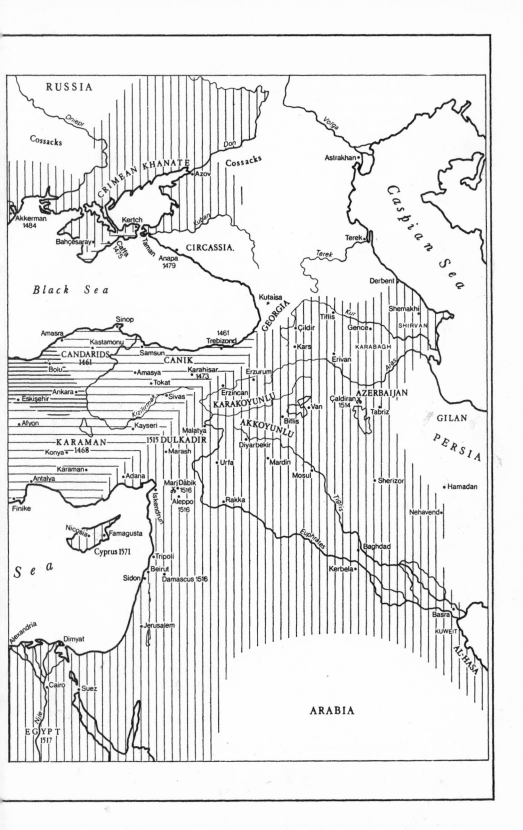

RUSSIA

Dniepr

Cossacks

CRIMEAN KHANATE

Don

Cossacks

Azov

Astrakhan

Volga

Caspian Sea

Akkerman
1484

Kertch

Kuban

Bahçesaray

Caffa
1475

Taman

Anapa
1479

CIRCASSIA.

Terek

Terek

Derbent

Shemakhi

Black Sea

Sinop

Kutaisa

GEORGIA

Tiflis

Kur

SHIRVAN

Amasra

Kastamonu

Trebizond
1461

Çıldır

Gence

KARABAGH

CANDARIDS
1461

Samsun

CANIK

Kars

Erivan

Aras

Bolu

Amasya

Karahisar
1473

Erzurum

Ankara

Tokat

Çaldiran
1514

AZERBAIJAN

Eskişehir

Sivas

Erzincan

Van

Tabriz

GILAN

Kızılırmak

KARAKOYUNLU

Bitlis

Afyon

Kayseri

Malatya

AKKOYUNLU

PERSIA

KARAMAN

1515 DULKADIR

Diyarbekir

Konya

1468

Marash

Urfa

Mardin

Mosul

Sherizor

Hamadan

Karaman

Antalya

Adana

Marj Dâbik
1516

Rakka

Nehavend

Finike

Iskenderun

Aleppo
1516

Euphrates

Tigris

Baghdad

Nicosia

Famagusta

Cyprus 1571

Tripoli

Beirut

Kerbela

Sea

Sidon

Damascus 1516

Basra

KUWEIT

Jerusalem

Alexandria

Dimyat

AL-HASA

Cairo

Suez

Nile

EGYPT
1517

ARABIA

In the Ottoman camp the dispute continued between Çandarlï, who maintained that the siege would not be successful and should be raised immediately, and the sultan and the military group whose future depended upon its success. The conflict again came into the open at a council of war, held when news came that Venice and Hungary had mobilized their forces. When the emperor refused to surrender, the Ottomans planned a final assault for 29 May. Zaganos organized the preparations for the attack. On the morning of 29 May, overcoming all resistance, the Ottoman army entered the city through a breach in the wall. The sultan did not wish for the sack of his future capital, but the Religious Law required him to grant three days of pillage. The city had been taken by force and, therefore, according to the şerîat, movable property was the lawful booty of the soldiers and the population could be legally enslaved. On the first day of the conquest, Mehmed entered the city in procession, stopped the pillage, and went to the Hagia Sophia and prayed. He converted the church into a mosque and proclaimed 'Hereafter my capital is Istanbul'.[1]

The young conqueror now sat on the throne of the Caesars. His conquests in the Holy War surpassed those of all other Muslim sovereigns, and he saw in himself limitless authority. Immediately after the conquest, Çandarlï was arrested, charged with treason and executed, leaving the power in the hands of his rivals. To suppress rival claims to the throne, such as had endangered the unity of the empire for half a century, Mehmed the Conqueror found and executed Orhan, and had his younger brother, Ahmed, strangled.

In the following quarter century, the Conqueror undertook one campaign after another, establishing a centralized empire in Rumelia and Anatolia. There is no evidence to support the claim that his conquests followed a predetermined plan, but he did claim to be the legitimate ruler of all the former territories of the Eastern Roman Empire, since he now possessed the Byzantine throne. Pius II maintained that for his claim to be legitimate he would have also to be a Christian.[2] According to the contemporary writer Ibn Kemâl, the Conqueror adopted the principle of executing any Greek of royal blood with a claim to sovereignty.

Mehmed fully understood the strategic importance of Istanbul, believing that if he stationed his fleet in Istanbul he could rule the world.[3]

Just as he had blockaded the Bosphorus in 1452 by building the fortress of Rumeli Hisarï, in 1463 he brought the Dardanelles under his control by constructing two fortresses at Çanakkale, on either side of the straits. By fortifying Bozcaada (Tenedos) he further strengthened this system of defence which safeguarded Istanbul and the straits from attack and secured communications between Anatolia and Rumelia. In the 1470s the war fleet grew from thirty to ninety-two galleys.

In 1454 the Ottoman fleet sailed into the Black Sea, compelling all the governments on its shores – the Genoese colonies, the Comnene kingdom of Trebizond and Moldavia – to pay tribute in recognition of Ottoman suzerainty.

The Ottomans established the Danube as the empire's natural northern frontier. It became the Conqueror's policy to prevent any foreign state from establishing itself in the Balkan peninsula south of the Danube, and to annex any that already had a foothold there; this became evident with the conquest of the Morea in 1460, northern Albania in 1464–79, and Bosnia in 1463. Since there was always a danger that local governments and dynasties would cooperate with the enemy in case of invasion, Mehmed sought to remove all local dynasts from the Balkans by dismissing them with a pension or by sending them to remote areas as governors. After the conquest of the Morea, for example, he gave Demetrios Palaeologus a pension of 300,000 akçes. He was later to eliminate totally the Comneni of Trebizond and the King of Bosnia, whom he considered dangerous.

Mehmed's main task in the Balkans was to undermine Hungarian influence. In 1451 the Despot of Serbia, Branković, with Hungarian aid, seized the Kruševac region, thus extending Hungarian influence across the Danube towards the heart of the Balkans. After the conquest of Istanbul, Mehmed, in four campaigns, brought Serbia into subjection, finally annexing it in 1459. In 1456, however, the Hungarians had forced him to abandon the siege of Belgrade. In 1461 the Prince of Wallachia, Vlad Drakul, made an alliance with the Hungarians and attacked the Ottomans on the Danube. In the following year the Conqueror replied by invading Wallachia, deposing Drakul in favour of Radul, and thus reducing the Hungarian threat. In the Balkans, Venetian influence threatened Ottoman supremacy in the Morea and Albania.

In the Morea, a struggle had broken out between the Palaeologi, Demetrios seeking aid from the Ottomans and Thomas from the Venetians. The Venetians, meanwhile, had occupied the ports of Argos, Nauplia, Coron and Modon.

In two campaigns in 1458 and 1460, the Conqueror annexed the despotate of the Morea, where the Venetians and the Ottomans now confronted each other directly. In the mountains of northern Albania, Iskender Beg and the lords who had joined him, with aid from Venice, the Pope and the King of Aragon, successfully resisted the Ottomans. Taking advantage of the situation, the Venetians occupied Scutari (Shkodër) and Durazzo (Durrës); but the Venetians, supreme on the sea, and the Ottomans, supreme on the land, avoided any decisive engagement. The siege of Salonica from 1423 to 1430 had already shown how such an encounter could prolong itself indefinitely. But when, with the aid of the city's Greek bishop, the Ottomans took Argos, this intermittent struggle became a full-scale war, lasting from 1463 to 1479. The Hungarians reacted to Mehmed's invasion of Bosnia and Herzegovina in 1463 by entering Bosnia and occupying its capital, at the same time signing a treaty with Venice. The pope urged other Christian rulers to join the alliance. In Albania, Iskender Beg co-operated with Venice, while the Venetians sought allies in the east. In the autumn of 1463 they opened negotiations with the Akkoyunlu ruler, Uzun Hasan, the Ottoman's greatest rival in eastern Anatolia. When a struggle for the throne of Karaman broke out in 1464, Uzun Hasan intervened in central Anatolia affairs. Although Mehmed occupied Karaman in 1468, he was unable to subjugate a number of Turcoman tribes living in the mountains which extend to the Mediterranean coast. These tribes were not subdued for the next fifty years, and from time to time rose in revolt around pretenders to the throne of Karaman.

After the Ottoman occupation of Karaman, Uzun Hasan adopted a more aggressive policy; by 1471 the problem of Karaman had become a serious threat to Ottoman power. Uzun Hasan, now ruler of Iran as well as eastern Anatolia, had become as terrible an enemy as Timur. He had an alliance with the Venetians and, establishing contact with the Knights of Rhodes, the King of Cyprus and the Bey of Alanya, he promised to send them thirty thousand troops. He also intended to establish direct contact with Venice by marching on the Mediterranean coast through the Taurus mountains, then controlled by the Turcoman tribes. Although a few Venetian ships landed a force on this coast, equipped with the firearms Uzun Hasan lacked, they could not find Uzun Hasan's men. While a crusader fleet was attacking the Ottoman coasts in 1472, Uzun Hasan's army, with Karamanid reinforcements, drove the Ottomans from Karaman and marched on Bursa.

Under the terms of the treaty between Uzun Hasan and Venice, Uzun Hasan was to acquire all Anatolia, on the conditions that he did not construct fortresses on the coastline or close the seas to Venetian ships. Venice could regain the Morea, Lesbos, Euboea and Argos; it was even projected that Venice should occupy Istanbul.

Mehmed was equal to the situation. He repulsed the invasion of Uzun Hasan and the Karamanids, and took extraordinary measures against Uzun Hasan, collecting a force of some seventy thousand men. He levied, in addition to the regular army, extra paid troops from his Muslim and Christian subjects, and took two men from each Christian village in the Balkans. He met Uzun Hasan on the Euphrates and crushingly defeated him at the Battle of Başkent on 11 August 1473. Venetian hopes were shattered, and Mehmed turned the offensive directly against Venice, laying siege to Scutari in Albania in 1474.

In 1478 Mehmed came to direct the siege in person; Venice's lines of communication by sea were cut; and the aid promised from Hungary never materialized. According to the terms of the peace treaty of 25 January 1479, Venice surrendered Scutari, ceded the places she had lost during the war – Maina in the Morea and the islands of Limni and Euboea – restored the places which she had occupied; and agreed to pay an annual indemnity of ten thousand ducats. The sultan granted the Venetians freedom of trade and permitted a Venetian ambassador to reside in Istanbul.

Mehmed emerged from these wars victorious. His empire in Rumelia and Anatolia was now larger than Bâyezîd's. In Anatolia he had annexed Karaman and, in 1461, the Candarid principality in Kastamonu, extending the empire's borders to the Euphrates. In the Balkans he had established the Danube from Belgrade to the Black Sea as the northern limit of the empire; but Venice still occupied important points on the coasts of the Morea, and Albania, and in the Aegean. The Hungarians still occupied Belgrade and northern Bosnia; in the Aegean, the Knights of Rhodes, and on the Black Sea and the lower Danube Stephen the Great of Moldavia, supported by Poland, still threatened Ottoman supremacy.

Having consolidated his empire in Anatolia and Rumelia, Mehmed the Conqueror turned his attention elsewhere. The Knights of Rhodes not only prevented his access to the Mediterranean but formed, under papal command, a permanent vanguard for a crusader attack. In 1480 Mehmed sent an army against Rhodes under the command of the Vizier Mesîh Pasha; at the same time Gedik Ahmed Pasha sailed against southern Italy from Avlonya (Vlorë) on the Albanian coast. Mesîh retreated, but Gedik Ahmed took Otranto on 11 August 1480, establishing an Ottoman bridgehead there. He returned to Rumelia to collect a large army for the invasion of Italy. The Pope, preparing to flee from Rome to France, summoned all the western Christian states to his aid. In the following spring Mehmed crossed to Anatolia at the head of a large army, but died at the second camp-site.

Mehmed the Conqueror was the true founder of the Ottoman Empire. He established an empire in Europe and Asia with its capital at Istanbul, which was to remain the nucleus of the Ottoman Empire for four centuries. He used the title 'Sovereign of the Two Lands' – Rumelia and Anatolia – 'and of the Two Seas' – the Mediterranean and the Black Sea. He was a warrior who strove for world dominion but who was at the same time a man of tolerance and culture. He ordered Gennadius, whom he had appointed as Orthodox patriarch, to compose a treatise summarizing the principles of the Christian religion. Members of the ulema came to his Palace on certain days of the week to give him instruction. He received humanists and Greek scholars, at his court; he invited Gentile Bellini from Venice to paint frescos for the Palace and to paint his portrait. But those who rank Mehmed among contemporary Renaissance sovereigns exaggerate. He was, above all, an Islamic gâzî sovereign, whose rule aimed to transform his state into the world's most powerful empire.[4]

A terrible Janissary revolt, a struggle for the throne between his sons Cem and Bâyezîd, and a general reaction against his administrative policies followed Mehmed II's death in 1481. His excessively bellicose policy had exhausted the country. He had been a harsh ruler with unlimited authority, but the Janissary army, weary of campaigns which continued even in winter, had grown mutinous. To finance his great undertakings he had increased customs duties and some of the taxes paid by peasant farmers; he had repeatedly debased the silver coinage and tightened financial controls. Finally, he brought some twenty thousand villages and farms, previously held as vakıf or emlâk, under state control and distributed them as timars. This measure caused widespread discontent, especially among old and influential families, the ulema and the şeyhs and dervishes. The disaffected began a propaganda campaign and rallied around Mehmed's eldest son, Bâyezîd. On Mehmed's death they instigated a Janissary revolt. The Conqueror's grand vizier was assassinated, and measures taken to bring Bâyezîd to the throne. Bâyezîd's partisans could count on the support of Gedik Ahmed, the idol of the Janissaries; they called this great warrior, in the midst of preparations for his Italian campaign, to Bâyezîd's side. Gedik Ahmed defeated Cem and brought Bâyezîd to the throne, but the effective power remained in the hands of Gedik Ahmed and his father-in-law, Ishâk Pasha.

Various pressures forced the new sultan to renounce his father's policies. Vakıfs were restituted and emlâk, which had been converted into timars, reverted to private ownership; but the reaction was not confined to social and political life. A powerful body demanded the restoration of the şerîat in all spheres of life, proclaiming the new sultan as the champion of justice and the şerîat. It was at this time that Bellini's frescos were broken up and sold in the bazaar. Some people even claimed that Mehmed had gone too far in his conquests and advised the new sultan to return to the policy of Murâd II.

Gedik Ahmed Pasha, however, wished to continue the attack on the western Christian world and censured the new sultan. Bâyezîd arranged his assassination and dismissed his father-in-law, Ishâk Pasha. Gedik Ahmed's comrades-in-arms at Otranto had already surrendered on 11 September 1481, some of them even taking service with Italian princes as mercenaries. To pacify his troops and establish his own authority, Bâyezîd led a campaign against Moldavia, which Mehmed had never completely subjugated. He won a brilliant victory, seizing Akkerman and Kilia in 1484. A long and exhausting campaign against the Mamlûk sultan, ruler of Egypt and Syria, and the most respected sovereign in the Islamic world, followed the victory in Moldavia. The Mamlûks claimed sovereignty over southern Anatolia, regarding themselves as suzerain not only of the Turcoman principality of Dûlkâdir but also of the Akkoyunlus and Karamanids. Rivalry between the Ottomans and the Mamlûks had begun with the Ottoman conquest of Karaman in 1468, and again broke out when the Ottomans tried to extend their influence over the principality of Dûlkâdir. Furthermore, the Ottomans maintained that, since Mehmed the Conqueror was the greatest gâzî, they had primacy in the Islamic world and hence a superior claim to these buffer principalities on their frontier. It is possible that Mehmed's unfinished Anatolian campaign aimed to subdue the Mamlûks.

After his defeat by Bâyezîd in 1481, Cem had fled to Egypt but, in 1482, he entered Anatolia with Mamlûk assistance and civil war broke out again. Bâyezîd defeated him and he took refuge on Rhodes. In 1485 Bâyezîd again opened hostilities against the Mamlûks but with no decisive results. By 1491 six great campaigns had exhausted both sides and they signed a treaty confirming the prewar situation. This lack of success led Bâyezîd to reform his army and modernize it by increasing the number of firearms.

Bâyezîd's domestic and foreign policies were cautious and conciliatory a course dictated by the fact that the Knights of Rhodes could, on an order from the Pope, unleash a civil war by releasing Cem, the pretender to the throne. Bâyezîd paid first the knights and then the pope forty-five thousand ducats annually to keep Cem in prison.

After Cem's death on 25 February 1495, Bâyezîd's European policy became less cautious and he declared war on Venice. In alliance with Venice, Hungary attacked Serbia, but in the Morea the Ottomans seized the Venetian ports of Lepanto, Modon and Coron. The Venetian war of 1499-1502 indicated that the Ottoman fleet could now challenge Venice on the open seas. During the war the Ottomans constructed two warships of 1,800 tonilato, the largest then known.

The Ottoman Empire began at this time to play a part in European politics. In the Italian wars, any defeated state threatened as a last resort to seek Ottoman aid against their enemy. The Ottomans took the side of Milan and Naples against the Franco-Venetian alliance. Bâyezîd promised to send an army of twenty-five thousand men to assist the Neapolitans but wanted Otranto in return. The Ottoman role in European struggles was to become increasingly important.

In the years following 1500, Bâyezîd's mild administration encouraged disaffected elements in Anatolia – the old landowning families, former soldiers who had lost their livelihood and, especially, nomad groups – to rebel against Ottoman authority. Strong Turcoman groups in the central Anatolian steppes, the Taurus mountains and the highlands of Tokat and Sivas were opposed to the centralizing tendency of Ottoman administration. In an attempt to protect the settled population and maintain its revenues from agriculture, the administration sought to take these tribes under its control, recording them in its cadastral registers and subjecting them to systematic taxation. The Ottoman regime was incompatible with a nomadic economy and tribal customary law. The tribes adhered fanatically to dervish orders which professed a form of Islam profoundly modified by tribal customs and shamanistic beliefs, while the Ottoman regime upheld the cause of *sunni* orthodoxy. The tribes clothed their anti-Ottoman social and political aspirations in the garments of heterodox religious belief, becoming known as *kïzïlbaş* – red head – from the red head covering which they wore.

Turcomans such as these had formed the basis of the Akkoyunlu state in eastern Anatolia, and after his defeat of Uzun Hasan in 1473 Mehmed the Conqueror had suppressed them ruthlessly. In about 1500, Ismaîl Safavî, the descendant of a family of sheikhs from Ardabil and a blood-relative of Uzun Hasan, wrested power from the Akkoyunlus in eastern Anatolia, Azerbaijan and Iran. As the leader of a heterodox religious order, he extended his influence over all the Anatolian Turcomans. His agents preached his cause throughout Anatolia and even in Rumelia. Thousands of Ottoman subjects followed Ismaîl and he became the religious and political leader of all the Turcomans. For the Ottoman government, the kïzïlbaş movement had become more than a domestic problem.

Like Timur and Uzun Hasan before him, Ismaîl proclaimed that he would make Anatolia part of his Iranian Empire. The Ottomans, thus threatened in the east, sought to end the war with Venice. Ismaîl was later to seek an alliance with Venice, making a special request for artillery. Bâyezîd adopted a conciliatory attitude towards Ismaîl's challenge, but in 1511, in the last years of his reign when the Ottoman princes were in conflict for the throne, the kïzïlbaş in the highlands of western Anatolia rose in revolt around one of Ismaîl's agents. Burning and destroying everything in their path, they marched on Bursa. It is worth noting that sipâhîs, dispossessed of their former timars, led the revolt.

It was clear that the aged and sick sultan could no longer control the situation. Prince Selîm, who had from the first demanded strong action against Ismaîl, won the support of the Janissaries, and on 24 April 1512 forced his father to abdicate.

The reign of Bâyezîd II was a period of great economic development in conditions of stability and security. Edirne and Bursa continued to develop rapidly, assuming, with their mosques, caravanserais and other great buildings, the character of imperial cities. The contemporary historian Ibn Kemâl declared that Bâyezîd was not a great conqueror like his father but rather that he consolidated the conquests of his father's reign.

This period of development created the conditions necessary for the great conquests of Selîm I and Süleymân I. Bâyezîd also modernised the Ottoman army and navy; it was largely the use of firearms which enabled Selîm to achieve his decisive victories against Ismaîl in Iran and against the Mamlûks of Egypt.[5]

Selîm I (1512–20) one by one eliminated his brothers who were his rivals for the throne. He imprisoned and executed some forty thousand partisans of Shah Ismaîl in Anatolia and then attacked Ismaîl himself, denouncing him as a *shiite* heretic. Ismaîl replied, as Uzun Hasan had done, by reminding Selîm of Timur. Selîm caught up with Ismaîl's army in eastern Anatolia and won a decisive victory at Çaldïran on 23 August 1514. This victory temporarily subdued the kïzïlbaş threat and allowed Selîm to annex to the Ottoman Empire the mountainous region from Erzurum to Diyarbekir. In 1516–17 the local dynasties and tribal chieftains in this area recognized Ottoman suzerainty.

Anatolia was now secure against invasion from the east, and the routes to Azerbaijan, the Caucasus and Baghdad were open to the Ottomans. But at the same time, Turcoman tribes from Anatolia, in particular from eastern Anatolia, began a mass migration to Iran and Azerbaijan, where they served as the main force in the Safavid armies.

Selîm's invasion of the principality of Dulkadir in the following year made a conflict with the Mamlûks of Egypt inevitable. The Mamlûk rulers, a military caste descended from Turkish and Circassian slaves, who had ruled Egypt and Syria for two and a half centuries, were at this time hard pressed in the south by the Portuguese and requested naval aid from the Ottomans.

The entire Arab world, alarmed by Portuguese attacks in the Red Sea, fixed their hopes on the Ottoman sultan, the great gâzï ruler. In 1516 the Sherif of Mecca, a descendant of the Prophet Muhammad, proposed to send a delegation to Selîm I. Al-Ghawrî, the Mamlûk sultan, prevented it; but it is likely that at that time the Arab lands were prepared to accept Ottoman rule, and when Selîm marched against the Mamlûks he announced to the Arabs that he came to free them from the Mamlûk yoke and to protect the Islamic world.

Selîm marched first against Aleppo. The city's governor and people deserted to the Ottomans, and on 24 August 1516 Selîm destroyed Al-Ghawrî's army at Marj Dâbik. The Mamlûk sultan died on the battlefield. In the great mosque of Aleppo, in the presence of the Abbasid caliph Al-Mutawakkil, Selîm received the title 'Servant of

Mecca and Medina'. (The Mamlûk sultans had borne the title 'Protector of Mecca and Medina'.) The Ottoman army overcame the resistance of the remaining Mamlûk forces and took Damascus and Jerusalem.

In Egypt, Tuman Bay, who had proclaimed himself sultan, refused to submit to the Ottomans. Thereupon, Selîm crossed the Sinai Desert with his army, announcing thất he would grant amnesty to the people and peasantry of Egypt and that his campaign was directed only against the Mamlûks. Tuman Bay, defeated in the battle of Reydaniyya on 22 January 1517, wished to continue the resistance by guerrilla methods but he was captured and executed. Shortly afterwards, on 17 July 1517, the Sherif of Mecca sent Selîm the keys of the Holy Cities and announced his submission. Syria, Egypt and the Hejaz now recognized Ottoman sovereignty, and at the same time Selîm laid claim to parts of the Yemen. Appointing Hayra Bay, the former Mamlûk governor of Aleppo, as governor of Egypt, Selîm returned to Istanbul.

The addition of the Arab lands, and especially of Mecca and Medina, to the Ottoman Empire, marks the beginning of a new era. The empire was no longer a frontier state but an Islamic caliphate, and the Ottoman sultans now considered themselves protectors not only of the frontiers but of the entire Muslim world. The political advantages of this concept of state became clear in the reign of Selîm's successor.

One result of the new consciousness of the Ottoman rulers was to raise the religious law of Islam to a position of prime importance in the administration of the state. An equally important result of Selîm's conquests was that the Ottomans now controlled the world's richest centres of the transit trade. Ottoman state income doubled, the reserve treasury in the Palace was overflowing, and with these resources Süleymân I (1520–66) was able to support his plans for world-wide conquests.

CHAPTER V

THE OTTOMAN STATE AS A WORLD POWER
1526–96

Up to 1596 there was no question of international politics which did not somehow involve the Ottomans.

In 1519 the Habsburg Charles v and Francis i of France were candidates for the crown of the Holy Roman Empire, and both promised to mobilize all the forces of Europe against the Ottomans. The Electors considered Charles v more suited to the task, and shortly after the election, in March 1521, these two European rulers were at war with each other. Europe, to the great advantage of the Ottomans, was divided, and Süleymân i chose this time to march against Belgrade, the gateway to central Europe. Belgrade fell on 29 August 1521. On 21 January 1522 he captured Rhodes, the key to the eastern Mediterranean, from the Knights of St John.

When Charles v took Francis prisoner at Pavia in 1525, the French, as a last resort, sought aid from the Ottomans. Francis later informed the Venetian ambassador that he considered the Ottoman Empire the only power capable of guaranteeing the existence of the European states against Charles v. The Ottomans too saw the French alliance as a means of preventing a single power dominating Europe. Francis i's ambassador told the sultan in February 1526 that if Francis accepted Charles' conditions, the Holy Roman Emperor would become 'ruler of the world'.

In the following year Süleymân advanced against Hungary with a large army. The Ottoman victory at Mohács on 28 August 1526, and the occupation of Buda, threatened the Habsburgs from the rear. The Ottomans withdrew from Hungary, occupying only Srem, and the Hungarian Diet elected John Zapolya as King. At first the Ottomans wished to make Hungary a vassal state, like Moldavia, since it was considered too difficult and too expensive to establish direct Ottoman rule in a completely foreign country on the far side of the Danube. But the Hungarian partisans of the Habsburgs elected Charles v's brother, Archduke Ferdinand, King of Hungary, and in the following year he occupied Buda and expelled Zapolya. Süleymân again invaded

Hungary, and on 8 September 1529 again enthroned Zapolya in Buda as an Ottoman vassal. Zapolya agreed to pay an annual tribute and accepted a Janissary garrison in the citadel. Although the campaigning season was over, Süleymân continued his advance as far as Vienna, the Habsburg capital. After a three-week siege, he withdrew.

In 1531 Ferdinand again entered Hungary and besieged Buda. In the following year Süleymân replied by leading a large army into Hungary and advancing to the fortress of Güns, some sixty miles from Vienna, where he hoped to force Charles v to fight a pitched battle. At this moment Charles' admiral, Andrea Doria, took Coron in the Morea from the Ottomans. Realizing that he now had to open a second front in the Mediterranean, the sultan placed all Ottoman naval forces under the command of the famous Turkish corsair and conqueror of Algiers, Hayreddîn Barbarossa, appointing him *kapudan-i deryâ* – grand admiral – with orders to cooperate with the French. Since 1531 the French had been trying to persuade the sultan to attack Italy and now they sought a formal alliance. In 1536 this alliance was concluded. The sultan was ready to grant the French, as a friendly nation, freedom of trade within the empire.[1] The ambassadors concluded orally the political and military details of the alliance and both parties kept them secret. Francis' Ottoman alliance provided his rival with abundant material for propaganda in the western Christian world. French insistence convinced Süleymân that he could bring the war to a successful conclusion only by attacking Charles v in Italy. The French were to invade northern Italy and the Ottomans the south. In 1537 Süleymân brought his army to Valona in Albania and besieged Venetian ports in Albania and the island of Corfu, where a French fleet assisted the Ottomans. In the following year, however, the French made peace with Charles. Francis had wished to profit from the Ottoman pressure by taking Milan, and when the emperor broke his promise he reverted to his 'secret' policy of alliance with the Ottomans.

In the Mediterranean Charles captured Tunis in 1535, but in 1538 Barbarossa defeated a crusader fleet under the command of Andrea Doria at Préveza, leaving him undisputed master of the Mediterranean.

When Francis again approached the sultan in 1540 he told Charles' ambassadors, come to arrange a peace treaty, that he was unable to conclude a peace unless Charles returned French territory. There was close cooperation between the Ottomans and the French between 1541 and 1544, when France realized that peaceful negotiations would not procure Milan.

In 1541 Zapolya died, and Ferdinand again invaded Hungary. Süleymân once again came to Hungary with his army, this time bringing the country under direct Ottoman rule as an Ottoman province under a beylerbeyi. He sent Zapolya's widow and infant son to

Transylvania, which was then an Ottoman vassal state. Since 1526 Ferdinand had possessed a thin strip of Hungarian territory in the west and north, to which the Ottomans, as heirs to the Hungarian throne, now laid claim. In 1543 Süleymân again marched into Hungary with the intention of conquering the area, and at the same time sent a fleet of 110 galleys, under the command of Barbarossa, to assist Francis. The Franco-Ottoman fleet besieged Nice and the Ottoman fleet wintered in the French port of Toulon. In return, a small French artillery unit joined the Ottoman army in Hungary. This cooperation, however, was not particularly effective. With the worsening of relations with Iran Süleymân wanted peace on his western front. As in 1533, he concluded an armistice with Ferdinand, which included Charles. According to this treaty, signed on 1 August 1547, and to which Süleymân made France a party, Ferdinand was to keep the part of Hungary already in his possession in return for a yearly tribute of thirty thousand ducats.

Three years later war with the Habsburgs broke out again when Ferdinand tried to gain control of Transylvania. The Ottomans repulsed him, and in 1552 established the new *beylerbeyilik* of Temesvár in southern Transylvania.

When the new king, Henry II, came to the throne in France, he realized the need of maintaining the Ottoman alliance in the struggle against Charles V. The French alliance was the cornerstone of Ottoman policy in Europe. The Ottomans also found a natural ally in the Schmalkalden League of German Protestant princes fighting Charles V. At the instigation of the French, Süleymân approached the Lutheran princes, urging in a letter that they continue to cooperate with France against the pope and emperor. He assured them that if the Ottoman armies entered Europe he would grant the princes amnesty. Recent research[2] has shown that Ottoman pressure between 1521 and 1555 forced the Habsburgs to grant concessions to the Protestants and was a factor in the final official recognition of Protestantism. In his letter to the Protestants, Süleymân intimated that he considered the Protestants close to the Muslims, since they too had destroyed idols and risen against the Pope. Support and protection of the Lutherans and Calvinists against Catholicism would be a keystone of Ottoman policy in Europe. Ottoman policy was thus intended to maintain the political disunity in Europe, weaken the Habsburgs and prevent a united crusade. Hungary, under Ottoman protection, was to become a stronghold of Calvinism, to the extent that Europe began to speak of 'Calvino-turcismus'. In the second half of the sixteenth century the French Calvinist party maintained that the Ottoman alliance should be used against Catholic Spain, and the St Bartholomew's Day Massacre of the Calvinists infuriated the Ottoman government.

It should be added that at first Luther and his adherents followed a passive course, maintaining that the Ottoman threat was a punishment from God, but when the Turkish peril began to endanger Germany the Lutherans did not hesitate to support Ferdinand with military and financial aid; in return they always obtained concessions for Lutheranism. Ottoman intervention was thus an important factor not only in the rise of national monarchies, such as in France, but also in the rise of Protestantism in Europe.

Charles v, following the example of the Venetians, entered into diplomatic relations with the Safavids of Iran, forcing Süleymân to avoid a conflict with the Safavids, in order not to have to fight simultaneously in the east and west.

In 1533, however, Sheref Khan, the local lord in Bitlis in the frontier region, placed himself under Persian protection; at the same time, the shah's governor in Baghdad came to an agreement with the Ottomans and war became inevitable. Süleymân signed an armistice with Ferdinand and marched on Iran at the head of his army. In this campaign of 1534–5 the Ottoman sultan took Tabriz and Baghdad and annexed Azerbaijan and Iraq. The local dynasts in the silk-producing areas of Gilan and Shirvan also recognized Ottoman suzerainty. In 1538 the Emir of Basra tendered his submission. By gaining mastery of the Persian Gulf, as well as of the Red Sea, the Ottomans controlled all the routes leading from the near east to India. By 1546 they had made Basra their second base after Suez for equipping fleets against the Portuguese; but in 1552 an Ottoman expedition failed to oust the Portuguese from the island of Hormuz which controlled the Persian Gulf.

When the Ottomans renewed the war in central Europe, the Persians counterattacked, and in 1548 Süleymân, for the second time, marched against Iran. This war lasted intermittently for seven years. By the Treaty of Amasya, signed on 29 May 1555, Baghdad was left to the Ottomans.

These Ottoman enterprises resulted, in the mid-sixteenth century, in a new system of alliances between the states occupying an area stretching from the Atlantic, through central Asia, to the Indian Ocean. In this way the European system of balance of power was greatly enlarged.

In the mid-sixteenth century the Russian Tsar, Ivan iv, occupied the Volga basin as far east as Astrakhan, threatening not only the Ottomans but also the khanates of central Asia. The Ottomans and the Uzbeks were drawn closer together. The central Asian khanates, unable to establish contact with the near east via Iran, usually used the route passing north of the Caspian Sea and leading to the Crimean ports. When the Russians gained control of this route, the central Asian khanates, and in particular the Khan of Khwarezm, made repeated calls to the Ottoman sultan to free this pilgrimage and trade route from Russian control.

The Ottomans had not regarded the great expansion of Muscovy, which until the 1530s had been a second-rate power in eastern Europe, as a danger in the north and had even supported an alliance between Muscovy and the khanate of Crimea against the Jagellonians, who threatened Ottoman sovereignty in the Crimea. In 1497 they had granted the Muscovites freedom of trade in the Ottoman Empire. But when in the 1530s the Grand Duke of Muscovy and the Khan of the Crimea went to war over the succession to the former territories of the Golden Horde in the Volga basin, the khan sought to awaken the Ottomans to the danger. It was only in the mid-sixteenth century that the Ottomans came to realize that the Russian advance threatened their position in the Black Sea basin and the Caucasus. After Ivan IV had assumed the title of tsar in 1547, he conquered and annexed the Muslim khanates of the Volga basin – Kazan in 1552 and Astrakhan in 1554–6 – advancing as far as the Terek river in the northern Caucasus, laying the foundations of the Russian Empire. In this region the tsar found allies among the Circassians and the Nogays; in the west in 1543, Petru Raresh, the voivoda of Moldavia, had sought the protection of Moscow; and finally, in 1559, the Cossack chieftain Dimitrash attempted to capture the fortress of Azov, the northernmost outpost of the Ottoman Empire. Following these successes, the tsardom of Muscovy succeeded the khanate of the Golden Horde as a first-class power in eastern Europe, spreading its influence into Ottoman domains in the Caucasus and the Black Sea region.

The Ottomans were able to turn their attention to the north only after 1566, when the war with the Habsburgs was no longer pressing. They conceived the bold plan of conveying an Ottoman army and fleet up the Don to the place where it flows closest to the Volga, where they would dig a canal between the two rivers, allowing the fleet to sail on Astrakhan down the Volga. The army and navy would cooperate in ousting the Russians from Astrakhan, the fleet then entering the Caspian Sea to assist the Ottoman army in Iran. The plan thus aimed to drive the Russians from the Volga basin and encircle Iran. This common danger united the two powers. In the winter of 1568 the tsar sent an envoy to Iran proposing an alliance against the Ottomans, and at the same time Pope Gregory XIII included the tasr and the shah in his plans for a crusade against the Ottomans. In 1569 the Ottoman attempt to dig the canal and besiege Astrakhan failed. The grand vizier, Sokollu Mehmed Pasha, had formulated the plan, and his rivals now proposed that the empire should concentrate its forces in the Mediterranean rather than continue the expensive and difficult war in the north. The tasr, for his part, knew that for the time being he could not hope to challenge the Ottomans.

To preserve his position in the Volga basin, the tsar adopted a peaceful and even friendly policy towards the sultan. The sultan left Kazan and Astrakhan in Russian hands but claimed Ottoman sovereignty over the khanate of the Crimea, the Circassian lands and the Caucasus. He demanded that the Russians withdraw from these areas and keep open the route from central Asia to the Crimea. But the sultan did not pursue this policy consistently or forcefully, since at this point he opened hostilities with western Europe in the Mediterranean, capturing Cyprus in 1570 and meeting with a crushing defeat at Lepanto in 1571.

Although the pope urged Russia to join Austria and Poland in attacking the Turks, the tsar remained at peace. Once established in the Volga basin, his policy was one of procrastination. He never evacuated the fortresses he had built in the northern Caucasus.

The Ottoman government left the struggle against Russia to its two vassals, the Khan of the Crimea and the Prince of Erdel (Transylvania). When the tsar stood for election as King of Poland in 1572, the Ottoman supported first Henry of Valois and then their vassal Stephen Batori, the Prince of Erdel. They succeeded in winning the Polish throne for Stephen, who then began a merciless struggle against Moscow, recovering all the tsar's conquests in the west.

CHAPTER VI

THE DECLINE OF THE OTTOMAN EMPIRE

In an inscription dating from 1538 on the citadel of Bender, Süleymân the Magnificent gave expression to his world-embracing power:

I am God's slave and sultan of this world. By the grace of God I am head of Muhammad's community. God's might and Muhammad's miracles are my companions. I am Süleymân, in whose name the *hutbe* is read in Mecca and Medina. In Baghdad I am the shah, in Byzantine realms the Caesar, and in Egypt the sultan; who sends his fleets to the seas of Europe, the Maghrib and India. I am the sultan who took the crown and throne of Hungary and granted them to a humble slave. The voivoda Petru raised his head in revolt, but my horse's hoofs ground him into the dust, and I conquered the land of Moldavia.[1]

But in his final years international conditions became unfavourable to the Ottomans and Süleymân's attempt at world-wide domination met its first decisive failures.

The Peace of Cateau-Cambrésis in 1559 established Spanish hegemony in Europe, and as France was drawn into civil war she ceased to be the Ottomans' main ally in European politics. The withdrawal from Malta in 1565 and Süleymân's last Hungarian campaign in 1566 marked the beginning of a halt in the Ottoman advance into central Europe and the Mediterranean.

The conquest of Cyprus in 1570–71 was the last great Ottoman military success. The capture of this heavily fortified island required cutting the lines of communication of the most powerful Christian fleet in the Mediterranean, transporting a vast army to the island and maintaining it there. This victory, achieved by the cooperation of the army and the fleet, was the greatest feat of Ottoman arms; but the creation of a Christian alliance during the course of the campaign was a realization of the Ottomans' greatest fears. The strong allied fleet, under the command of Don John of Austria, defeated the Turkish fleet at Lepanto on 7 October 1571, in the greatest battle ever fought on the Mediterranean. Four hundred and thirty-eight vessels took part; the Ottomans lost two hundred out of two hundred and thirty ships, and losses on both sides amounted to fifty-nine thousand men. All Europe celebrated this great victory as the end of the Turkish peril. Spain, Venice, and the Papacy, bound by a three-year alliance, even considered a direct attack upon Istanbul; but when they sailed against Cyprus they encountered a newly constructed Ottoman fleet. During the winter all the Ottoman dockyards had laboured ceaselessly to replace the ships destroyed at Lepanto. Seeing this, Venice made peace with the Ottomans on 7 March 1573, renouncing all rights to Cyprus and paying a huge war indemnity.

In the quarter century between 1578 and 1606 the Ottomans waged a series of exhausting wars against the Persians in the east and the Habsburgs in central Europe. In the Persian wars, between 1578 and 1590, the Ottomans annexed all the western provinces of Iran, from the Caucasus to Nehavend. In 1588 the Ottoman's central Asian ally, the Uzbek khan, Abdullâh, invaded Khorasan. During this war the Ottoman commander in western Iran, Osmân Pasha, with his headquarters in Derbend, received military aid from the Crimea through the northern steppes and also attempted to construct a fleet on the Caspian. But Russian attacks from the northern Caucasus on the reinforcements sent to Iran from the Crimea, and the renewal of Russo-Iranian diplomatic relations, caused the Ottomans considerable concern.

The Ottomans had always considered a small portion of Hungarian land still held by the Habsburgs as belonging to the sultan, and after the peace with Iran in 1590 they decided finally to solve this problem. Border incidents led the two empires to war in 1593. This war, long and full of surprises, showed how much world conditions had turned against the Ottomans. In the east the pope procured strong allies for the Austrians. Moldavia, Wallachia and the vassal state of Transylvania revolted against the Ottomans and fought on the Austrian side, while the Dnieper Cossacks, too, attacked the Ottomans along a wide front on land and sea. The Ottomans made great efforts, and their army in Hungary, under the personal command of the sultan, won a great victory at Mezökeresztes on 23–5 October 1596. But it had no lasting effects. The emperor's forces continued to attack, advancing and laying siege to Buda.

In 1599 Shah Abbâs the Great of Iran sent ambassadors to Europe and opened military and economic negotiations directed against the Ottomans. In Vienna the emperor received the delegation warmly. He informed them that he wished to form an anti-Ottoman alliance with the Russians and the Georgians in the east, and that he was working to unite the Christian kings of Europe in a Holy Crusade. In imitation of the Ottomans the shah added to his army new slave units equipped with firearms. In 1603 he passed to the attack. The Ottomans now had to fight simultaneously on their eastern and western fronts, at a time when civil disturbances were shaking the empire. Shah Abbâs drove their troops from Azerbaijan and the Caucasus into Anatolia. In this situation the Ottoman government considered itself fortunate to be able to make peace with the Habsburgs and, by the Treaty of Zsitva-Torok in 1606, it renounced all claims to those parts of Hungary in Habsburg hands and the Habsburgs discontinued payment of the annual thirty thousand ducat tribute. The war had thus demonstrated to the Ottomans their own military weakness and compelled them to seek a peace treaty several times since 1595.

The burden which the Persian and Austrian wars imposed was the main cause of the confusion and unrest which afflicted the Ottoman Empire at this period. Neither were the Ottomans able, after Lepanto, to preserve their previous supremacy on the Mediterranean. In Europe, Philip II of Spain had strengthened his position. In France, the Massacre of St Bartholomew exterminated those Calvinists who had supported the Ottomans. In the Netherlands, the Spaniards had intensified their campaign against the rebels, at the same time increasing their pressure against the English. In 1580 they annexed the kingdom of Portugal and her colonies. In spite of the truce made with Spain in 1578 – a step necessary in order to concentrate all the resources of the empire against Iran – the Ottoman sultan sent encouraging letters to the Dutch, attempted to establish friendly relations with the English by granting them capitulations, and showed an interest in efforts to revive the kingdom of Portugal. The destruction of the Spanish Armada in 1588 had important consequences in the Mediterranean. With the decline of her power, Spain, the great rival of the Ottoman Empire, was no longer capable of vast undertakings in the Mediterranean. But it was not the Ottomans who benefited.

With the loss of their supremacy in the Mediterranean, they also lost control of their north African provinces. Naval forces from Tripoli, Tunis and Algiers no longer formed a regular part of the sultan's fleets, but became corsairs acting on their own initiative. The defeat at Lepanto was the sign for increased Christian pirate activity in the eastern Mediterranean. After 1570 the Knights of Malta and the military order of St Etienne seriously began to menace Ottoman traffic in the eastern Mediterranean. English and Dutch pirates soon joined them, attacking not only Spanish but also Ottoman shipping, and it was only with difficulty that the Ottoman government could keep open its vital lines of communication with Egypt and Syria. In the early seventeenth century the influence of the local Mamlûks in Egypt increased, undermining the Ottoman administration, while in Lebanon Emir Fakhr al-Dîn began to act as an independent ruler. All this indicated that the central government was losing control over its distant provinces.

It was a hardly less disturbing symptom of decline that the Ottoman fleet was unable effectively to engage the Cossacks on the Black Sea. From the 1590s the Cossacks, descending the Dnieper in their fleets of small floats, intensified their raids on the Black Sea coasts. With increasing boldness, they burned Sinop in 1614 and Yeniköy on the Bosphorus in 1625. Between 1637 and 1642 they even held Azov. There was no security on the Black Sea, the lifeline of the Ottoman economy, and its trade and ports began to decline.

There are several reasons for the decline of Ottoman naval power. The Ottoman fleet at the Battle of Lepanto was still composed of galleys, which were ineffective against the enemy's tall ships, capable of firing powerful broadsides. This new type of warship was to dominate the Mediterranean, especially with the arrival of the Dutch and the English towards the end of the sixteenth century. In 1607 Sir Thomas Sherley noted that one English warship could defeat ten Turkish galleys. The Ottoman navy was to adopt the new ships only very late and only with great difficulty. Another essential factor was the difficulty of equipping and maintaining an Ottoman fleet powerful enough to face the combined navies of the Christian Mediterranean states. The extraordinary taxes levied to finance the fleet caused widespread discontent and unrest, and after Lepanto the provincial military forces did everything in their power to avoid participating in naval campaigns. The empire had, in fact, exceeded its material capabilities.

Throughout the sixteenth century the Ottomans fought the Portuguese on the Indian Ocean and were able to prevent them gaining absolute control of the trade between India and the near east. In the Indian Ocean after 1580 the Ottomans faced the forces of the King of Spain, the new ruler of Portugal. Philip II believed that he could strike a fatal blow against the Ottomans by cutting their trade-route in the Indian Ocean. The Ottomans attempted to take advantage of the disaster that had befallen the King of Portugal at the battle of Alcazar in 1578, and a small Ottoman fleet sailed from Suez, capturing one by one the Portuguese factories on the east African coast. In 1585 the Prince of Mombasa recognized Ottoman suzerainty. But these Ottoman successes did not last. Despatching a strong fleet, the Spanish and Portuguese punished the local chiefs who had recognized the Ottomans, and faced by a superior Portuguese force and a local Negro attack the Ottoman admiral had to surrender. The African project had ended in failure. Before long, the Dutch and the English, with their superior ships, came to dominate the Indian Ocean, as they had the Mediterranean, and the Ottomans, like the Portuguese and Spaniards before them, were driven from the sea. In 1613, Dutch and English pirates were operating on the Red Sea.

Towards the end of the sixteenth century the English were still buying pepper and other spices in Cairo, but with the foundation of the East India Company in 1600 they preferred to buy directly from India, since customs duties levied in Ottoman ports, and the greater expenses incurred on the land route, meant that pepper prices were three times as high in near-eastern ports.[2] The Ottoman historian Âlî attributes the decline in the number of ships arriving in the Red Sea from India each year – a drop from twenty to three or four – primarily to the rapacity of customs officials. From 1614 the English began to sell pepper from Java and Sumatra directly in Ottoman ports. In 1618 English ships began to bring Indian products to Mocha in the Yemen, and when the coffee trade gained importance they established a factory there. Eventually, none of the Indian trade with the west passed through the near east. Loss of superiority on the seas was thus an important factor in Ottoman economic decline.

In the same period the search for new routes for the export of Persian silk to Europe was another threat to the Ottoman economy. Asia Minor was the main transit route for Persian silk and European woollens. Until the end of the sixteenth century English cloths were sent through Asia Minor as far as central Asia, and it has been estimated that this transit trade alone assured the Ottoman Treasury of 300,000 ducats a year in customs revenue.

When Shah Abbâs 1 attacked the Ottomans in 1603 he prohibited the export of Persian silk to the Ottoman Empire, and to prevent a shortage of silver and gold in Iran he attempted to sell the silk directly to Europe, via the Indian Ocean. A Persian diplomatic mission to Lisbon in 1603 carried with it two hundred bales of silk and tried to prove that silk would be cheaper when shipped by sea. Only the English, in 1617, were persuaded by the shah, and two years later the first Persian silk, shipped via the Indian Ocean, arrived in England.[3]

The end of the war between the Ottoman Empire and Iran in 1618, and the English insistence on bartering woollens for silks instead of paying in silver or gold, prevented the total abandonment of the Ottoman markets as a centre of the silk trade. Nevertheless, with the English and Dutch trade, the port of Bandar Abbas on the Persian Gulf developed rapidly. In the same way as the Indian trade had been transferred to the Atlantic route, dominated by the Dutch and the English, the trade route between Europe and central Asia came under Russian control. The Ottoman Empire had become, politically and economically, a regional empire confined to Asia Minor, the Balkans and the Arab lands, and even within this area could defend her boundaries only with difficulty. The Christian world was everywhere assaulting her vital arteries – in the Mediterranean, the Red Sea and the Black Sea. Yet the chief causes of the Ottoman decline were internal.

Until the 1580s the Ottoman state and Ottoman society appeared to have achieved harmony and equilibrium within its own system and ideals. It was a society interested not in change but in preservation of the existing order. The empire's ruling classes – the military and the ulema – had secure, lasting and sufficient sources of income. Their consumption of luxury goods increased. Not only sultans and viziers but even less wealthy persons, commissioned great works of architecture and created vakîfs. The preservation for seventy years of the ratio between the silver akçe and the gold coinage is an indication of this economic and social stability. In 1510 one gold piece was valued at 54 akçes, in 1580 at 60. Thousands of people in government service – courtiers, soldiers, teachers, kâdîs and bureaucrats – received regular salaries or timar incomes, within a clear system of promotion. This society looked to the future with optimism. The productive class knew exactly what taxes were due and an effective central authority gave protection from local abuses. Government registers had for centuries recorded the members of all classes, and the state was able strictly to control this class structure. The empire was, at the same time, self-sufficient in all basic commodities, the main imports being luxury goods such as European woollens, Indian textiles and spices, Russian furs and Persian silk. The empire's rulers believed that they could conquer the world, and amidst a splendour which dazzled the eyes of foreigners they spoke of an empire that would last forever.

Yet twenty or thirty years later the whole magnificent edifice was shaken to its foundations. Amidst turmoil and confusion, and fearing for their livelihood and future, these same rulers began to oppose the sultan's authority, disregard the law, rob the state Treasury and plunder the property of defenceless people. As violence, profiteering, bribery and other abuses spread, civil disorders increased. Prophets of doom predicted the empire's fall. The contemporary historian Selânikî, bemoaning the prevailing anarchy, wrote that:

The reâyâ no longer obeyed the sovereign's commands; the soldiers turned against the sultan. There was no respect for the authorities and they were attacked not by words but blows. All acted as they pleased. As tyranny and injustice increased, people in the provinces began to flee to Istanbul. The old order and harmony departed. When these have finally collapsed, catastrophe will surely follow.

Those who prophesied that doomsday would fall on the thousandth anniversary of the hegira* felt their fears to be justified. But the modern historian must seek the causes elsewhere.

One of these was population growth. Archival research has shown that in the sixteenth century the population of the Ottoman Empire increased by 40 per cent in the villages and by 80 per cent in the towns.[4]

* This coincided with the Christian years 1591–2.

When, after 1570, the government sent thousands of landless and unemployed Anatolian peasants to Cyprus, it was aware of the population excess. In the state records from the second half of the sixteenth century, landless and unemployed youths, known as *levends* or *gurbet tâifesi*, are mentioned more and more frequently. There is an obvious relationship between the growing number of levends, who could not be transported to new areas of conquest, and the increase in brigandage in Anatolia.

The two fundamental institutions of the classical Ottoman Empire were the slave and timar systems. They defined the state's military and political order, taxation system and forms of land tenure, determining its whole social and political structure. Towards the end of the sixteenth century these institutions began to deteriorate rapidly and contemporary Ottoman commentators saw this decay as the fundamental cause of the empire's decline. They held that only the sultan's slaves should perform governmental and military service. From 1575, however, the reâyâ – tax-paying subjects – began to infiltrate their ranks and share their privileges, and in this way entered court and state service. Thus the basis of the slave system was destroyed and contemporary observers believed that this was the cause of the decline in obedience and discipline. The sultan's authority was undermined, and since the reâyâ preferred the sword to the plough, agricultural land was abandoned and income from taxes was reduced.

The timar system also suffered. Many timars were acquired by courtiers, who converted them into private property or vakîfs, so that the total number of timars decreased; others were granted to the reâyâ in return for bribes. Consequently the number of timar-holding sipâhîs, the backbone of the empire's army, was reduced, and those that remained were unfit for warfare.

Ottoman writers, seeking the causes of decline, realized that the institutions of the old Ottoman regime had deteriorated but attributed this deterioration to the decline and fragmentation of the sultan's authority. They maintained that formerly only the grand vizier had represented the absolute authority of the sultan, but that weak sultans had later delegated their authority to irresponsible persons; the state administration had thus lost its unity. Certain individuals had begun to use the sultan's authority for their personal ends; bribery and corruption had increased alarmingly. They regarded bribery as one of the chief causes in the decline of the organization and administration of the state.

In their analysis of the decline, most of these writers were guided by the traditional near-eastern concepts of state and society, which regarded the state and the ruler's authority as identical. They upheld those institutions which guaranteed the integrity and absolute character of this authority. Their suggested remedies did not go beyond this concept and the measures taken produced results opposite to what was intended. With no regard for the changed conditions, they maintained that the revival of the 'old laws and regulations' – meaning the classical Ottoman institutions – would arrest the decline. It was not until after the mid-seventeenth century that this view was seen to be wrong. The political thought of this period, influenced by Ibn Khaldûn's determinist view of history, claimed that it was possible only to prolong the period of the decline but not to arrest it altogether.

One cannot expect the Ottoman writers of the sixteenth century and the modern historian to attribute the same causes to the fundamental changes in the Empire. We shall begin by analysing the causes of the corruption of the timar system.

The timar-holding cavalry, armed with the traditional mediaeval weapons – bow and arrow, sword and shield – formed a mediaeval army whose day passed when it met the German infantry equipped with firearms. This cavalry regarded itself as forming a true military class in the mediaeval tradition and considered the use of firearms unbecoming to their sense of chivalry. The Ottoman government, therefore, sought other ways of creating an army capable of competing with the German infantry. From the time of Süleymân I it continually increased the number of Janissaries equipped with firearms. In Süleymân's time there were sixteen thousand Janissaries; by 1609 their number had reached thirty-seven thousand. In contrast to this, the number of sipâhîs, which in Süleymân's reign had been at least eighty-seven thousand, had by 1609 dropped to forty-five thousand. In 1630 Koçi Bey wrote that only about eight thousand sipâhîs remained.

As the *kapîkulu* army expanded, native Turks were admitted to the Janissary corps, a practice which undermined the *devşirme* system. At the same time the Ottoman government began to hire young Anatolians, who understood the use of firearms, as salaried troops. These cavalry and infantrymen, equipped with firearms and known as *sarîca* and *sekban*, were composed mainly of young, landless villagers who had left their homes.

Towards the end of the sixteenth century, the reâyâ in the Ottoman Empire began to make and use firearms, and the government organized these young sharpshooters from Anatolia into hundred-man sekban and sarîca companies, usually under the command of the sultan's slaves, employing them on the battlefields of central Europe. After 1590 they were to become the most effective units in the Ottoman army. Provincial governors began to use them in their personal retinues, and as a result the old military organization in the provinces fell into neglect. The sipâhî army was now mostly used only for building roads and fortifications. Other old organizations, such as the yayas, voyniks and *müsellems*, were abolished or assigned to other duties.

These changes in the classical military organizations, which had once held such an important place in the empire, had a profound effect on its political, economic and social life. Here we can give no more than a general outline of these very complex changes, considering first the changes in state finances and those forms of land tenure and taxation which had been fundamental to the timar system.

In order to pay the Janissaries their monthly salary and the sekban troops their daily wage, the state had to amass an ever-increasing amount of coin in the central Treasury. To meet these requirements, some of the lands assigned as timars were brought under direct Treasury control and the right to collect their revenue farmed out; but some of them passed, by fraudulent means, into the hands of palace and government officials, while others were converted into vakĭfs and their revenues lost to the government. The sums raised by taxation were inadequate and the Treasury faced a permanent deficit. In the 1580s the debasement of the silver coinage, and the subsequent increase of counterfeit and defective coin in circulation, further aggravated the financial crisis.

In the mid-sixteenth century Mexican silver flooded the European market, causing huge price increases, and in the 1580s this situation was repeated in the Ottoman Empire, where gold was cheaper in relation to silver. These relatively low gold prices encouraged the export of European silver to the empire, to such an extent that in 1584 it was reported that 'one of the main items of trade going to Turkey are Spanish reals sent by the chestful'.[5] European silver coins inundated the Ottoman market, and within a short time prices doubled. Fixed-income groups such as timar-holding sipâhîs, kapĭkulus, or those who derived their incomes from vakĭfs, were suddenly impoverished. Sipâhîs abandoned their timars rather than go on long campaigns which they found too costly, and the Janissary corps in the capital mutinied more and more often. Bribery and misappropriations increased among state officials, soldiers and kâdîs. The state sought to offset rocketing Treasury expenses by debasing and diminishing the akçe; but these panic measures only worsened the situation.

In 1534 the central Treasury's annual income had reached five million gold ducats, but by 1591 it was worth only half its original value since most of the taxes were levied in akçe. Depreciation brought with it an increase in counterfeit coin, speculation, an excessive increase in interest rates, usury and profiteering. The situation was exacerbated by the opening of hostilities with Austria in 1593, a war motivated partly by the desire to rid the capital of the mutinous Janissaries by sending them on campaign. But the war lasted far longer than was anticipated, and military and naval expenditure caused a huge and permanent deficit in the state budget. The government increased long-standing taxes – the *cizye*, for example, was increased four- or fivefold – but revenue was still insufficient. Taxes which had previously been raised only as extraordinary levies called *avâriz* were increased and converted into regular, annual taxes, payable in cash.

The sum which was to be met by the extraordinary levy was divided among the peoples of the empire, who for taxation purposes were separated into units. In 1576 each unit was assessed at 50, in 1600 at 280 akçes. Money taxes became a principal source of state revenue, a development which revolutionized the tax system. The commutation of taxes paid in kind for taxes paid in cash was a progressive step; but taxation was a heavy burden on the peoples of the empire, especially on its Christian subjects, and discontent was widespread.

Further measures intended to remedy the state's financial distress had disastrous results. In particular, beylerbeyis were granted authority to raise local taxes to pay for the enlistment of sekban troops. This encouraged minor military commanders, even commanders of sekban and sarïca units, to operate independently and plunder the people on their own account. Furthermore, when the state was unable to pay these troops the wages due for a campaign, or else discharged them from service, bands of them would roam the countryside, collecting provisions and money wherever they went. Anatolia was in the same situation as France after the hundred years war, with companies of discharged soldiers pillaging the land.

The Ottoman government took strong action against these brigands, proclaiming them *celâlîs* – rebels against the state. To combat them, it at first allowed the people to form their own militias, but this only worsened the situation since the militia-men more often than not joined the celâlîs. In the end the government could combat them only with sekban and sarïca units equipped with firearms. Sipâhîs, whose timars had been confiscated or yielded insufficient income, and nomads seeking plunder, joined the rebellious sekban and sarïca companies; towards 1598 the rebels' forces under the energetic leadership of Kara Yazïcï numbered some twenty thousand men. In 1602 government forces, with difficulty, defeated Kara Yazïcï and the brigands dispersed throughout Anatolia. The richer Anatolians began to migrate to the Balkans, the Crimea, Iran and the Arab lands; the land was left fallow, hunger and famine followed, and the Treasury lost its sources of revenue.

Between 1595 and 1610 these armed brigands wrought havoc in Anatolia. In 1603 Shah Abbâs took advantage of the prevailing anarchy to counter-attack, driving the Ottoman troops from the former Persian provinces back into Anatolia. The Ottoman government, before it could wage war against Iran, had to gather all its forces against the celâlîs in Anatolia. Between 1607 and 1610 Canbulatoğlu, the leader of all the Anatolian celâlîs, was defeated and thousands of brigands slaughtered. Many took refuge in Iran or fled to Syria and Iraq.

In the same period brigandry became widespread. Heavy taxes, corruption and insecurity led to the first large-scale rebellions of the reâyâ.

The celâlî period came at a time of great financial crisis, dragging the empire into a decline from which it never recovered. In 1607 the English ambassador wrote from Istanbul: 'As far as I can see, the Turkish Empire was in great decline, almost ruined.' Similar unrest was to recur in the seventeenth century, especially in times of war.

As a result of the celâlî rebellions, Janissaries were stationed in the provinces, where they came to represent a new upper class. The Janissaries and the sultan's standing cavalry, the main regular forces used against the celâlîs, were stationed in small as well as large towns and cities. As their numbers increased they joined the ulema, the guild masters and merchants, as the most influential class in provincial society, and used their influence and power to amass great fortunes, usually acquired by extortionate tax-farming. They acquired, by various means, large tracts of state lands, the villagers on these lands sinking to the status of share-croppers. As the central authority weakened in the provinces, their power and influence increased, and it was this class which was to provide many of the local dynasties which later appeared in the provinces, and to form the basis of the class which was to dominate the provinces in the eighteenth century.

The privileges of the kapîkulu troops – the salaried, standing army of the state – served to heighten the rivalry between them and the sekbans and sarîcas. Some of these even disguised themselves as kapîkulus so that throughout the empire, but especially in Anatolia, there were thousands of soldiers posing as Janissaries. The remaining sekban and sarîca troops gathered around rebellious leaders and mercilessly attacked the kapîkulus. Between 1623 and 1628, under the command of Abaza Mehmed Pasha, they controlled all eastern Anatolia.

The fundamental institutions of the classical Ottoman Empire had disintegrated under the impact of a new Europe and the Ottomans were unable to adapt themselves to the changed conditions. They failed to understand modern economic problems, remaining bound by the traditional formulae of the near-eastern state. Against the mercantilist economics of contemporary European powers, Ottoman statesmen clung to the policy of free markets, their main concern being to provide the home market with an abundance of necessary commodities. Unable to formulate a comprehensive economic policy for the Ottoman Empire, they saw no danger in extending the capitulations so that from the second half of the sixteenth century Europeans began to control even the carrying trade between the empire's Mediterranean ports. The

Ottoman government, bound by traditional concepts, encouraged the import of goods into the empire but discouraged exports. They taxed imports and exports at the same rate and prohibited the export of certain goods where this might cause a shortage in the home market. By preserving corporation restrictions they hindered development in some branches of industry and exports.

While a rapidly developing and humanistic Europe was ridding itself of all forms of mediaevalism, the Ottoman Empire clung ever more zealously to the traditional forms of near-eastern civilization, becoming by the time of Süleymân I, when these reached their full perfection, self-satisfied, inward-looking and closed to outside influences. Even if the Ottomans had throughout their history borrowed a number of discoveries in technology, medicine and finance, they adopted them only for military or other purely practical purposes. They never fully broke away from the values and outlook of near-eastern culture, sanctified by the şerîat, and never wished to understand the mentality that had created European implements and methods. As early as the fifteenth century there had been some European observers who sought to describe objectively the Ottoman state, religion and culture,[6] while the Ottomans, convinced of their own religious and political superiority, closed their eyes to the outside world.

Thus in the last decade of the sixteenth century the economic and military impact of Europe, and the subsequent profound crises, radically transformed the Ottoman Empire and opened a new era in its history. The institutions of the classical near-eastern state disintegrated, and efforts to adjust to the new conditions shook the empire to its foundations. When, in the mid-seventeenth century, it was again relatively calm, it was radically different from the empire of before 1600.

Part II

THE STATE

CHAPTER VII

THE RISE OF THE OTTOMAN DYNASTY

Historical records show Osmân Gâzî, the founder of the Ottoman dynasty, as a chieftain of the semi-nomadic Turcomans, fighting on the frontier, under the command of the Emir of Kastamonu. How he emerged as the founder of a dynasty is a central historical problem.

To become an indpendent leader in the Seljuk frontier organization, frontier tradition required that Osmân win a major victory over the Christians and receive the title of bey from the Seljuk sultan. According to Ottoman tradition, Osmân captured an important Byzantine fortress, and after the victory the sultan proclaimed him bey, sending him the traditional symbols of authority – a robe of honour, flag, horse and drum. The tradition attempts to show a legitimate Islamic origin for Osmân's authority. According to the same account, Osmân proclaimed his independence after his famous victory at Baphaeon in 1301, and had the *hutbe* read in his own name. This again is a later tradition, invented to legitimize the royal authority of the Ottoman dynasty; but there can be no doubt that this victory was the most important fact in bringing Osmân into the historical limelight.

At the same time, dervish orders dominated the spiritual life of the frontiers, and consequently a mystic origin was also sought for Ottoman political power. The earliest accounts show Osmân receiving sanctification from Şeyh Edebali, who was probably the head of an *ahî* fraternity. Predicting that Osmân's descendants would rule the world, Şeyh Edebali girded him with a gâzî's sword. Osmân also had the foresight to marry the daughter of Edebali, the most influential man on the frontier.

On Osmân's death, a meeting to choose his successor was held in the zâviye of Edebali's nephew, Hasan the Ahî. Orhan and his son Süleymân later created in newly conquered areas hundreds of vakîfs for these ahîs and other dervishes, confirming that the ahîs played an important part in the establishment of the Ottoman state and dynasty. Orhan, the true founder of Ottoman power, bore the title of sultan, and as a token of independence struck the first Ottoman coins.

55

As the small Anatolian principalities began to recognise the sovereignty of Orhan's son, Murâd, he assumed the title of 'Hudâvendigâr' – Emperor – and 'Sultan-i âzam' – the Most Exalted Sultan – which the Seljuk sultans before him had used and which clearly indicated his claim to the title of empire. His successor, Bâyezîd I, was the first Ottoman sultan whom contemporary western sources described as 'imperator' – emperor. In 1395 Bâyezîd sought from the Abbasid caliph in Cairo official recognition of his title Sultan al-Rûm – sultan of the Byzantine lands – which had been a special title of the Seljuk rulers of Anatolia. But soon afterwards, Timur was to lay claim to the former Mongol territories in Anatolia and demand the submission of the Ottoman ruler, whom he considered a mere frontier bey. Later Timur's son, Shâhrukh, was to make the same claim, which the Ottomans countered by producing a genealogy which connected their own line to the ancient Turkish khans of central Asia, and by claiming descent from the legendary Oğuz Khan. In this period the Ottomans consciously revived and adopted the Turkish traditions of central Asia. Writing in the time of Murâd II, the historian Yazïcïoğlu stated that 'Ertugrul, from the tribe of Kayï, his son Osmân Bey, and the beys on the frontier, held an assembly. When they had consulted each other and understood the custom of the Oğuz, they appointed Osmân khan.' The central Asian concept of khanship thus united with the Islamic concept of the sultan as a gâzî leader.

With the conquest of Constantinople, Mehmed II became the most prestigious Muslim ruler. The Ottomans regarded him as the greatest Islamic sovereign since the first four caliphs, and the Islamic world came to regard Holy War as the greatest source of power and influence. Mehmed the Conqueror saw himself as fighting on behalf of all the Muslims: 'These tribulations are for God's sake. The sword of Islam is in our hands. If we had not chosen to endure these tribulations, we would not be worthy to be called gâzîs. We would be ashamed to stand in God's presence on the Day of Resurrection.'[1] In his letter informing the Mamlûk sultan of his conquest of Constantinople, Mehmed wrote: 'It is your responsibility to keep the pilgrimage routes open for the Muslims; we have the duty of providing gâzîs.'

With the possession of Constantinople, the capital of the Eastern Roman Empire, Mehmed regarded himself as the only legitimate heir of the Roman Empire. Giacomo de Languschi reported him as saying 'The world empire must be one, with one faith and one sovereignty. To establish this unity, there is no place more fitting than Constantinople.'[2] The Greek scholars and Italian humanists at his court instructed him in Roman history: a Greek, George Trapezuntios, addressed him thus in a poem: 'No one can doubt that he is emperor of the Romans. He who holds the seat of empire in his hand is emperor of right; and Constantinople is the centre of the Roman Empire.'[3]

The Conqueror claimed to have united in his own person the Islamic, Turkish and Roman traditions of universal sovereignty, and with the object of making Istanbul the centre of a world empire he appointed Gennadius to the Greek Orthodox patriarchate in 1454 and brought to Istanbul the Armenian patriarch and the chief rabbi.

During the reign of Selîm I the status of the Ottoman sultan changed radically. By annexing Syria, Egypt and Arabia, the old heartland of the caliphate, to the empire, Selîm became more than simply a gâzî sultan on the frontiers of the Islamic world; he became at the same time protector of Mecca and Medina and guardian of the pilgrimage routes. This was more significant than his bearing the title of caliph, a title then in use by every Muslim ruler. Although Selîm sent to his Palace in Istanbul the holy relics of the Prophet, considered the symbols of the caliphate, it is not true that the Abbasid caliph, al-Mutawakkil, surrendered the office of caliph to Selîm, or that Selîm claimed to be, in the classical sense, caliph of the whole Islamic world. According to sunnî doctrine, the caliph had to be from the Kuraysh, the Prophet's tribe and, furthermore, the classical concept of a single caliph for the whole Islamic community had had no force since the thirteenth century.

When Süleymân I laid claim to the 'Supreme Caliphate' and used the title 'Caliph of the Muslims', he meant only to emphasize his pre-eminence among Muslim rulers and his protectorship of Islam. In a letter sent to congratulate Süleymân on his accession to the throne, the Sherif of Mecca wrote that his success in Holy War had exalted him above all other Islamic sovereigns. The Ottoman sultans always remained gâzî sultans but they extended the concept of gazâ to bring the whole Islamic world under their protection. They invested the institution of the caliphate with new meaning, basing their concept not on the classical doctrines but on the principles of gazâ – Holy War.

The Muslim world saw the Ottomans as the only power able to defend it from the attacks of western Christianity and readily accepted Ottoman overlordship. In 1517, while Selîm was still in Cairo, a Portuguese fleet entered the Red Sea to attack Jidda and Mecca. Gathering his wealth and property, the Sherif of Mecca prepared to flee to the hills, and the people of the Hejaz begged the Ottoman admiral, Selmân, not to abandon them. Selmân repulsed the Portuguese. When, in the mid-sixteenth century, Muslim rulers in Sumatra and India requested Ottoman aid against the Portuguese, they expressly used in their letters the Sultan's title 'Protector of Islam'. The khans of Turkestan made similar pleas to the sultan to prevent the Russians occupying the Volga basin and cutting their communications with the Holy Places of Islam through the Crimea. The sultan was to organize expeditions in India and the Volga basin, in order, he would claim, to keep the pilgrimage routes open. The Ottomans naturally sought to exploit this situation for their own political advantage. It was only in the eighteenth century, and again for reasons of political expediency, that they were to revive the classical doctrine of the caliphate.

When Süleymân assumed the protectorship of the Islamic world, this was only one aspect of his universal policy. In Europe he refused to recognize Charles v's right to the title of emperor, acknowledging him only as King of Spain, and encouraged any force which opposed Charles' claim to sovereignty over the whole of western Christendom.

CHAPTER VIII

THE MANNER OF ACCESSION TO THE THRONE

In six centuries of rule the Ottoman family produced thirty-six sovereigns, and it is impossible to imagine the empire without the dynasty. Dynastic change in England, for example, did not cause the dissolution of England as a state, but without the Ottoman family there could be no Ottoman Empire.

According to Islamic tradition, the sultan had to be a male of full age and sound mind, but there was no law or custom regulating succession to throne. According to old Turkish beliefs the appointment of the sovereign was in the hands of God and, therefore, to establish a fixed law of succession or actively to challenge the enthroned sultan was to oppose the will of God. Süleymân 1 told his son, Bâyezîd, who had plotted for the throne that 'in future you may leave all to God, for it is not man's pleasure, but God's will, that disposes of kingdoms and their government. If He has decreed that you shall have the kingdom after me, no man living will be able to prevent it.' Whichever Ottoman prince succeeded in securing the empire's capital, Treasury and archives and in winning the support of the Janissaries, ulema, bureaucracy and Palace officials, was the legitimate sultan. In practice after 1421 the support of the Janissaries became a fundamental factor in the succession.

The outcome of a fratricidal struggle for the throne was regarded as a divine decree. The defeated princes usually sought refuge in enemy lands, and consequently the Ottoman Empire faced the continual threat of civil war. In his *kânûnnâme*, therefore, Mehmed the Conqueror codified a practice which in fact had been general since the early years of the empire: 'For the welfare of the state, the one of my sons to whom God grants the sultanate may lawfully put his brothers to death. A majority of the ulema consider this permissible'. But even this did not prevent civil wars. A major cause of this was the ancient Turkish tradition whereby the sons of the sovereign, on attaining the age of puberty – in Islamic Law, twelve – were sent with their tutors as governors to the old administrative capitals of Anatolia, where they established palaces and governments modelled on those in the capital.

In Seljuk times these princes had been practically independent in their own provinces, but the Ottomans carefully selected the princes' tutors and other administrators from within the Palace, and these acted under orders from the central government. The princes received only the revenues assigned to them and were closely controlled.

While their fathers were still alive these princely governors attempted to secure governorship close to the capital and to win support within the Palace and among the kapïkulu troops. The princes' impatience sometimes led to civil war. In 1511 Selîm took arms against his brothers, and in 1553 and 1561 Süleymân executed his sons, Mustafa and Bâyezîd, for rebelling against his authority. Taking warning from these events, Selîm II (1566–74) and Murâd III (1574–95) sent only their eldest sons to governorships. On the death of their fathers, the latter ascended the throne unopposed and easily disposed of their brothers, who had been confined to the Palace. Murâd III's first act on entering the Palace was to strangle his five brothers; Mehmed III (1595–1603) had his nineteen brothers executed and ended the practice of sending princes to governorships. He confined them instead to specially appointed quarters within the *harem* of the Palace, which came to be known as the *kafes* – the cage. The princes could not leave the kafes and were prevented from fathering children. Living in constant fear of execution, most of them suffered psychological disorders. When Süleymân II (1687–91) was called to the throne he sobbed to the Palace officials who came to escort him from the kafes: 'If my death has been commanded, say so. Let me perform my prayers, then carry out your order. Since my childhood, I have suffered forty years of imprisonment. It is better to die at once than to die a little every day. What terror we endure for a single breath.'[1] He was taken with difficulty from the kafes and placed on the throne.

Previously, the princes in the provinces had contested openly for the throne and defeat was considered God's will. The kafes system was contrary to ancient Turkish tradition and, from this, it appears that by the late sixteenth century these traditions had lost their force. The sovereign had become the symbol of an indivisible realm and authority.

Palace intrigues, and especially those of the *vâlide sultan* – the reigning sultan's mother – came to play an important part in the destiny of the sultanate. Public opinion did not, however, sanction the murder of defenceless children. When, at the accession of Mehmed III, nineteen coffins containing the bodies of his brothers emerged from the Palace behind their father's bier, in the words of a contemporary historian, 'The angels in heaven heard the sighs and lamentations of the people of Istanbul.' On the death of Mehmed III his eldest son, Ahmed I (1603–17), came to the throne but he did not, after hearing the pleas of certain high officials, execute his mentally defective younger brother,

Mustafa. When Ahmed died, his sons had not yet reached maturity and Mustafa came to the throne; three months later he was deposed in favour of Ahmed I's son, Osmân II (1618–22).

Despite the example of Mustafa, royal fraticide continued during the seventeenth century. Before setting out on his Polish campaign, Osmân II secured a fetvâ sanctioning the execution of his eldest brother, Mehmed. In 1622 the Janissaries murdered Osmân, and his uncle, Mustafa, came to the throne again. Mustafa was in turn deposed and Osmân's brother reigned as Murâd IV (1623–40). Murâd executed three of his brothers, sparing the fourth, Ibrahîm, because he himself had no children. On Murâd's death, Ibrahîm became sultan. When Mehmed IV (1648–87) was enthroned at the age of seven, he spared his brothers Süleymân and Ahmed. On Mehmed's deposition, Süleymân became sultan, succeeded, on his death, by Ahmed II (1691–5). They did not execute Mehmed IV's children, who reigned as Mustafa II (1695–1703) and Ahmed III (1703–30). Thus succession by seniority replaced the customary passage of the sultanate from father to son; but no formal regulation governed the succession until the promulgation of the first constitution in 1876.

When a sultan died all appointments and legal regulations were considered null and void until the new sultan confirmed them, and since there was then no legally constituted authority the kapïkulu troops would obey no one and give themselves up to plunder and destruction. Sometimes the interregnum lasted for as long as two weeks and the Palace sought to conceal the fact of a sultan's death until the new sovereign had been enthroned. The introduction of the kafes system, naturally, ended this situation.

The historian Selânikî described Mehmed III's enthronement in 1595, and a summary of his description will serve to show the manner of accession to the throne. When Murâd III died the vâlide sultan hid the fact and, secretly, sent word to her son Mehmed, then governor in Manisa. Mehmed hastened to Istanbul, and when he entered the Palace a cannon salute announced to the city the new sultan's accession. A command sent to the mosques ordered that Mehmed's name be mentioned in the hutbe. All dignitaries of state were summoned to the Palace, and after prayers they took the ceremonial oath of allegiance to the sultan. While the sultan, dressed in mourning, sat on a throne before the Gate of Felicity at the entrance to the Inner Palace, the çavuşes saluted him, crying 'My Sultan, may you and your realms endure a thousand years.' The dignitaries of state, the ulema and commanders of the kapïkulu divisions, one by one came forward and offered their allegiance, prostrating themselves before the throne. Then the sultan retired and changed his mourning clothes. He was present at his father's obsequies and burial. Members of the late sultan's family – twenty-seven daughters, seven pregnant concubines, and concubines with whom the late sultan had shared his bed – were removed to the Old Palace together with their tutors and eunuchs. The officials who had accompanied the new sovereign from Manisa received most of the important functions in the palace. Three days after accession, 1,300,000 gold ducats, drawn for the traditional accession gratuity from the Inner Treasury, were distributed to the sultan's army, 550,000 ducats going to the Janissaries. (After the enthronement of Selîm II each Janissary had received two thousand akçes and each of the sultan's cavalry a thousand akçes as an accession gratuity.) The senior pages of the Inner Service received posts outside the palace. To show himself to his subjects the sultan attended the Friday prayer at the mosque of Hagia Sophia.

A new government was established. The sultan appointed Ferhâd Pasha grand vizier, replaced the *defterdârs* – the heads of the Treasury Department – and made his tutor a vizier. Two weeks after his succession the new sultan, accompanied by the ministers of the realm, proceeded in state up the Golden Horn to the tomb of Eyyûb Ensârî, a Companion of the Prophet, there to be girt with the Sword of Osmân. Sacrificial sheep were distributed to the poor. Returning by land, the sultan visited the tombs of his ancestors Selîm I, Mehmed II, Prince Mehmed, Süleymân I and Bâyezîd II. The recital of prayers and the distribution of alms concluded the coronation ceremonies.

With the *bîat* – the oath of allegiance – the sultan was considered legally enthroned. The bîat, an old Islamic institution, signified the recognition of a new caliph and a solemn promise of obedience by a group representing the community of Muslims. A new Ottoman sultan informed foreign rulers of his accession in bombastic letters, and the *fermâns*, which he sent to the governors and kâdîs in his empire, usually contained the formula:

With God's help, I have gained the sultanate. On this date, with the perfect concurrence of the viziers, ulema, and people of all stations, high and low, I have ascended the throne of the sultanate that has come down to me from my forefathers. The hutbe has been recited and coins struck in my name. As soon as you receive this decree, proclaim my enthronement to the people in all cities and towns, have my name mentioned in the hutbes in the mosques, have cannon salutes fired from the citadels, and festively illumine the cities and towns.

Then all diplomas of title were renewed in the name of the new sultan and a general cadastral survey was ordered, showing the sources of taxation throughout the empire, the legal status of all subjects, and their tax-exemptions.

Various powerful factions within the empire, such as the frontier forces, the Janissaries, the ulema or Palace cliques, were instrumental in the selection of who was to occupy the throne. The ahîs in the period when the empire had been a frontier principality, and the frontier lords during the interregnum of 1402–13, had been important in this respect. Later, Murâd II's uncle and brother were to challenge him for the throne but the young Murâd, through the support of the Janissaries and the influential Şeyh Emir Sultan of Bursa, and through his winning over the frontier lords, defeated his two rivals. In 1446 the Janissaries, at the instigation of the grand vizier, Halîl Pasha, forced Mehmed II to abdicate but Murâd returned to the throne only when convinced that this was the wish of the Janissaries. In 1481 the Janissaries, acting on the orders of Ishâk Pasha and Gedik Ahmed Pasha, were instrumental in placing Bâyezîd II on the throne, forcing him to accept a number of conditions for the administration. During the struggle for the throne in 1511 each of the princes sought to win the Janissaries to his cause with promises of increased salaries. Although the sultan and the grand vizier preferred Prince Ahmed, it was Selîm, who had the support of the Janissaries, who finally forced his father to abdicate and seized the throne.

To preserve their authority, sultans and grand viziers had to gain the good-will of the Janissaries, whom only strong-willed sultans such as Mehmed the Conqueror or Selîm I could effectively control. On the other hand, grand viziers such as Çandarlı Halîl, Gedik Ahmed or Yemişçi Hasan, who had the support of the Janissaries, could exercise unchallenged authority.

With the institution of the kafes, the Janissaries came to be tools in the intrigues of the vâlide sultan and the *harem ağası* – the chief black eunuch of the Palace – and the grand viziers became the playthings of these two forces. From the seventeenth century the *şeyhülislâms* and the ulema often made common cause with the Janissaries, gaining the power to overthrow viziers and sultans. To give their revolts a semblance of legality, the Janissaries needed the şeyhülislâm's fetvâ. The şeyhülislâm was sometimes merely an instrument in these power struggles but their fetvâs usully reflected public opinion. The deposition of Sultan Ibrahîm (1640–48) is a case in point.

Ibrahîm came to the throne after long imprisonment in the kafes, and to demonstrate his authority he began to issue excessively arbitrary commands. The crisis in the Venetian war and his mad excesses turned public opinion against the sultan and stirred the Janissaries into revolt. With the şeyhülislâm at their head, the ulema went to the mosque of Sultan Ahmed, and joining forces with the rebels took the government into their own hands and chose a grand vizier. The vâlide sultan in the Palace had no choice but to support the insurgents. Going to the Palace, the ulema invited Ibrahîm to abdicate. In a fetvâ they accused him of violating the şeriat, of devotion to his own pleasures to the neglect of affairs of state, of tolerating corruption, of inaction in the face of the enemy, of unlawfully seizing the wealth of merchants, of unjust executions and allowing the harem to influence government. They claimed that in Islamic law these offences rendered Ibrahîm ineligible as caliph (Mehmed ıv, Ahmed ııı and Selîm ııı were later accused and deposed in the same manner). With the cooperation of the vâlide sultan they placed Ibrahîm's seven-year-old son on the throne as Mehmed ıv. Ibrahîm resisted, crying out to the şeyhülislâm who had deposed him, 'Did I not appoint you to this high office'. The şeyhülislâm replied, 'No, God appointed me.' The sultan turned for help to the ağa of the Janissaries, who merely told him that all the people had turned against him; Ibrahîm was left imprecating, 'Oh my God, suppress these tyrants. They have united against me and rebelled.' They confined him to a narrow room in the Palace and later obtained from the şeyhülislâm a fetvâ approving his execution, since they feared that Palace officials might try to bring him to the throne once more. The ulema came to the Palace again, where the courtiers, wishing to have no part in the matter, wept and took flight. With the Koran in his hand, Ibrahîm cried out, 'Behold! God's book! By what writ shall you murder me?' The executioners hesitated in carrying out the order, but urged by the ulema finally strangled the sultan with the bowstring.

CHAPTER IX

THE OTTOMAN CONCEPT OF STATE AND THE CLASS SYSTEM

As the empire developed, the Ottoman concept of state changed accordingly. We have already shown how the Ottomans extended the concept of frontier gazâ – the empire's fundamental and unchanging principle – and it is natural that a state which considered the defence and extension of Islam as its most important function should meticulously observe the şerîat. When the empire was still a frontier principality, governmental and legal affairs were in the hands of ulema who had come from the sophisticated centres of the hinterland. The first Ottoman viziers were from the ulema, and Ottoman documents from the first half of the fourteenth century show that already in this period the bureaucratic traditions of near-eastern states had found a place in Ottoman administration and were to become increasingly dominant towards the end of the century. In the early fifteenth century an anonymous chronicle, written in accordance with the traditions of the frontier, severely criticized the bureaucratic developments of Bâyezîd ı's era – the application of registration and accounting systems, a financial policy aimed at increasing Treasury revenue, and the adoption of the kul-slave-system. In this period, administrators came from old Seljuk centres in Anatolia and from Iran and Egypt, firmly implanting ancient near-eastern concepts of statecraft and administration in this new and rapidly developing empire. This concept of state had developed in the pre-Islamic period and passed to the Abbasid caliphate through the employment of Persian and Christian scribes. Modified between the eleventh and thirteenth centuries by the Turco-Mongol traditions of central Asia, it passed to the Ottomans.

According to the Arab historian Tabarî,[1] the Sassanid king, Peroz (459–84), when accused of reducing the people to poverty by heavy taxation, replied, 'After God, it is wealth and troops which support the ruler and ensure his strength.' Chosroes ı (531–79 AD) expressed a different opinion: 'With justice and moderation the people will produce more, tax revenues will increase, and the state will grow rich and powerful. Justice is the foundation of a powerful state.' A work entitled

65

Kutadgu Bilig,[2] written in 1069 for the Turkish ruler of the Karakhanids in central Asia, expresses this same concept of state, which was to find its way into all Islamic works on political theory: 'To control the state requires a large army. To support the troops requires great wealth. To obtain this wealth the people must be prosperous. For the people to be prosperous the laws must be just. If any one of these is neglected the state will collapse.'

Justice, in this theory of state, means the protection of subjects against abuse from the representatives of authority and in particular against illegal taxation. To ensure this protection was the sovereign's most important duty. The fundamental aim of this policy was to maintain and strengthen the power and authority of the sovereign, since royal authority was regarded as the corner-stone of the whole social structure.

The need to increase the state's revenues and power required the reign of justice, which the Sassanid kings and Muslim caliphs dispensed in a number of ways. The sovereign could at fixed times convene an imperial council, where surrounded by his high officials he would listen to the complaints of the people against the authorities and pass immediate judgement. If he was hunting or on campaign he could receive the written complaints of the people. Or he could send secret agents to the provinces to investigate cases of oppression, every oriental government maintaining as one of its basic institutions an elaborate secret service. More dramatically to display this form of justice, the Sassanid rulers used for two days in every year to stand as ordinary persons before the Great Magi – the religious leader – and hear any grievances against their rule. A thousand years later we find the same institution maintained by the Seljuk sultans of Anatolia, who for one day a year would go to the kâdî's court of justice in the capital. If there was any plaintiff against the Sultan, he would stay before the kâdî.

An early Ottoman folk epic in the gâzî tradition reflects the same concept of state. The dervish Sarï Saltuk advises Osmân Gâzî; 'Be just and equitable; do not provoke the curses of the poor; do not mistreat your subjects ... keep watch over your kâdîs and governors. Act justly, so that you may stay in power and retain the obedience of your subjects.' The Ottomans received this concept of state in a form modified since the eleventh century by the Turco-Mongol traditions of the Seljuk and Ilkhanid empires.

The Persian traditions of state regarded justice as a grace and favour of the sovereign's absolute authority, and the equity of the government as depending ultimately on the sovereign's ethical qualities. The Turkish traditions of central Asia, on the other hand, regarded justice as the impartial application of the *törü* or *yasa* – a code of laws which the founder of the state had established. Sovereignty and törü are two inseparable concepts. According to the Gök-Türk inscriptions, written in 735 AD, the ideal government is one administered in accordance with the törü. Even after their conversion to Islam, the Mongol khans of Iran reverently preserved in a special depository Genghis Khan's yasa – code – seeking its guidance in affairs of state.

The ancient Turkish traditions of state, adapted to life in the steppes, also took a different attitude to finance and taxation. *Kutadgu Bilig*[3] gives this advice to the sovereign: 'Open your treasury and distribute your wealth. Make your subjects rejoice. When you have many followers, make Holy War and fill your treasury' for 'the concern of the common people is always with their bellies . . . Do not withhold their food and drink.' The eighth-century Gök-Türk inscriptions express the same view, and Turkish sovereigns regarded it as their duty to offer their subjects, as a symbolic gesture, huge outdoor banquets. Sovereigns who did not hold these feasts were held in low esteem. Old Ottoman sources relate that in the Ottoman Palace 'at the time of the afternoon prayer, the band played so that the people might come and eat.' The royal kitchens dispensed food to anyone who came to the Palace. Mehmed the Conqueror's grand vizier is quoted as saying that 'the state must amass wealth, but the ruler must act lawfully so as not provoke his troops by withholding money from them.' Thus the Ottoman concept of state, while basically derived from the ancient near east, perpetuated certain old Turkish traditions.

The old Indo-Persian *Mirror for Princes* literature usually likens the sovereign to a shepherd and his subjects to a flock. God entrusts the subjects to the shepherd so that he may protect them and guide them on the right path, and absolute obedience to this sovereign is the duty of the subjects.

The Ottoman sultans, like all Islamic rulers, considered their subjects, Muslim or non-Muslim, as reâyâ – meaning 'flock' – and their fermâns frequently reiterate that God had given them the reâyâ in trust. It was the sultan's duty as head of the Islamic community to lead the reâyâ along the path of the şerîat, the path of God's decree. The theory of the caliphate as propounded by Muslim jurists is in many respects the same as the ancient near-eastern theory of state; but in making the observance of the şerîat a principal duty of the sovereign it wrought a fundamental change in near-eastern concepts. The aim of government was now to realize the ideals of Islam and authority ceased to be an end in itself. In practice, however, Islamic governments adhered to the older traditions of the near-eastern state which the bureaucrats, who effectively controlled the government, always perpetuated. In the second half of the fifteenth century, an Ottoman bureaucrat and historian, Tursun Bey, wrote that:

Government based on reason alone is called sultanic *yasak*; government based on principles which ensure felicity in this world and the next is called divine policy, or şeriat. The Prophet preached şeriat. But only the authority of a sovereign can institute these policies. Without a sovereign men cannot live in harmony and may perish altogether. God has granted this authority to one person only, and that person, for the perpetuation of good order, requires absolute obedience.[4]

Tursun Bey equates the state with the absolute authority of the sovereign and regards justice as essential for its endurance. State and society rest upon law and justice, which Tursun Bey defines as observing moderation in all things and ending oppression. A society without justice cannot survive.

The fundamental principles of the near-eastern theory of state had thus remained unchanged down to Ottoman times, despite the influence of the şeriat and of Greek political thought. Ottoman administration was based on these principles, which are evident in all its government offices and in all its state activities.

Six articles attributed to the Sassanid King Chosroes I summarizes the principles of equitable government.[5] These were to levy taxes according to the peasant's capacity to pay and to prevent abuses in their collection; to prevent the privileged oppressing the weak and interfering with the lives and property of the people; to guard the public highways, to construct caravanserais and bridges and to encourage irrigation; to form an army; to appoint just governors and judges to the provinces; and to prevent attack by foreign enemies.

To fulfil these duties the Sassanids established four branches of the administration – the political branch, the Judiciary, the Treasury and the Chancery – but the most important part of government was the sovereign's assembling the imperial council to hear complaints against the authorities and to rectify injustices. These basic functions of the near-eastern state remained unchanged down to the time of the Ottoman Empire.

The same concepts regulated the class system in the near-eastern state. Society fell into two distinct divisions: first, the ruler and the ministers and governors to whom he delegated his authority, and secondly, the taxpayers, the reâyâ. Nasîr al-Dîn of Tus (1201–74), following the old Persian traditions, further divided the ruler's servants into two groups – the military class, who held political power, and the bureaucrats. These groups did not pay taxes. The tax-payers were subdivided, according to their economic activity, into farmers, merchants or herdsmen, to which some added the urban artisans. '*Kalîlah and Dimnah*', a work of Indian origin maintained that if this division of the classes were not rigidly maintained disaster and anarchy would ensue. According to Nizâm al-Mulk's *Siyâsetnâme*,[6] a twelfth-century manual of statecraft, the government could prevent anarchy only by each person's remaining within his own class as recorded in official registers. Supporting his view with quotations from the Koran and the Traditions of the Prophet, the Muslim jurist Ibn Taymiyya (1263–1328) sought to incorporate this view of social stratification into the şeriat.

The Ottomans maintained the same class divisions, dividing the peoples of a newly conquered region, Muslim or non-Muslim, into the military class and the reâyâ. In the Balkans in the fifteenth century they accepted thousands of Christian cavalrymen into the military class despite their religion. Military groups in the Anatolian principalities annexed to the empire similarly received the privileges of the Ottoman military class; but those engaged in trade and agriculture, whether Christian or Muslim, in the Balkans or Anatolia, were considered reâyâ and paid reâyâ taxes.

The military class comprised all who were directly in the sultan's service, all military groups not engaged in production, men of religion and bureaucrats, and their families, relatives, dependents and slaves. A class known as the 'exempted reâyâ' received certain tax exemptions and privileges in return for particular services to the state.

Release from reâyâ status and entry into the military class required a special and rarely granted decree from the sultan. For the son of a peasant to enter the military class he normally had to have certain connections with that class or to fight as a volunteer on the frontier or in the sultan's campaigns. In appreciation of his services the sultan could issue a diploma granting him military status. Süleymân 1, however, revoked the tax exemptions formerly granted to those who had entered the military class in this way and not by descent from military ancestors. For a man to pass from reâyâ to military status was considered a breach of the fundamental principles of state, since the reâyâ were essential as producers and tax-payers. Ottoman writers of the early seventeenth century regarded the abandoning of this principle as the main cause of the empire's decline.

CHAPTER X

LAW: SULTANIC LAW (KÂNÛN) AND RELIGIOUS LAW (ŞERÎAT)

According to Tursun Bey, writing in the late fifteenth century, the sultan could make regulations and enact laws entirely on his own initiative. These laws, independent of the şerîat and known as *kânûn*, were based on rational and not religious principles and were enacted primarily in the spheres of public and administrative law.

Some Islamic jurists, including Ibn Khaldûn, considered kânûn – law based solely on the sultan's decree – unnecessary, maintaining that the şerîat – the religious law of Islam – could solve all legal problems. Other jurists maintained that kânûn was both necessary and legal, provided that the şerîat made no statement on the case in question; that the law conformed to a generally accepted custom or principle that could serve as a basis for analogy; that it was necessary for the welfare of the Islamic community; that the sovereign could effectively enforce the law; and that it contained nothing contrary to the şerîat.

The preface to the kânûnnâme, attributed to Süleymân I but actually codified towards the end of the fifteenth century, states that 'the sultan has commanded the codification of Ottoman kânûn, since these regulations are essential for prosperity in the affairs of the world and for the regulation of the affairs of the people.'[1]

With the spread of Turkish rule in the mid-eleventh century, the principle of kânûn became firmly established in Islamic legal practice, since in Turkish tradition, sovereignty and the establishment of a royal code of laws – törü – were intimately related. Furthermore, rulers did not wish to recognize any limitation to their political authority. Kânûn was already an established principle in the near east, in the period immediately before the rise of the Ottomans.

Ottoman kânûn originated as fermâns – 'Whatever the sultan decrees is the sultan's law' – and was thus a set of regulations which individual sultans had issued as circumstances required. They had, therefore, to be confirmed whenever a new ruler came to the throne. The fundamental and immutable law was the şerîat, the religious law of Islam. Fermâns always contained a formula stating that the enactment conformed with the şerîat and previously established kânûn.

There were three categories of kânûn. First, there were decrees, in the character of laws, which sultans had issued on specific topics. Scattered collections of documents contain thousands of these legal decrees, which constitute the bulk of Ottoman kânûn. Secondly, there were decrees which concern a particular region or social group.[2] Thirdly, there were general kânûnnâmes applicable to the whole empire.

The central government, usually in response to administrative problems or needs, issued most of these laws, which secretaries formulated as fermâns. After checking and initialling these documents, the grand vizier and the *nişancı* formally presented them to the sovereign and after his oral or written confirmation they became law. The same procedure was followed in the issuance of all laws, regardless of who proposed them in the first place. There are, however, some rare instances where the sultan promulgated laws directly, without the intermediate steps. The compilation of a kânûnnâme, or the exposition of a point of law, was always within the nişancı's sphere of competence.

Tax and population surveys in particular gave rise to suggestions for new laws. When the Ottomans undertook such a survey in a newly conquered region, their first step was to ascertain the pre-conquest laws and customs of the area. They did not seek to annul all the laws, customs and institutions of conquered territory but preferred to maintain many local usages, hoping thereby to avoid the unrest that might follow the sudden introduction of a new system. Furthermore, experience had taught them that drastic change brought a decrease in tax revenues. In these areas the commissioner of the survey merely abolished those practices which were contrary to the şerîat and Ottoman legal principles. The others he recorded and forwarded to the capital for the sultan's approval. In later surveys, alterations might be made or Ottoman laws replace the old regulations. After the conquest of eastern Anatolia in 1517–18, and of Iraq in 1537, the Ottomans preserved the laws of the Akkoyunlu ruler, Uzun Hasan. They similarly maintained the laws of the Mamlûk sultan, Kayitbay, in Egypt and Syria. After 1540, however, typically Ottoman regulations replaced the Akkoyunlu code. Although the tax regulations for Hungary in the second half of the sixteenth century were essentially Ottoman, some of the principal taxes were nevertheless survivals or adaptations from the times of the Hungarian kings. After the conquests of Cyprus and Georgia, as had largely been the case in Hungary, Ottoman laws were immediately introduced. However, it is certain that in the earlier periods local practices had held a more prominent place in the Ottoman regulations and, indeed, had had a great influence in the development of the typically Ottoman kânûn.[3]

71

The Ottomans also preserved, unchanged from the pre-conquest period, regulations governing the status of certain groups. In Serbia and Bosnia, the old Ottoman mining statutes, and decrees concerning the organization of the Vlachs, were exact translations of the earlier native laws. When in the mid-sixteenth century the region was no longer on the frontier, the Vlachs became subject to the normal Ottoman reâyâ laws.[4]

The commissioner of a survey could write to the sultan, recommending the abolition or revision of a law, showing due cause. The need for this usually arose from the complaints of the local population or from the need to increase revenue. If the sultan accepted the proposals and issued a fermân, the laws of the region would be amended accordingly. The new surveys were thus crucial in establishing and modifying the legal regulations of a region.

There was a survey register for each *sanjak*[5] – the principal administrative unit of the Ottoman Empire – and from the time of Bâyezîd II it became customary to preface each of these registers with the kânûn-nâme of that sanjak, according to which local disputes could be settled. The main purpose of the sanjak kânûnnâmes was to show the rates and manner of collection of the taxes in the timars. In this connection they described the laws of land-tenure and transfer, and the legal status and exemptions of the reâyâ. Less frequently they included separate lists showing the market and customs dues in the cities. They rarely contained criminal laws or laws governing the status of the military class.

Although each sanjak had its own regulations, they all conformed in their essentials to the kânûn-i osmânî. There was in fact a legal system peculiar to the Ottomans, and fundamental to the régime, and the Ottomans considered any customs contrary to this system as unjust innovations. The two kânûnnâmes of Mehmed the Conqueror systematized this body of law – the kânûn-i osmânî – for the first time.

The first of these compilations, issued immediately after the conquest of Constantinople, concerns the reâyâ. The first section contains a code of criminal law applicable to all reâyâ, but the section regulating taxation treats Muslims and Christians separately. It deals primarily with the taxes due from the reâyâ to timar-holders, systematizing them, in conformity with the survey registers, as reâyâ taxes, tithes, labour services and, finally, market dues. This kânûnnâme is a codification of laws which had been in force up to the time of Mehmed the Conqueror and it is therefore natural to find in it strong local influences.

The Conqueror's second kânûnnâme of about 1476 dates from the last years of his sultanate and concerns state organizations. The nişancï who compiled it wrote in the introduction that he had, by royal command, collected the laws of the sultan's forefathers and that the sultan himself had made several additions. Mehmed's written order at the beginning of the work confirms the codification and, at the end, he wrote, 'This far has the state been ordered. Let my sons who follow me strive for its improvement.' The kânûnnâme shows the chief officials of the government and Palace, together with their powers, promotions, ranks, salaries and pensions, protocols and punishments. It strongly reflects the concept of the sultan as the centre of government and the source of all authority, with a system of protocol based on the degree of proximity to the sultan as its framework. These concepts and forms are entirely Turco-Islamic and not, as has sometimes been thought, Byzantine.[6]

Apart from these two general kânûnnâmes, the Conqueror issued a number of legislative decrees concerned with mining, the circulation of coin, the mint, customs, monopolies and the collection of certain taxes, and regulations governing the status of certain groups.[7] These laws and regulations, which remained in force with minor revisions until the seventeenth century, display strong local influences.

Although later additions and modifications widened its scope, the Conqueror's kânûnnâme governing the status of the reâyâ remained the nucleus of the kânûn-i osmânî. The first major additions must have been made before 1501, in the time of Bâyezîd II.

The fundamental principles of the kânûn-i osmânî had been formulated by the end of the fourteenth century, even before their codification in the kânûnnâme of Mehmed the Conqueror and the sanjak kânûnnâmes of Rumelia and Anatolia. In the sixteenth century the kânûnnâmes for the beylerbeyiliks of Anatolia and Rûm (Amasya-Sivas) were extended to include the provinces of eastern Anatolia, Syria, Cyprus and Georgia. The sanjak kânûnnâmes of Rumelia similarly formed the basis of legislation in Hungary.

According to the late fifteenth century kânûnnâmes, the basic principle of the kânûn-i osmânî was that 'the reâyâ and the land belong to the sultan'. Thus no one had any right or could exercise any authority over the land and peasantry without a specific mandate from the sultan. This principle secured the sultan's absolute sovereignty in the empire, eventually eliminating all forms of legal lordship in the provinces. It allowed him to establish the timar system and to exercise some control over vakîfs and private estates. It was in fact the cornerstone of the autocratic and centralizing Ottoman regime.

The kânûn-i osmânî, in principle, condemned forced labour and services, commuting them in most cases for cash levies. It introduced a system of taxation which was in general simpler and less liable to abuse than the earlier systems of feudal services.[8] Emergency provisions were to be levied and forced labour exacted only when this was in the imperial interest and only after the sultan had issued a special decree; at all other times the functionaries bought provisions from the reâyâ at market prices. These regulations aimed to prevent the military class oppressing the peasantry and, therefore, assessment according to means and collection according to law were the governing principles of the tax system. The kânûn-i osmânî attached great importance to the establishment of the rate of each tax and the time and manner of its collection, and contained provisions to prevent the collection of a tax twice under different names. It exempted unpaid priests, the aged and infirm, and women and children.

The criminal code was applicable throughout the empire. It was a code of kânûn, which the kâdîs administered, supplementing the şerîat. For severe crimes, such as murder, rape, robbery with violence or highway robbery, it prescribed execution or mutilation and forbade the public authorities to accept money fines in their place. Separate chapters deal with adultery, physical assault, wine-drinking and various categories of theft, prescribing as punishments fines or the bastinado. The penal code was drawn up according to principles such as the *lex talionis*, which also formed the basis of şerîat law, and fixed fines and punishments which the şerîat did not clearly prescribe. For example a horse-thief had his hand amputated, or paid an equivalent fine, fixed at two hundred akçes – about five gold ducats. For wine-drinking, the kâdî decreed a certain number of bastinado blows and the sultanic law fixed a fine. Adulterers were fined according to their means – three hundred akçes for the rich, two hundred akçes for the middle-income group, and one hundred akçes for the poor. For illegal sexual relations, unmarried persons were fined one hundred, fifty, forty or thirty akçes, according to their means.

The usual forms of corporal punishment were amputation of a hand or leg, condemnation to the galleys and the bastinado. Beatings or, in their place, money fines, were the penalties for minor crimes. The authorities used torture to force criminals to confess and deaths from torture were not subject to inquiry. If a criminal was not found the whole community, such as a village, could be punished. The severity of the punishment varied according to whether the guilty party was male or female, free or slave, married or unmarried, Muslim or non-Muslim, the second member of each of these pairs paying half the amount of the fine.

The imperial council in the capital, or councils under the presidency of the head of the military organization to which they belonged, tried members of the military class. On matters concerning public order the sultan, his viziers or other representatives of his authority could impose sentences or grant pardons unrestricted by the kânûnnâme. A bloodless execution by the bowstring was reserved for members of the dynasty and high-ranking officials.

Ottoman law attached great importance to precedent and gave wide discretionary powers to the judges, whom fermâns frequently instruct simply to act in accordance with 'the law that is customarily applied'. The kânûnnâme of Silistra, dating from the period of Süleymân I, states that:

In a situation concerning which the kânûnnâme contains no clear, written command, the kâdî should officially refer the matter to the capital. Acting in accordance with the command that arrives, he should make a decision solving the problem. He should record this decision in his register and act according to it in similar situations.

The sultan's official diploma appointed the kâdîs to administer and execute both şerîat and kânûn. They had at their disposal collections of sultanic kânûn, which did not have to be officially certified copies. The kâdîs merely recorded in their official registers the legislative orders which they had received and with which they were required to act conformably. They could if they wished indicate these modifications in the copies of the kânûnnâmes in their possession. Ottoman law was thus in a state of continuous development, and the hundreds of annotated kânûnnâmes that have come down to us are a valuable source for its history.

No accused person could be punished without the kâdîs written judgement. The enforcement of sentences was the sole right of the beys, but without the kâdî's judgement they could not exact even the smallest money fine. The law even required that kapïkulus, come to administer a punishment on the sultan's orders, should bring the accused into the kâdî's presence and obtain his judgement.

In civil law cases within the scope of the şerîat, even the sultan had to respect the kâdî's decisions. For example, in inheritance cases where there were no apparent heirs the inheritable property remained in the hands of the executor for one year and the Treasury could claim it only after this period. The kâdî recorded and held for safe keeping the property of any deceased non-Muslim foreigner until an heir appeared. The law forbade the Treasury to confiscate such property.

This is a description of the ideal forms of Ottoman law. The sultans, in fact, had sometimes to issue *adâletnâmes* – rescripts redressing the malpractices of provincial authorities. These deal most frequently with cases where kâdîs and other officials had imposed forced labour or unlawful levies of provisions on the reâyâ, or illegally increased the rates of fines and dues.

CHAPTER XI

THE PALACE

In the near eastern state the degree of proximity to the sovereign determined the importance of lands and persons. The provinces were the ruler's 'well-protected realms' and the city where he resided was 'the foot of his throne' or 'the abode of his sultanate'. His Palace was the source of all power, favour and felicity. Government was conducted at his gate and its officials were his slaves.

The Ottoman Palace in Istanbul, like those of Ctesiphon and Baghdad before it, gave brilliant expression to this idea. The Turks, like the Byzantines, never considered an imperial candidate to be the legitimate sovereign until he had secured the capital or the region believed to be the abode of sacred power. With the capture of Constantinople – the seat of the Byzantine emperors – Mehmed the Conqueror considered himself as the legitimate heir to the rulership of the Roman Empire, announcing, as he entered the city, 'Henceforth my throne is Istanbul'. He ordered the immediate construction of a Palace in the centre of the city on the site of the forum Tauri. From 1326 to 1402 Bursa in Asia, and from 1402 to 1453 Edirne in Europe, had been the Ottoman capitals. The new capital bridged the two continents.

The Palace was completed in 1455; but the Conqueror soon came to dislike it, feeling insecure in the midst of the city, and in 1459 commanded the construction of a new Palace on a promontory overlooking the Bosphorus and the Sea of Marmara. By 1464 the main part of the Palace was complete and by 1478 the surrounding walls. The new Palace formed almost a separate city, with gardens, hunting grounds and pavilions, and was for four centuries to remain the residence of the Ottoman sultans.

In plan the Palace resembled the old royal residence at Edirne, consisting of an Inner – *enderûn* – and Outer – *bîrûn* – section. Over the imperial council room was erected a tower called the 'Mansion of Justice', to symbolise the idea that the ruler should see all injustices committed against his subjects.

76

The sultan spent his private life in the Inner Palace, a wide courtyard which the harem and other apartments surrounded on all sides. All the services and organizations regulating the sultan's relations with the outside world occupied the second court. Joining the two courts was a portal called the 'Gate of Felicity' where the sultan received the people, dispensed justice, conducted government and observed ceremonies from a throne which was set up on these occasions. To the right of the 'Gate of Felicity' was the domed chamber where the imperial council met; behind it was the throne room where the sultan received state dignitaries and foreign ambassadors.

The sultan's Palace was the real centre of government. Governors, military commanders and all who exercised the royal authority came from the Palace and were the sultan's slave-servants. Thus the Palace was more than a royal residence. In it the sultan's slaves received a special education, after which they were appointed to the high offices of state. This system, known as the kul – slave – system, was the foundation stone of the Ottoman state. Writing in 1537, P. Giovio described a kul as 'one who, blindly and unquestioningly obeys the will and commands of the sultan'.

As in the Abbasid Empire and the Islamic sultanates in Egypt and Iran, the Ottomans, too, created a slave army and entrusted administrative positions to specially educated slaves, since the sultan, by delegating authority only to those who owed him unquestioning allegiance, assured his own absolute rule. 'He – the sultan – can elevate them and destroy them without danger.'

In ancient Iran the dominant Achaemenid tribes had possessed large slave armies, and the Turkish and Mongol rulers of central Asia employed the leaders of defeated tribes in their personal retinues.

The Ottomans adopted the slave system in an intelligent and thoroughgoing manner. Already in the 1430s the scholar Yazÿcïoğlu could write that a sultan could secure his position only by possessing a Treasury and slaves. At the beginning of the next century Ibn Kemâl was to note that since all the slaves in the sultan's service were equal, no one of them could dominate the other or covet the sultanate. In Europe, Machiavelli correctly observed that the Ottoman Empire was an absolute monarchy dependent on slavery.

Pre-Ottoman Islamic states used slaves mainly for military service. The bureaucracy, from whom the viziers were chosen, remained in the hands of native Muslims, particularly ulema. The Ottomans followed the same principle until the middle of the fifteenth century, when Mehmed the Conqueror began to delegate his royal authority mainly to slaves. His grand viziers were all of slave origin until the appointment of Nişancï Mehmed, a bureaucrat from an old Konya family, who appointed bureaucrats and members of the ulema to vizierates. On the death of the Conqueror, however, the Janissaries, incited by the old pashas of slave origin, murdered Nişancı Mehmed and dragged his corpse through the streets. They forced the new sultan to accept the condition that henceforth he would elevate only men of slave status to the grand vizierate.

In the fourteenth century most of these slaves had been prisoners-of-war, since according to the şerîat one-fifth of all prisoners-of-war were the property of the sultan. At the same time children of noble families in newly conquered regions were sometimes taken to the Palace as hostages. The slave markets were another source. According to one estimate, in the seventeenth century twenty thousand captives a year came into Istanbul alone. However, in the fifteenth and sixteenth centuries a levy on the sultan's subjects – the devşirme – provided most of the slaves and contemporary records show that this system was in operation already at the end of the fourteenth century.

In the sixteenth century, when a levy was to be made the sultan's fermân first appointed a commissioner and a Janissary officer for each district. Under the supervision of the local kâdî and sipâhî, at each village the commission summoned all male children between the ages of eight and twenty, and their fathers, choosing those children who appeared to be fit. The levy included only the children of Christian villagers engaged in agriculture, excluding urban children and any only child. The commission recorded each child's name and description in a register and sent the boys in groups of a hundred to a hundred and fifty to the ağa of the Janissaries in Istanbul.

An Ottoman source of the early seventeenth century[1] explains the exemption of Muslim Turks from the devşirme: 'If they were to become slaves of the sultan, they would abuse this privilege. Their relatives in the provinces would oppress the reâyâ and not pay taxes. They would oppose the sanjak beyis and become rebels. But if Christian children accept Islam, they become zealous in the faith and enemies of their relatives.' It was only in Bosnia that families converted to Islam provided children.

The government considered the devşirme as an extraordinary levy on the reâyâ, not as the enslavement of its own subjects. It was indeed a harsh measure, and although some families especially in poor, mountain districts, gave their children of their own accord, sources indicate that people usually sought to avoid the devşirme. There were levies every three to seven years, according to need. One source estimates the number of boys taken annually in the devşirme in the sixteenth century as a thousand; another source sets it at three thousand annually.

When the youths arrived in Istanbul the best of them were selected as *içoğlans* – pages – for the Palace, with the sultan himself sometimes presiding at the selection. The içoğlans then went to Palaces in Istanbul and Edirne to receive a special training, while the remainder were hired out, at one or two gold ducats, to Turkish villagers in Anatolia before entering the Janissary corps. According to Ottoman sources, Mehmed the Conqueror established this practice, which was intended to teach the boys the Turkish language and Turkish customs. Under the strict discipline of the eunuchs, for two to seven years the pages received instruction from their Palace tutors and then underwent a second selection, called *çikma*. The most able entered the service of the two chambers in the sultan's Palace – the Greater and the Lesser Chambers – while the remainder joined the kapïkulu cavalry divisions. In the sixteenth century there were as many as seven hundred pages in the two Chambers of the Palace. These continued their education, at the same time receiving instruction in horsemanship, archery, fencing, wrestling and jereed. Each one also learned the craft or fine art for which he showed an aptitude.

European observers record that the temperament and capabilities of each boy were carefully considered.[2] Those who showed an ability in the religious sciences prepared for the religious professions; those proficient in the scribal arts prepared for a career in the bureaucracy. The sultans, particularly Bâyezîd II who sometimes came to examine them personally, took a great interest in their education.

According to Menavino, who had himself been an içoğlan, the Palace education aimed to produce 'the warrior statesman and loyal Muslim who at the same time should be a man of letters and polished speech, profound courtesy and honest morals.' But its fundamental aim was to instil complete obedience and loyalty to the sultan. All means, Rycaut observed, were used to inculcate this ideal in the young men who were studying at the Palace school and destined to fill the highest offices of the empire. They learned that death in the sultan's service was the greatest blessing.

The *ak ağas* – white eunuchs of the Palace – strictly supervised and disciplined the pages. Every minute of the pages' day was regulated. They woke, slept, ate, rested and played at fixed times; they could not converse wherever and whenever they wanted; they were denied access to the world outside the Palace. They led bachelor lives, remaining in the Palace normally until they were twenty-five or thirty. Their every activity was controlled, infractions of rules bringing punishments suited to the offence – reprimand, bastinado, expulsion or death.

At the time of Selîm I there were forty ak ağas, serving under the *kapï ağasï* – the chief white eunuch – who was supervisor of the whole Palace and the sultan's absolute deputy there. He made recommendations to the sultan for all Palace appointments and promotions and was in his confidence in affairs of state. However, with the increasing influence of the Palace women, the harem ağasï – the black eunuch of the harem – became independent of and at times more powerful than the kapĭ ağasĭ.

The pages normally received four years training in one of the Chambers and then after another selection the most suitable went to the Chambers reserved for the personal service of the sultan while the remainder went to the cavalry units.

There were four Chambers in the sultan's service – the *hâs oda* (Privy Chamber), *hazîne* (Treasury), *kiler* (Larder) and *seferli oda* (Campaign Chamber). Pages graduating from the Lesser and Greater Chambers served in one of the last three Chambers, and could then after another review rise to the Privy Chamber. The forty pages of the Privy Chamber attended directly on the sultan, being responsible for his toilet, clothing and weapons, and standing guard at night. The *hâs oda başĭ* – the chief of the Privy Chamber – was the person closest to the sultan, never leaving his side. He was, after the kapĭ ağasĭ, the most important functionary in the Palace. In 1522 Süleymân I even elevated his hâs oda başĭ, Ibrahîm, to the grand vizierate.

Beneath the hâs oda başĭ in the Privy Chamber were the *silahdâr*, who accompanied the sultan with his sword; the *rikâbdâr*, the sultan's stirrup-holder; the *çuhadâr*, who kept the sultan's outer garments; the *dülbend oğlanĭ*, who kept his linen; and the *sĭr kâtibi*, his confidential secretary.

Sixty pages normally staffed the Treasury Chamber, which housed the sultan's valuables. The larder had a staff of thirty, raised to thirty-four after 1679, who prepared and served the sultan's meals. The Campaign Chamber was created in the early seventeenth century by bringing together in one Chamber laundrymen, bath-house attendants, barbers, musicians, singers and others. By 1679 this group totalled 134 people. After serving in these Chambers the most capable of the pages entered the Privy Chamber, while the others joined the sultan's cavalry.

The pages who finally graduated as senior ağas from the Privy Chamber were appointed to provincial governorships, to the direction of service groups in the Outer Palace, or to commanderships in the Janissaries or the sultan's cavalry. The pages in these Chambers numbered 80 in 1475, 488 in 1568, and 900 in 1612.

No matter whether the boys were in origin Greek, Serbian, Bulgarian, Albanian, Hungarian or Russian, they severed all ties with their past. In the Palace they received a thorough Muslim and Turkish education, their teachers all being Muslim Turks. Above all, they were slaves of the Ottoman sultan, forming around him an imperial group and completely dependent on him for all things. They did not consider Anatolian Turks or any other group as their equals. For them, as for the dynasty, Holy War was the highest ideal, a kind of uniting ideology.

The Outside Service comprised all the organizations regulating the sultan's relations with the outside world, comprising governmental and ceremonial offices and the sultan's standing army. The officers of the various groups were the *mîr alem*, the *kapîcî başî*, the *kapîcîlar kethüdâsî*, the *mîrahûr*, the *çakîrcî başî*, the *çaşnigîr başî*, and the *çavuş başî*. There were in addition the military commanders – the ağa of the Janissaries, the *siphâhî bölükleri ağalarî* – commanders of the sultan's cavalry divisions – the *cebeci başî* – chief armourer, and the *topçu başî* – chief gunner. The others are described below.

The mîr alem was custodian of the sultan's symbols of sovereignty – the standard, horse-tails, tents and military music. It was he who ceremonially presented newly appointed governors with the standard and horse-tails, symbolic of the sultan's authority. At the beginning of the seventeenth century he had 1,063 grooms serving under him, 835 of them as tent grooms.

The kapîcî başî – the chief gate-keeper – was commander of the gate-keepers who guarded the outer entrances to the Palace. This group, organized as military units, comprised five hundred men in 1510 and 2,007 in 1660. His lieutenant, the kapîcîlar kethüdâsî, together with the çavuş başî, had the duty of maintaining order and protocol at meetings of the imperial council. It was he who summoned and ushered the plaintiffs into the imperial council, and administered bastinado sentences. Under him came the commanders of the units, also known as kapîcî başîs. The government employed these on embassies; to convey orders to governors; as inspectors; and to administer punishments.

The mîrahûr and his assistant, the lesser mîrahûr, had responsibility for the animals, stables, carriages and sedan chairs, both inside and outside the Palace. His organization numbered 2,080 in 1540, rising to 4,322 by the beginning of the seventeenth century, and included among others grooms, saddlers, shoeing-smiths, veterinary surgeons and muleteers. In 1547 there was a sister organization in the provinces, employing several thousand people, and responsible for maintaining pasture land and breeding transport and riding animals.

The çakîrcî başî – the chief falconer – headed an organization responsible for the royal hunting birds. In addition to the three divisions in the Palace there was a large associated organization in the provinces. The reâyâ, who worked for this organization, were exempt from taxation in return for capturing and training falcons. In 1564 they numbered about 3,500.

The çaşnigîr başî – chief taster – and the men under him served meals to the members of the imperial council, who took breakfast and lunch in the council room, and waited at banquets given in the council room for foreign ambassadors.

Table 1

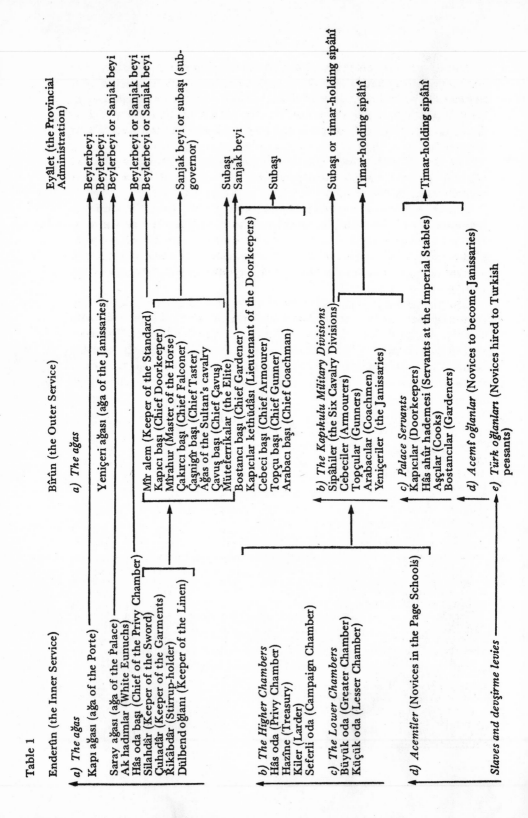

Enderûn (the Inner Service)

a) The ağas
Kapı ağası (ağa of the Porte)

Saray ağası (ağa of the Palace)
Ak hadımlar (White Eunuchs)
Hâs oda başı (Chief of the Privy Chamber)
Silahdâr (Keeper of the Sword)
Çuhadâr (Keeper of the Garments)
Rikâbdâr (Stirrup-holder)
Dülbend oğlanı (Keeper of the Linen)

b) The Higher Chambers
Hâs oda (Privy Chamber)
Hazîne (Treasury)
Kiler (Larder)
Seferli oda (Campaign Chamber)

c) The Lower Chambers
Büyük oda (Greater Chamber)
Küçük oda (Lesser Chamber)

d) Acemîler (Novices in the Page Schools)

Slaves and devşirme levies

Bîrûn (the Outer Service)

a) The ağas
Yeniçeri ağası (ağa of the Janissaries)

Mîr alem (Keeper of the Standard)
Kapıcı başı (Chief Doorkeeper)
Mîrahur (Master of the Horse)
Çakırcı başı (Chief Falconer)
Çaşnigîr başı (Chief Taster)
Ağas of the Sultan's cavalry
Çavuş başı (Chief Çavuş)
Müteferrikalar (the Elite)
Bostancı başı (Chief Gardener)
Kapıcılar kethüdâsı (Lieutenant of the Doorkeepers)
Cebeci başı (Chief Armourer)
Topçu başı (Chief Gunner)
Arabacı başı (Chief Coachman)

b) The Kapıkulu Military Divisions
Sipâhiler (the Six Cavalry Divisions)
Cebeciler (Armourers)
Topçular (Gunners)
Arabacılar (Coachmen)
Yeniçeriler (the Janissaries)

c) Palace Servants
Kapıcılar (Doorkeepers)
Hâs ahûr hademesi (Servants at the Imperial Stables)
Aşçılar (Cooks)
Bostancılar (Gardeners)

d) Acemî oğlanlar (Novices to become Janissaries)

e) Türk oğlanları (Novices hired to Turkish peasants)

Eyâlet (the Provincial Administration)

Beylerbeyi
Beylerbeyi
Beylerbeyi or Sanjak beyi
Beylerbeyi or Sanjak beyi
Beylerbeyi or Sanjak beyi
Sanjak beyi or subaşı (sub-governor)
Subaşı
Sanjak beyi
Subaşı
Subaşı or timar-holding sipâhî
Timar-holding sipâhî
Timar-holding sipâhî

The çavuş başỉ commanded the çavuşes, who numbered 300 in the sixteenth century and 686 in 1670. They oversaw discipline and protocol in meetings of the imperial council and Palace ceremonies; on campaign they supervised military discipline; they served on embassies and as couriers; they conveyed orders to the provinces and effected awards and dismissals.

The sons of pashas and vassal lords formed a separate group in the Outside Service known as *müteferrikas*, receiving a daily wage and participating in ceremonies with their dazzling uniforms.

These six officers, together with the ağa of the Janissaries and the commanders of the sultan's cavalry divisions, enjoyed the privilege of riding to campaign beside the sultan, and hence were known as 'ağas of the stirrup'. When they received posts outside the Palace they became sanjak beyis or beylerbeyis, while their retinues received timars in the provinces.

Groups of the second rank in the Outside Service included the gardeners who served in the Palace gardens in Istanbul, the cooks who worked in the Palace kitchens, tailors and other craftsmen. Tables 1 and 2 give an idea of the relative importance of these various groups.

Members of the various groups could at fixed intervals be promoted or transferred, at a çỉkma. In the sixteenth century, these promotions

TABLE 2 A COMPARISON OF THE PALACE ORGANISATIONS AT VARIOUS DATES

Year	1480	1568	1609	1670
The Janissaries	10,000 men	12,789 men	37,627 men	53,849 men
Acemî oğlanlar (Novices)	?	7,745	9,406	4,372
Bostancılar (Gardeners)	?	?	?	5,003
Cebeciler (Armourers)	?	789	5,730	4,789
Topçular (Gunners)	100	1,204	1,552	2,793
Top arabacılarî (Drivers of cannon-carriages)	?	678	684	432
Ahur hademeleri (Stable Boys)	800	4,341	4,322	3,633
Aşçilar (Cooks)	120–160	629	1,129	1,372
Ehl-i hiref (Craftsmen)	?	647	947	737
Terziler (Tailors)	200	369	319	212
Çadır mehterleri (Tent-pitchers)	200	620	871	1,078
Alem mehterleri (Standard-bearers)	100	620	228	102
Sipâh (Cavalry)	3,000	11,044	20,869	14,070
Kapıcılar (Doorkeepers)	400(?)	?	2,451	2,146
Kapıcı başıları (Head door-keepers)	4	?	?	83
Müteferrikalar (The Elite)	?	40	?	813
Çavuşlar (Pursuivants)	400	?	?	686
Tersâne neferleri (Arsenal employees)	?	?	2,364	1,003
Şikâr halkı (Hawkers)	200	?	592	?
Çaşnigîrler (Tasters)	20	?	?	21
Sakkâlar (Water-carriers)	?	25	?	30

and transfers took place every two to five years, and in the following century once every seven or eight years. At the accession of each new sultan there was a çĭkma involving most of the Palace staff. When Mehmed IV came to the throne in 1649 some three thousand pages were transferred. Table I is a diagram of transfers at the time of a çĭkma.

A detailed system of protocol and promotion established every person's place within this organization. Seniority was the general rule for promotion but it was possible for a person of outstanding ability to rise more rapidly. Each person received a daily stipend according to his rank. In the sixteenth century a novice in a Chamber received eight akçes daily, while the hâs oda başĭ received seventy-five. Clothes were distributed four times a year. Ağas who had reached a certain age retired on a pension.

Ağas who served as provincial governors gained experience and skill in administrative and military matters. The most distinguished of them could rise to become beylerbeyi of Rumelia, the senior provincial governorship, whence they could be promoted to the rank of vizier in the imperial council in Istanbul.

Lutfî Pasha, one of Süleymân I's grand viziers, described, in an autobiographical sketch, life in the Palace organizations :

The writer of this treatise is the weakest of God's slaves, Lutfî Pasha, son of Abdulmuîn. Through the bounty of the sultans, I, this humble one, was brought up in the Inner Palace from the time of the late Sultan Bâyezîd (whose abode is Paradise). At the threshold of this Ottoman dynasty, I was well disposed towards them for God's sake, and while I was in the Inner Palace I studied many kinds of science. On the accession of his Excellency Sultan Selîm, I left the post of çuhadâr and entered the Outside Service as a müteferrika with 50 akçes daily. Then the posts of kapĭcĭ başĭ, mîr alem, sanjak beyi of Kastamanu, beylerbeyi of Karaman and Ankara and, finally, in the time of our Sultan Süleymân, the posts of vizier and grand vizier were bestowed on me. When I, this humble and imperfect one, had left the Palace, I consorted with many ulema, poets and men of culture and sought to the utmost of my ability to refine my character with the acquisition of the sciences.

Lutfî Pasha's loyalty was typical. Until the seventeenth century a disobedient pasha was a rare exception and then, if the kapĭcĭ başĭ came with an order for his execution, he would perform his prayers and with resignation surrender his neck to the executioner, knowing that neither the local people nor the sultan's slaves in his suite would risk a hair on his behalf.

The slave system required all, including the sultan, to respect absolutely its rules and traditions, which received the same esteem as the kânûns of former rulers. Like the pages, the sultan himself studied with tutors on certain days of the week. He had meticulously to observe ceremony, customary usage determining even the words he had to use on certain occasions. Not even in the harem was he free. With the exception of such forceful men as Mehmed the Conqueror, Selîm I or Murâd IV, the Ottoman sultans were little more than cogs in a machine.

Pages in this over-regulated slave system attempted to make their own intelligence and capacity conspicuous among those of their equal, enduring the life in the hope that one day they would reap great rewards. Brought up in the belief that they laboured in God's path, they felt it their duty to make God's word reign in the world. These beliefs gave meaning to their lives.

The Palace staff followed the sultan on campaign, with no changes in its organization. The pages received weapons and horses, and each group in the Outside Service was in fact already organized as a military division. At the Battle of Mezökeresztes in 1596 the intervention at the last moment of the ten-thousand-strong Palace contingent decided the outcome of the battle.

From the time of Machiavelli the autocracies of Europe began to take an interest in the Ottoman slave system. In 1624 M.Baudier wrote that 'the order and method with which these youths are trained is proof that the Turks have retained nothing of barbarism but the name.' In describing the Ottoman slave system in 1688 Rycaut wrote of it as, 'if well considered and weighed, one of the most Politic Constitutions in the world, and none of the meanest supports of the Ottoman Empire'. Lybyer's view that this system perhaps developed under the influence of Plato's Republic is totally without foundation.[3]

The harem – the section reserved for the sultan's women and family – formed a Palace within a Palace, and was, as in every Turkish household, a private place, forbidden to all strangers. Its organization complemented the slave system, an aspect of its character forgotten amidst a proliferation of fanciful tales, and paralleled the page organization.

Women for the sultan's Palace were carefully selected from among prisoners-of-war, or from the slave markets. Women were not, however, subject to the devşirme. In 1475 there were 400 female slaves in the Topkapï Palace and 250 in the Old Palace, and these girls, like the pages, passed through a long period of education and training. When they first came to the Palace they lived together in two large rooms, the Greater and Lesser Chambers, and were known as *acemîs* – novices. Under the strict supervision of the *kâhya kadîn* – a woman superintendent – they grew up as refined and skilful women. They learned the principles of Islam, at the same time acquiring such skills as sewing, embroidery, dancing, singing, playing musical instruments, puppetry or story-telling, each according to her capabilities. The acemîs in time attained the ranks of *câriye*, *şâgird*, *gedikli* and *usta*. (It is worth noting that this hierarchy and the last three terms are the same as in the guild organizations, and were used also in the bureaucracy. It was the Ottoman practice that any skill or craft should be learned through an apprentice-master system.) In the same way as pages received promotion from the Larder to the Privy Chamber, the ustas too were selected from the ranks of the gediklis to perform a specific service for the sultan. Women from this group whom the sultan chose for his bed were distinguished with the title *hâs odalık* or *hâseki*.

Until the time of Süleymân I, Ottoman sultans also took the daughters of foreign rulers as canonically legal spouses. Süleymân contracted a religious marriage with the Russian slave-girl, Roxelana, known as Hurrem Sultan, but in the period between 1574 and 1687, when the influence of the vâlide sultans came to dominate the Palace, the sultans no longer contracted canonically legal marriages. The vâlide sultans themselves were not legal wives according to the şerîat. In the seventeenth century Osmân II and Ibrahîm I were the exceptions who contracted legal marriages. Nevertheless, four of the hâsekis – four being the canonically legal number of wives in Islam – were distinguished by the title of *kadın* and received special treatment.

A hâseki who bore the sultan's child received special privileges. Ceremonially crowned and dressed in sable, she went to kiss the sultan's hand, and a private apartment was set aside for her use. The first woman to give birth to a son took precedence over all the others, with the title *baş kadın*. The staff of the harem, like the pages, received a daily stipend and a clothing allowance, each group having its own special uniform. Women above the rank of usta adorned their clothes with fur.

The vâlide sultan had absolute authority within the harem, and the chief black eunuch – the harem ağası or *dârüssaâde ağası* – stood in the same relationship to her as the chief white eunuch – the kapı ağası – did to the sultan. As the influence of the vâlide sultans increased after 1574, so too did that of the chief black eunuch, who came eventually to be the most important officer in the Palace.

It is related that when the women in the harem heard the sultan's silver-nailed slippers they at once hid from sight, since it was an offence to meet him face to face. Any woman who disrespected the rules or the hierarchy of the harem was punished, since if a novice were to win the sultan's heart this would undermine the rights of the senior ustas and the authority of the vâlide sultan. The vâlide sultan herself carefully chose the ustas who were to consort with the sovereign. Tradition relates that in 1536 Roxelana, Süleymân's favourite wife, had the harem transferred from the Old to the New Palace, and henceforth

gained an increasing influence over the sultan and over affairs of
state.

Wishing to secure the throne for her own children, Roxelana con-
trived the execution of her rival's son, Mustafa. Some of the letters
which she wrote to Süleymân have survived in the Palace archives,
and in one of these she wrote:

My Lord, your absence has kindled in me a fire that does not abate. Take
pity on this suffering soul and speed your letter, so that I may find in it at
least a little consolation. My Lord, when you read my words, you will wish
that you had written more to express your longing. When I read your letter,
your son Mehmed and your daughter Mihrimâh were by my side, and tears
streamed from their eyes. Their tears drove me from my mind ... You ask
why I am angry with Ibrahîm Pasha. When – God willing -- we are together
again, I shall explain, and you will learn the cause.[4]

Most of the Palace girls went as wives to the pages when these left
the Palace for the outside services.

Finally, it should be noted that not only the sultan but all ranks of
the military class adopted the slave system. The sultan's palace provided a model for the residences of viziers and statesmen in the capital
and of governors in the provinces. The law required that in the provinces beylerbeyis, sanjak beyis, subaşїs, and even sipâhis in the villages
should maintain retinues in proportion to the income received from their
fiefs. To increase their influence some pashas maintained more than
the obligatory number of kapїkulus, Rüstem Pasha, for example,
having 1,700 slaves at the time of his death.

After a campaign pashas would recommend to the sultan the confer-
ment of timars on their slaves who had performed outstanding services.
The slave thus left the pasha's retinue to become a sipâhî. The pages
of some viziers were taken, on their master's death, directly into the
imperial Palace. Slaves belonging to persons of the military class also
had military status.

In Ottoman society, to be a slave of the sultan was an honour and
privilege, and in fact the translation of 'kul' as 'slave' is misleading.
Islamic law normally considered freedom as fundamental, and slave-
dom as a transitory condition. It regarded the manumission of slaves
as a meritorius act which religion encouraged. Canonically legal
marriage with a female slave was possible. Although the Turkish
traditions of family and tribal ties shaped Ottoman society in its
formative period, slaves gradually grew in importance. The mothers
and tutors of the Ottoman sultans usually had slave origins, and Ducas
reported that Murâd 11 treated his slaves as brothers[5]. Former owners,
however, still possessed certain rights over their manumitted slaves,
notably the right of inheritance, and this was an important factor in
the spread of the slave system. Merchants preferred to use their actual

or manumitted slaves as commercial agents, and kâdîs' registers indicate that manumitted slaves formed the richest and most influential group in the great Ottoman cities.

The slave system was important in cultural as well as in political and economic life. The Palace school produced artists and scholars as well as soldiers and administrators, and craftsmen working for the sultan created some of the finest and most original works of Ottoman civilization. The Palace was the principal creative source in Ottoman culture. The great architect Sinan (1490?–1588), for example, came originally as a devşirme boy from Kayseri. He received all his professional training in his many years' experience in the army and the architects' office at the Palace, eventually becoming the sultan's chief architect and author of many works throughout the Empire, including such masterpieces as the Süleymâniye and Selîmiye mosques in Istanbul and Edirne. There grew up in the Palace an Ottoman artistic style and aristocratic way of life which the sultan's slaves diffused to all corners of the empire.

Classical Ottoman literature and architecture developed as Palace arts. From the fifteenth century Palace architects erected buildings in a distinctive Ottoman style throughout the empire, from Konya to Sarajevo. Most poets and writers had some connection with the Palace; Bâyezîd II's account books show that about twenty poets regularly benefited from the sultan's largesse. Historiography received similar encouragement. Side by side with the folk histories, written in the early period in simple Turkish, Palace poets and writers in the service of Mehmed the Conqueror composed works in high literary Persian. It did not take long for Palace histories to appear, written in Turkish but imitating this ornate Persian style and, in time, a peculiarly Ottoman school of historiography came into being.

Ottoman culture remained essentially a Palace culture and became sterile for this reason. In the sixteenth century it reached its classical perfection, but confined to the service of the Palace and closed to outside influences it gradually lost its vitality.

CHAPTER XII

THE CENTRAL ADMINISTRATION

THE IMPERIAL COUNCIL (DÎVÂN-I HÜMÂYÛN) AND ITS MEMBERS

In the near-eastern state the administration of justice was considered the most important function of government. Although the great divan – the ancestor of the Ottoman *dîvân-i hümâyûn* – which met at fixed times to hear complaints of the people and set right injustices, was in origin a high court of justice, it was at the same time the supreme organ of government. This institution conformed with the near-eastern concept of state and had retained its importance since Sassanid times. In Seljuk Anatolia, the example closest to Ottoman practice, the sultan came twice a week to the great divan to hear the complaints of the oppressed. Cases within the scope of the şerîat were referred to the kâdî, while administrative matters were referred to members of the divan. Bâyezîd I's Egyptian physician, Shams al-Dîn, wrote:[1]

Early in the morning the Ottoman ruler would sit on a wide, raised sofa. The people stood some distance away, in a place whence they could see the sultan, and anyone who had suffered wrong would come to him and state his complaint. The case was judged immediately. Security in the land is such that nowhere will anyone touch a fully-laden camel whose owner has left it and departed.

Bertrandon de la Brocquière visited Murâd II's Palace in Edirne and describes how the divan assembled in that period:[2]

We passed through the first gate. The door opened inwards and was guarded by about thirty slaves, all armed with staves. Should any person wish to enter without permission, they warn him once to withdraw; if he persists, they turn him back with their staves ... When the said ambassador [of Milan] entered, they made him sit beside the gate. Whenever an ambassador arrives, which happens almost daily, 'il fait porte'. 'Faire porte' in France would be called 'to be received into the king's presence'. What we call the 'Court du Roy', the Turks call the 'Porte du Seigneur'. When the sultan entered he went to a side gallery, where his seat had been prepared. This was a kind of couch, upholstered in velvet and mounted by four or five steps.

He sat on this, according to their custom, in the manner of tailors when they are at work. Then the pashas, who had waited in another place beside the gallery, came and passed in front of the sultan. When they had entered the gallery, everyone else who customarily attended the divan took their places. They posted themselves along the walls of the gallery as far from the sultan as possible.

The term *kapı* or *dergâh-i âlî* – the Sublime Porte – referred originally to the place where the sultan heard suits and conducted governmental business, and eventually came to mean the Ottoman government.

In about 1475 Mehmed the Conqueror ceased to preside in person over meetings of the imperial council. However, since he could not neglect the sultan's fundamental duty of personally hearing complaints he had a grated window opened in the 'Mansion of Justice', overlooking the council chamber. Through this he could follow suits and discussions.

A western source described the window:[3]

There is, at the end of a secret gallery, a small square window which serves as a listening post. It is a wicker-work grille, with a curtain of crape or black taffeta, and is called the 'dangerous window', because the prince may, whenever he wishes, listen to and see all that takes place, without being seen and without anyone knowing whether he is there or not. It would be extremely dangerous to try to conceal or hold back anything, because in these sessions they discuss all kinds of business, public and private.

When the dignitaries had taken their places in the imperial council, complainants received permission to enter and business began. The imperial council always preserved its original character of a high court. Murâd III once left the listening post to take a seat in the council itself when he saw the people's affairs neglected; he thus assured that they received prompt attention. Ahmed I arranged that the council's deliberations should on some occasions take place in his presence and made the senior ulema attend the trial, in the imperial council, of Kâsim Pasha, who was accused of oppressing the people.

In the eighteenth century the imperial council ceased to meet in the Palace and transacted all governmental business in the grand vizier's residence. In 1766, however, Mustafa III commanded that it meet in the Palace at least once a week, since 'the imperial council was first established so that the sultan could hear the complaints of those who had suffered injustices'.

When going to the Friday prayer, riding to the hunt or setting out on campaign, the Ottoman sultans would listen in person to the complaints of the people, since 'the people should feel that the sultan is concerned with their welfare'. On the day of *nevrûz* – the vernal equinox – in 1591, when Murâd III was residing in his summer Palace on the sea-shore, a group of residents from Galata approached in their caiques and presented their complaint against the kâdî of Galata. The sultan at once dismissed the kâdî. (In ancient Iran the sovereigns held a great council on nevrûz, a sacred day, to hear the people's suits.)

Anyone, regardless of his social status, could petition the imperial council directly, and for important matters the reâyâ would send delegations to Istanbul. As a result, justice and security were greatest in the regions nearest the capital. In distant areas plaintiffs went to the court of the local kâdî, who recorded their grievances in his register and addressed a formal letter of complaint to the sultan or, if the case were urgent, sent a spokesman to Istanbul. The investigation of complaints and the rectification of grievances were considered the most important of the imperial council's duties. Complaints usually concerned the heavy burden of taxation, abuses in the collection of taxes, or oppression by the local authorities. The sultan sometimes sought to please the people with grandiose gestures, sweeping aside the formalities of law and disregarding the interests of the Treasury. Thus the people, whether they were Anatolian Turks or Balkan Christians, had to look upon the sultan as the highest representative of justice and as a symbol of mercy who could remove all injustices.

In 1661 a group of people in Denizli sent a delegation to Istanbul to complain of oppression by a local notable. But the members of the imperial council, influenced by the defendant, ignored the charges, until the plaintiffs cried, 'If justice is not done here, where else we go?' The sultan, listening from behind the curtain, ordered a special meeting of the imperial council for the next day. The plaintiffs were found to be in the right and the defendant was immediately executed.

Foreigners too had recourse to the sultan as a last resort. For example, in 1648, when the English wished to complain about the increase in customs duties and the viziers had denied them direct access to the sultan, they burned pitch in copper buckets attached to the masts of seven English ships so that the fires were visible from the Palace. The sovereign saw the fires and sent his çavuş başî to hear the complaint.

It was possible, too, to appeal to the imperial council against the decisions of local kâdîs. In this case, depending on its nature, the suit was referred to the same court for a re-hearing or transferred to another court in the same district. The imperial council heard directly complaints against government administrators.

In the execution of justice the sultan would often have recourse to other methods typical of the near-eastern state, including the despatch of inspectors and secret agents and the proclamation of adâletnâmes.

Sometimes a sultan would disguise himself and personally carry out inspections. Süleymân I used to dress as a sipâhî and Ahmed II as a *mevlevî* dervish, and thus disguised they would mingle with the people.

Murâd IV, on his incognito tours, had many trouble-makers mercilessly executed, hoping thereby to strengthen the people's confidence in the royal and his own authority.

A principal duty of the grand vizier was from time to time to check security in the capital and to inspect market prices, reporting the situation to the sultan. The sovereign kept the army and the provinces under scrutiny by secretly despatching palace slaves to gather information. In the provinces, however, the local kâdîs were usually empowered to carry out official inspections and were required to submit reports.

Adâletnâmes, another instrument of justice, were general declarations by the sultan, enumerating and forbidding under threat of severe punishment abuses which the authorities had perpetrated in a particular region or throughout the empire. They were publicly announced to the people and anyone who wished could obtain a copy from the kâdî.

Janissaries and sipâhîs, too, had the same rights of complaint, and would gather before the Palace to make known their grievances against the men of state. These protest gatherings sometimes even threatened the sultan's throne. When in 1588 the sipâhîs were paid in debased coin whose value had fallen by half, they obtained a fetvâ from the şeyhülislâm, proving this an injustice, and then went to the Palace to demand the death of Mehmed Pasha, the author of the financial reform. Listening at his curtained window the sultan heard this complaint and wished to ignore it, but when his ministers informed him that this would be too dangerous he ordered the execution of Mehmed Pasha and the chief defterdâr.

The use of force to obtain justice set a dangerous precedent. In 1632 the kapĭkulu troops rose in revolt and entered the Palace. A throne was set up before the Gate of Felicity, whence the sultan could hear the complaints of his troops. All the state dignitaries, ulema and military commanders stood about the sultan's throne to discuss the causes of the revolt, but the soldiers declared that the grand vizier was a traitor to the sultan and the state and cut him to pieces before the sovereign's eyes. This act was a violation of the sultan's authority since only he had the power to dispense high justice.

After Mehmed II had ceased to preside in person over the deliberations of the imperial council, the authority to review grievances and hear cases passed normally to the grand vizier, whom the *kâdîaskers* of Rumelia and Anatolia, also members of the imperial council, assisted in cases within the scope of the şerîat. After meetings of the imperial council, the sultan received the council members in the chamber behind the Gate of Felicity to approve and confirm their decisions. They entered his presence in a fixed order. The first to enter was the ağa of the Janissaries, followed after his departure by the kâdîaskers.

Next came the grand viziers and the other viziers, the defterdârs and the nişancĭ. The defterdârs left after reporting on financial affairs, leaving the grand vizier to give an account of the day's business and receive the sultan's confirmation of particularly important appointments and decisions.

In this same Chamber the sultan received foreign ambassadors and newly appointed governors, military commanders and kâdîs. At other times, whenever he wished to read an order directly, he wrote it in his own hand and sent it to the grand vizier through the kapĭağasĭ. Before taking important decisions the sultan would summon the grand vizier or the şeyhülislâm to the Palace for discussions, either by themselves or with others whom he trusted. In 1597, for example, after the dispersal of the council, Mehmed III summoned the grand vizier and another vizier to a pavilion by the sea where they discussed the war with Austria. Apart from these secret consultations the sultan could, before taking important decisions, convene consultative councils over which he or the grand vizier would preside. He would summon the şeyhülislâm, the senior viziers and military commanders, and other advisers, all of whom could express their views freely. Before his attack on the Mamlûks, Selîm I held such a meeting, where the decision for war was taken. If the grand vizier wished to hold such a meeting he had first to obtain the sultan's permission. However, certain extraordinary consultative councils took the decision to depose the sultan and form a transition government.

Since the government's most important function was the administration of justice, the imperial council was essentially a high court, but in the Ottoman state it served also as a sort of cabinet which discussed and took decisions on all governmental affairs and appointments.

In conformity with the traditional near-eastern concept of state, the principal activities of government fell within the spheres of three separate departments – the political, judicial and financial. To preserve the state's authority, to maintain internal security and to defend the realm from foreign enemies were essentially political matters and the responsibility of the viziers. The two kâdîaskers represented the judicial, and the defterdârs the financial authority. Beside these was the nişancĭ, representing the Chancery, who certified that orders and letters issuing from the imperial council conformed to established practice and were in accord with state regulations. It was he who fixed the *tuğra* – the sultan's official monogram – to a document to confirm its legality. The holders of these four offices, known as the 'Pillars of the Realm', represented the royal authority in the imperial council and had the right of personal access to the sultan. They were responsible only to him and could be tried in a kâdî's court only in civil lawsuits. Only the sultan could pass judgement on them in their public capacity. In 1596 a suggestion that the chief defterdâr be tried for accepting bribes was rejected on the grounds that 'the chief defterdâr acts on the sultan's authority and is director of the Treasury in the sultan's name. To date there has never been an inquiry into this office.'

The beylerbeyi of Rumelia, originally the commander of all timar-holding sipâhîs in the provinces, had always had the privilege of sitting with the viziers in the imperial council and participating in discussions. Süleymân I confirmed the privilege. Sometimes the grand vizier held this post.

In the second half of the sixteenth century, as the fleet grew in importance, the kapudan-i deryâ – the grand admiral – came to be chosen from among the viziers and thus gained permission to sit in the imperial council. The ağa of the Janissaries and other military commanders, and the şeyhülislâm, took part only in extraordinary meetings.

The şeyhülislâm had no political authority. Once, during the reign of Selîm I, the şeyhülislâm Alî Cemalî went of his own accord to the imperial council, when the death penalty for a hundred and fifty guilty Treasury officials was under discussion. Maintaining that this sentence was contrary to the şerîat, he requested an audience with the sultan. The şeyhülislâm's interference enraged the authoritarian Selîm I, who told him that his words were 'a violation of the sultan's authority' and that 'no one had the right or competence to question what the sultan commands or forbids'.

Thus in the classical period of the empire the sultan delegated his political and executive authority only to the viziers. Only they had the right, when in the provinces or on campaign, to establish of their own accord an extraordinary council to hear suits. They could impose sentences, including even the death penalty. In the imperial council, they used their authority with the consent or order of the grand vizier. On the grand vizier the sultan conferred the right to act as his absolute deputy in the exercise of his political and executive authority.

The kânûnnâme of Mehmed the Conqueror describes the grand vizier thus:[4]

Know that the grand vizier is, above all, the head of the viziers and commanders. He is greater than all men; he is in all matters the sultan's absolute deputy. The defterdâr is deputy for the Treasury but under the supervision of the grand vizier. In all meetings and in all ceremonies the grand vizier takes his place before all others.

Viziers, ulema, governors, military and reâyâ presented their petitions and requests to the grand vizier who, if he deemed it necessary, transmitted them to the sultan to secure his approval. He then issued an order bearing the sultan's seal. All appointments had first to be submitted to the grand vizier. As the sovereign's absolute deputy he could take certain decisions without consulting the sovereign: 'No one, not even the other viziers, must be privy to the grand vizier's dealings with the sultan and to his secret decisions.' The ruler entrusted him with his own signet, as a symbol of his function as absolute deputy, repossession of the signet tokening his dismissal. When the grand vizier was commander-in-chief of a campaign his powers reached their height, since he could then take decisions without consulting the sultan and make appointments and dismissals at will.

The grand vizier's status as military commander and the sultan's absolute deputy in civil administration, which would have been abnormal in the earlier Islamic states, was normal in the Ottoman Empire. The first grand vizier to possess these powers was Çandarlï Hayreddîn in the reign of Murâd I. Mehmed II was to create the classical type of Ottoman grand vizier, by selecting his grand vizier from his slaves and entrusting them, as his own deputies, with an absolute authority and a central position in the state. The first example was Mahmûd Pasha, who held the post continuously from 1455 to 1468. There was, during the reign of Murâd II, a rivalry between Halîl Pasha, a bureaucrat from the ulema, and the beylerbeyi of Rumelia who commanded the provincial army. Mehmed the Conqueror was for some time to unite the offices of grand vizier and beylerbeyi of Rumelia in the person of Mahmûd Pasha.

However, a number of checks on the authority of the grand vizier safeguarded the position of the sultan. Two grand viziers were in fact executed allegedly for coveting the sultanate – Ibrahîm Pasha in 1536 and Nasûh Pasha in 1614 – and a powerful grand vizier could cause a Sultan's deposition. But his authority was not unlimited. Before making an important decision the grand vizier had absolutely to consult with the other members of the imperial council; a factor in the condemnation of Ibrahîm Pasha was his habit of acting without consulting the other viziers. Furthermore, the heads of the financial and judicial branches of the government were in their own spheres the direct representatives of the sultan, who had absolute control of appointments to these posts. Murâd III appointed one of his close associates, Üveys Pasha, to the post of defterdâr, to counteract the excessive influence of the grand vizier Sokollu. The grand vizier had the right to supervise the defterdâr but, in the words of the kânûnnâme of Mehmed the Conqueror, 'Unless the defterdâr orders it, not a single akçe will enter or leave the Treasury.' The defterdâr, on the other hand, had to present a monthly report to the grand vizier. A request for the defterdâr's dismissal had to be made directly to the sultan.

On afternoons following meetings of the imperial council at the Palace, the grand vizier, the defterdâr and the kâdîaskers held councils in their own residences to discuss the business of their own offices.

The grand vizier did not command the Janissaries, the most important military corps. The ağa of the Janissaries, whom the sultan appointed directly, held a separate council at his own residence where he dealt with Janissary affairs and heard suits involving the troops. He had, on the other hand, to inform the grand vizier beforehand of any petitions which he would present to the sultan. Furthermore, the grand vizier selected the clerk of the Janissaries, who acted as a personnel officer to the corps, and this gave him some administrative control. When a sultan did not go on a campaign in person, some of the Janissaries remained behind; only very rarely were all the Janissaries placed under the command of the grand vizier.

From the second half of the sixteenth century the kapudân-i deryâ also presided over a separate council which dealt with naval matters and lawsuits arising in the fleet, and made nominations, appointments and dismissals. The grand vizier, however, had the right to visit and inspect the Arsenal from time to time.

The kapï ağasï supervised the Palace staff and administration independently of the grand vizier, making all Palace appointments and promotions by directly petitioning the sultan. The grand vizier, however, could petition the sultan for the dismissal of a kapï ağasï and the appointment of his own nominee.

The ulema represented the greatest power within the state independent of the grand vizier. The kâdîaskers of Anatolia and Rumelia were the government functionaries responsible for the administration of the religious law, possessing the power to appoint and dismiss kâdîs and religious dignitaries. They gave the final decision in lawsuits within the scope of the şerîat. The şeyhülislâm – the head of the ulema – was not considered a member of the government; nevertheless, he came in time to exercise a great influence in affairs of state. For the appointment of a new şeyhülislâm the grand vizier petitioned the sultan, who did not however have to accept the nomination. Thus in 1598, despite the grand vizier Yemişçi Hasan's strong pressure to appoint his own candidate, the sultan brought his tutor to the post. Hasan Pasha was in continual conflict with the şeyhülislâms, successfully manipulating the dismissal of one of them, Sun'ullâh. On the other hand, the grand vizier, Cerrâh Mehmed, seeking to preserve harmony, consulted with the şeyhülislâm on all important state matters. Accusations in a şeyhülislâm's fetvâ brought about the deposition of sultans and, equally, the downfall of many grand viziers.

The şeyhülislâm was the head of the ulema. He petitioned the grand vizier for the appointment, promotion and dismissal of medrese staff, and from the sixteenth century he acquired the authority to propose the nomination and dismissal of the kâdîs of important regions, thus effectively gaining control of the entire organization of ulema. In

the same way as the grand vizier was the absolute representative
of the sultan's executive authority, the şeyhülislâm became absolute
representative of the sultan's religious authority.

These various checks prevented the grand vizier's gaining power
equal to the sultan's; but in his capacity as absolute deputy of the
sovereign he had the right to supervise and inspect all state departments,
thus maintaining the independence of his administration and the unity
of his control. No appointments or dismissals could be made in any
office, nor any order of the sultan issued, without the grand vizier's
confirmation; and it became the custom that the sultan should not
reject any decision of the imperial council which the grand vizier submitted for his confirmation. The independence of the first vizier was an
immutable principle of the near-eastern state.

In a decree, written in his own hand, appointing Murâd Pasha to the
grand vizierate, Ahmed I stated, 'Accepting no one's recommendation
or request, I have conferred on you the grand vizierate and sent you my
seal.' It is said that in 1656 Köprülü Mehmed accepted the grand
vizierate on the conditions that the sultan would not reject any proposals
which he might submit; that he alone would make all the appointments
and dismissals; that the sultan would take no consultant on state affairs
other than the grand vizier; that the Palace would protect none of his
rivals; and that all calumnies against him would be ignored.

The second vizier was customarily the candidate for the grand
vizierate, but the kapï ağasï, the vâlide sultan or the sultan's tutor
usually played an important part in the actual selection. The new grand
vizier, unable thus to preserve his independence, relied for support on
the Janissaries or the ulema, or sought to extend his term of office by
ingratiating himself with an influential Palace clique.

The grand viziers of autocratic sultans such as Selîm I remained in
the shadows, while others such as Gedik Ahmed (grand vizier 1474,
vizier 1481–2) or Köprülü Mehmed (1656–61) had dictatorial powers.
Gedik Ahmed's source of strength was the Janissary corps, and Köprülü
Mehmed's the Palace. Until the introduction of the kafes system a new
sultan would arrive at the capital with the men who had served in his
Palace during his term as a provincial governor. Their attempts to
transfer political power into their own hands greatly influenced Ottoman
domestic policy. Mehmed the Conqueror's tutor, Zaganos, vigorously
opposed the grand vizier Çandarlï Halîl and encouraged the new ruler
to besiege Constantinople. After the conquest, Zaganos had his rival
executed and replaced him as the grand vizier. When Selîm II came to
the throne he embarrassed the old grand vizier, Sokollu, by acting on
the advice of his old tutor. Between 1579 and 1599 the tutor of Murâd
III and Mehmed III, Sa'deddîn, was the main voice directing the state's
domestic and foreign policies, the official court historian commenting

that, 'the affairs of the sultanate were totally dependent on his opinion'. With the institution of the kafes system, the opinion of the vâlide sultan became the main factor in the appointment of viziers. In 1596 Ibrahîm remained grand vizier only on the insistence of Mehmed III's mother, Safiye Sultan. But none of the vâlide sultans was as influential as Ahmed I's wife, Kösem Sultan, who in alliance with a faction of Janissaries played a vital part in all changes of grand vizier and in all accessions to the throne until the accession of Mehmed IV. Until Mehmed IV's mother, Turhan Sultan, had her strangled in 1651, she controlled all the strings of government.

The sultan's şeyh was another hidden influence determining the government's decisions. Each sultan had a şeyh who served as his spiritual mentor and who, it was believed, could foretell the future and secure God's aid, like the shamans who had served the pagan Turkish rulers of central Asia. During the seige of Constantinople, Mehmed II constantly sought the spiritual guidance of his şeyh, Akşemseddîn. When he could not forecast the date of the conquest, the şeyh wrote that the soldiers lacked faith and urged the appointment over them of a harsh and severe commander.[5] So influential was Murâd III's spiritual advisor, şeyh Şüccâ – a member of the *halvetî* order of dervishes – that anyone seeking high office had necessarily to visit him first.

The most famous of these men was Ahmed I's şeyh, Hüdâî Efendi, who not only encouraged the sultan's religious fervour but also interfered in politics. He recommended, for example, that a peace settlement be made with the Russian ambassador on the condition that the Russians relinquish the fortresses of Terek, Astrakhan and Kazan; he urged the release of imprisoned kâdîs; and advised that Ahmed Pasha be appointed governor of Egypt.

Public opinion, too, had a greater influence in determining Ottoman policy than has generally been recognised. Already in the second half of the sixteenth century there was an alliance of interest between the numerous kapîkulu troops and the artisans. Many of the kapîkulus had themselves become artisans or traders; others had invested their money in trading ventures and usury. The populace of Istanbul were always ready to riot, such disturbances occurring usually at times of financial and economic distress. Public opinion would support these uprisings and a fetvâ of the şeyhülislâm would give legal expression to this popular sanction. Typical of this were the uprisings which led to the deposition of Sultan Ibrahîm in 1648, Mehmed IV in 1687, Mustafa II in 1703, Ahmed III in 1730 and Selîm III in 1807.

Popular uprisings could usually be successful only with the cooperation of the kapîkulu troops. In 1651, however, the people of Istanbul rose against the power of the Janissary junta. Until the seventeenth century peasant revolts in the provinces were rare since the law forbade the reâyâ to carry arms. But the peasants leaving the land and dispersing was a form of passive resistance which caused the government as much anxiety as uprisings, since by depriving the state of its sources of revenue and the timar-holders of their sources of income it undermined the military strength of the empire. Threatened by this flight of peasants from the land, the government often had to take measures favourable to the reâyâ, sometimes even lowering taxation.

The Ottoman sultans' desire to attract the good-will of the public was a force determining them to act justly. If a ruler was unpopular, the people would start rumours that he did not respect the şeriat or that he drunk wine or committed other unlawful acts. The tyrannical Murâd IV was a habitual drinker, and at the same time the most ruthless supporter of the prohibition against alcohol. In order to appear faithful to the şeriat, the sultans would from time to time issue general orders to punish those who neglected their prayers or broke the Ramadan fast, and closed down taverns and brothels. They never failed to attend the mosque on Fridays and frequently to distribute alms to the poor and to the dervishes. On the annual Feast of the Sacrifice, thousands of sheep – three thousand in Istanbul alone – were ritually slaughtered and distributed to the poor. The sultan sent a yearly gift worth tens of thousands of gold ducats to Mecca and Medina, and the departure of this treasure train and its procession along the route to the Holy Places occasioned great ceremonies and display.

The sultans always feared religious leaders, especially the popular şeyhs and dervishes whom they sought to make dependent on their own goodwill or to subdue with stern measures. These şeyhs and dervishes were usually the principal propagandists of opposition movements. For example, during the reign of Mehmed III the sermons of a şeyh in Istanbul so aroused the people that the government banished him from the city, but popular demonstrations forced it to permit his return. In 1639 Murâd IV executed a şeyh of the nakşbendî order of dervishes, called Mahmûd, who had grown too influential, and in Ilgïn he put to death the şeyh of Sakarya who had attracted some seven or eight thousand followers.

The grand vizier's loss of independence was the main cause of the political crisis in the first half of the seventeenth century. In 1656 Köprülü Mehmed was appointed grand vizier with dictatorial powers, and his son Ahmed followed him in office (1661–76). Under the Köprülü administration, government business was conducted at the grand vizier's residence, and meetings of the imperial council at the Palace lost their old importance. Written reports kept the sultan informed. He returned these after adding in his own hand his commands and wishes.

With the removal of the effective government to the grand vizier's residence, the viziers of the imperial council passed into the background, while three officials, directly in the service of the grand vizier, came to the fore. These were the *kâhya bey*, the grand vizier's agent in political and military affairs; the çavuş başî, who received complaints and lawsuits in the imperial council; and the *reîsülküttâb*, who had for a long time been chief secretary to the imperial council and guarded state treaties and regulations. In meetings at the grand vizier's residence each of these officials actually became a member of the government, achieving the status of vizier after 1720. In the nineteenth century these offices were to become respectively minister of the interior, minister of justice and minister for foreign affairs.

At the same time the defterdâr's residence developed to become a large, independent department. On certain days of the week the defterdâr would take part in meetings held at the grand vizier's residence. Before taking important decisions the grand vizier would hold general consultative councils.

THE BUREAUCRACY

Ottoman administrative and bureaucratic practice originated from and continued the ancient traditions of pre-Islamic near-eastern states. The division of functions within the administration was in accord with these traditions. Islamic political theory recognized the 'Men of the Pen', beside the 'Men of the Sword' and the 'Men of Religion', as a pillar of the administration, and in pre-Ottoman Muslim states the head of the government, with the title of vizier, was usually someone who had achieved distinction in the state's Chancery or Exchequer.

The scribal art was considered one of the practical sciences. Within the profession there were two main branches – correspondence and finance – each with its own specialized skills and requiring special training. The clerk received his training in the bureaus themselves, which were organized on an apprentice-master system like any craft guild. For security reasons the scribal profession was in many eras a closed body. In Umayyad and Abbasid times only local Christian and Persian scribes had sufficient experience in the techniques of finance and administration and for a long time monopolized the public affairs of the caliphate.

Kalkashandî (1355–1418) distinguished three categories of scribe: those who drew up the orders sent to governors and officials; those who collected state income and ascertained its sources; and those who supervised the appointments and salaries of men engaged in defending the country and the social order. These bureaucratic categories corresponded to Ottoman practice. The first group of clerks served under the reîsülküttâb and his suite, the second worked in the Exchequer and the third under the nişancĭ.

The head of the Chancery, the nişancĭ, often stemmed from the ulema. Many of the clerks of the imperial council were graduates of the Palace, but Ottoman writers of the sixteenth century criticized this practice, regarding the introduction of slaves into the bureaucracy as contrary to tradition and regulations. It was usually the relatives and dependants of clerks who entered the bureaus as şâgirds – apprentices. Here they served for a long time under a *kalfa* – senior secretary – acquiring the necessary skills and knowledge and developing a particular speciality. There were also professional secretarial manuals, the oldest of which had been written by Persian secretaries in Abbasid service. The secretaries completed their education in the religious and legal sciences by attending courses at the mosques.

The departmental heads – *hâcegân* – corrected the kalfas' work, helping them to develop their own skills. The apprentice, as in a guild, became a secretary after he had passed an examination and received the approval of his superiors, who then entered his name in the register of *mülâzims* – candidates. There was a fixed number of secretaries in each office. A regulation of 1732, for example, establishes the secretarial staff of the imperial council at fifty secretaries, twenty apprentices and thirty candidates. If a secretary died, his son, if he was suitable, took his place; otherwise one of the mülâzims received the post. The most important condition for selection was the demonstration of professional ability to the senior secretaries of the bureau. They would then submit the name of their nominee to the grand vizier, who in turn submitted it to the sultan. When approval was received, the issue of a royal warrant concluded the formalities of appointment. In 1537 there were eighteen secretaries directly employed in drawing up edicts in the imperial council, of whom eleven specialized in political and administrative commands and seven in financial decrees. The bureaus employed both full secretaries and apprentices. By 1568 there were 222 secretaries in the Exchequer departments, with over seven hundred by the end of the eighteenth century.

Outside the central government a number of commissionerships, such as those of the Mint, customs or cereals, and a number of military organizations, such as the Janissary corps, gun-foundry or arsenal, had their own offices. In the provinces, governors, kâdîs' courts and numerous important vakĭfs had their own secretarial staff, and in each fortress there was a clerk to handle the garrison's accounts and personnel matters. A responsible commissioner, with a secretary to assist him, was appointed for all state undertakings, whether construction, mining, manufacture or agriculture. Thus the total number of secretaries was far greater than the limited body who worked in the offices of the central government. At the end of the sixteenth century Âlî Efendi wrote that a number of secretaries earned a precarious living by writing petitions and copying manuscripts. The thousands of registers and literally millions of documents still preserved in Turkish archives are proof that the Ottoman Empire was a bureaucratic state.

As in all Islamic states the secretaries in the Ottoman Empire were the essential elements of the administration. It was they who formulated the ruler's decrees, suggested administrative measures, prepared laws and regulations, and supervised their application. The head of the Chancery, the nişancï, had always been a member of the imperial council, and there are several examples of nişancïs rising to the grand vizierate. After 1699, when the Ottoman Empire pursued a peaceful, reformist policy and attached a growing importance to diplomacy, an increasing number of grand viziers stemmed from the secretarial class. Before this period most of the grand viziers had been from the military class.

A nişancï's career usually followed a particular pattern. He would serve for a long time as *tezkereci* – one of the secretaries who wrote the edicts of the imperial council – and gain experience by reading petitions, following discussions and writing drafts of fermâns. He would then receive promotion to the bureau of the reîsülküttâb, the head of the offices attached to the grand vizierate. Thence he would rise to become nişancï.

In the service of the viziers there were confidential secretaries, well versed in the traditional principles of statecraft, and it was these who were really responsible for the success of several great Ottoman statesmen. In the reign of Süleymân 1, for example, the renowned Celâlzâde, a member of the secretarial class, became confidential adviser to the grand vizier Ibrahîm Pasha and, later, as nişancï from 1525 to 1557, he was very active in the administration and in the drafting of laws. The famous grand vizier Sokollu Mehmed (1564–79) took no decision on matters of state without first consulting his confidential secretary, Ferîdûn, who was to serve as nişancï between 1573 and 1581. A secretary called Şâmîzâde Mehmed was to advise the Köprülüs. The sultan's confidential secretaries, however, never became so influential as they had been in Mamlûk Egypt, since it was an essential principle of Ottoman government that there should be no intermediary between the sultan and the grand vizier.

It was the secretaries who were generally responsible for introducing the traditional near-eastern principles of administration to the Ottoman Empire. They represented the political and secular interests of state, as against the ulema who represented the şerîat, and their chief concerns were to maintain the independence of political authority and centralization of government, to increase revenue and to protect the reâyâ.

In the period of the empire's decline it was they who, despite the opposition of the ulema, instituted reforms and regarded the adoption of European ideas, in the administration and in all other spheres, as the only way of saving the empire. The reforming grand viziers Koca Râgib, Halîl Hamîd and Mustafa Reşîd were all professional bureaucrats.

In the Ottoman Empire, as in all Islamic states since the Umayyads and Abbasids, bureaucrats were required to possess an encyclopaedic knowledge, and for this reason they displayed an interest in all fields of practical and useful knowledge – literature, language, calligraphy, law, history and philosophy or geography, the principles of the calendar, surveying and agriculture. The ulema had no direct interest in these subjects, and the most important Ottoman writings in these fields are the work of professional secretaries. Kâtip Çelebi (1608–57), the greatest Ottoman encyclopaedic scholar, was a secretary in the imperial council. It is the historical and political works composed by members of the bureaucracy which best express the near-eastern traditions of state, and these men, together with the slaves educated in the royal Palace, played a vital role in the creation of Ottoman culture.

The bureaucrats, however, did not always act in the best interests of the state. From the end of the sixteenth century bribery became widespread, even in the highest grades of the administration. Falsification of fermâns became punishable by amputation of a hand or by death, but despite these severe penalties a major cause of the disorder in the system was secretaries' granting, in return for bribes, several patents for a single fief. At the same time a steady decline in the value of the akçe, without a corresponding rise in wages, encouraged bribery. In 1595 two of the clerks to the Treasury were hanged and six dismissed for accepting bribes; and in 1598 the grand vizier castigated the secretaries, saying 'With your many treacheries, you aim to undermine the good order of the state.'

CHAPTER XIII

THE PROVINCIAL ADMINISTRATION AND THE TIMAR SYSTEM

THE PROVINCIAL GOVERNMENT

From the earliest period the Ottoman sultans had always appointed two authorities to administer a district – the bey, who came from the military class and represented the sultan's executive authority, and the kâdî, who came from the ulema and represented the sultan's legal authority. The bey could not inflict any punishment without first obtaining the kâdî's judgement, but the kâdî could not personally execute any of his own sentences. In his decisions and his application of the şerîat and kânûn, the kâdî was independent of the bey. He received his commands directly from the sultan, whom he could also petition directly. The Ottomans considered this division of power in the provincial government as essential to a just administration.

When it was no more than a frontier principality the Ottoman realm was divided into the 'sovereign's sanjak' and the sanjaks which he entrusted to the government of his sons. The sanjak was an administrative unit under a military governor – sanjak beyi – who had received from the sovereign a 'sanjak' (standard) as a symbol of authority. With the rapid expansion of Ottoman territory in the Balkans after 1361, it became necessary, in order to maintain control, to appoint a beylerbeyi over all the sanjak beyis. Murâd I appointed his trusted tutor, Şâhîn, to this position, thus creating in Rumelia the first beylerbeyilik.

Murâd I later established his son, Bâyezîd, in Kütahya as governor of the newly conquered districts in the east. When Bâyezîd I crossed to Rumelia in 1393 he felt the need to create a beylerbeyilik of Anatolia, with its capital at Kütahya and including all of western Asia Minor. He also created a third beylerbeyilik with its capital at Amasya, and this too became the seat of an Ottoman prince. These were, until the middle of the fifteenth century, the three beylerbeyiliks of the Ottoman Empire, and they always constituted the backbone of the empire.

We have seen that during the period of conquest the establishment of Ottoman administration in European districts was a gradual process. Between the area organized as sanjaks under direct Ottoman rule, and the area open to Holy War, was a buffer zone, either a frontier region or a vassal state. The beys on the frontier were more independent of the central government than those closer to the capital and came from families like the Evrenuz oğullarĭ or the Mihal oğullarĭ who held their governorships on an hereditary basis. The position of these beys within the Ottoman Empire was similar to the position of Osmân Gâzî under the Seljuks. The sipâhîs in their regions were usually their own slaves or servants. In vassal states the Ottomans sometimes granted the dynasties autonomy in domestic affairs, but forced them to pay an annual tribute and to provide auxiliary forces for campaigns. Some regions they preferred to maintain as frontier *beyliks* or vassal principalities.

In the fifteenth and sixteenth centuries, however, the government usually placed newly conquered areas under the direct administration of sanjak beyis, over whom it would eventually appoint a beylerbeyi. Thus new beylerbeyiliks came into being. The formation of new beylerbeyiliks was almost always a long process, and one governed by military considerations. For example, it took from 1463 to 1580 before the province of Bosnia, previously a dependency of Rumelia, became a separate beylerbeyilik, established against Austria. The beylerbeyilik of Özü was created at the end of the sixteenth century from the sanjaks of the western Black Sea region, as a bulwark against the Cossacks. In 1520 there were only six beylerbeyiliks in the empire; by the end of Süleymân's reign there were sixteen.

In 1533, the beylerbeyilik of Algiers was created and conferred upon Hayreddîn Barbarossa in an attempt to unify all naval forces against Charles v. As kapudan-i deryâ – grand admiral – Barbarossa united under his administration Algiers, which he himself had conquered, and the thirteen sanjaks on the shores and islands of the Mediterranean. After the 1590s the beylerbeyiliks, now known as *eyâlets*, were limited in size. Towards 1610 there were thirty-two eyâlets in the empire. These are shown on p. 106.

The government could implement the timar régime only in those areas where the sanjak system, Ottoman law and Ottoman administration were firmly established. The timar system was not in force in the provinces of Egypt, Baghdad, Abyssinia, Basra and Lahsâ, which therefore preserved some local autonomy. The sultan stationed Janissary garrisons in each of these provinces and appointed a governor, defterdâr and kâdî. The provincial revenues were not distributed to sipâhîs as timars, but the governor, after paying all the military and administrative expenses of the province, had to remit to the capital a fixed annual sum, known as *sâlyâne*. These provinces came to be known as sâlyâne provinces.

The administration of the hereditary sanjaks belonging to the tribal chieftains in some areas of eastern Anatolia was, again, different.

TABLE 3

Beylerbeyilik	Capital	Date of conquest	Date of formation of beylerbeyilik
Rumeli (Rumelia)	Edirne; later Sofia and Monastir	1361–85	c.1362
Anadolu (Anatolia; western Asia Minor)	Ankara and Kütahya	1354–91	1393
Rûm	Amasya and Sivas	1392–7	1413
Trabzon (Trebizond)	Trabzon	1461	c.1578
Bosna (Bosnia)	Saraybosna (Sarajevo)	1463	1580
Karaman	Konya	1468–74	1468–1512
Kefe	Caffa	1475	1568
Dulkadir (Zûlkâdiriyye)	Maraş	1515	1522
Erzurum	Erzurum	1514	1533
Diyarbekir	Diyarbekir	1515	1515
Musul (Mosul)	Mosul	c.1516	1535
Haleb (Aleppo; northern Syria)	Aleppo	1516	1516
Şam (Damascus; southern Syria)	Damascus	1516	1517–20
Trablus-Şam	Tripoli (Lebanon)	1516	c.1570
Mısır (Egypt)	Cairo	1517	1517–22
Yemen (with Aden)	Zabîd, San'a	1517–38	1540
Cezâir-i bahr-i sefîd (the Aegean Archipelago)	Gallipoli	1354–1522	1533
Cezâir-Garb (Algeria)	Algiers	1516	1533
Kars	Kars	1534	1580
Bağdâd (Baghdad)	Baghdad	1534	1535
Van	Van	1533	1548
Tunus (Tunisia)	Tunis	1534	c.1573
Basra	Basra	1538–46	1546
Lahsâ (al-Hasâ)	al-Katîf	c.1550	1555
Budin (Hungary)	Buda	1526–41	1541
Trablus-Garb	Tripoli (Libya)	1551	1556
Tamışvar	Temesvár	1552	1552
Şehrizor	Shehrizor	1554	?
Habeş (Abyssinia)	Suakin and Jidda	1555–7	1557
Kıbrıs (Cyprus)	Nicosia	1570	1570
Çıldır	Çıldır	1578	1578
Rakka	Ruha	1517	c.1600

In these sanjaks, known as *hukûmet* – government – sanjaks, all the revenues belonged to the hereditary tribal bey, who was however required, on the sultan's command, to contribute a fixed number of troops to the army. In the important cities of the region the sultan appointed a kâdî and stationed a Janissary garrison.

There were thus a number of autonomous provinces distinct from those under direct Ottoman rule. These were the sâlyâne and hukûmet provinces; the Christian vassal principalities of Moldavia, Wallachia, Transylvania, Dubrovnik, Georgia, Circassia and, in the seventeenth century, the Cossack hetman; and finally the subject Muslim principalities – the khanate of the Crimea, the sherifate of Mecca and, for a time, Gilan. Tripoli, Tunisia and Algeria preserved their original character as frontier provinces.

In the sixteenth century the Ottoman government claimed theoretical sovereignty over Venice, Poland and the Habsburg Empire, all tribute-paying states, and over France when Francis I requested Ottoman aid and formed the Ottoman alliance.

But the typical Ottoman province was one where the timar system was in force. The need to support a great imperial army on the foundations of a mediaeval economy gave rise to this system, which was to shape the provincial administration of the empire and its financial, social and agricultural policies. All these were formulated in answer to the military needs of the state.

Shortage of coin was a fundamental problem of near-eastern empires. Gold and – even more important – silver were the basis of the money system, and faced with a scarcity of these metals the state had difficulty in financing its great undertakings and, especially, in maintaining a large standing army. It was impossible, under these conditions, for the peasant to pay his principal tax, the tithe, in cash, and so he paid in kind. But the mediaeval state had practically no means of collecting, and converting into cash, taxes paid in kind, and therefore usually sold these sources of revenue to tax farmers. In this way the state lost income and did not collect the funds necessary to pay military salaries. It therefore became the established practice to assign state agricultural revenues to the troops, who collected them directly, in place of salary. This system of distributing revenues from lands was an old-established practice in near-eastern Islamic empires. Similar military fiefs in the Byzantine Empire were known as pronoia, whose Persian equivalent is timar.

Under this system the cavalryman – sipâhî – resided in the village that was itself his source of income, and was easily able to collect the tithe, a tax on crops, paid in kind. Thus the soldier replaced the tax farmer, and on him fell the responsibility of converting the tithe into cash. One advantage of the system was that the cavalryman, the chief element in the mediaeval army, was easily able to maintain his horse in the village where he lived.

In the Byzantine Empire and its successor states, the peasant was required to give the fief-holder annually a waggon-load each of wood and fodder and half a waggon-load of hay. He owed, in addition, labour on the fief-holder's land and services with his cart. This was the system which the Ottomans found when they conquered the Balkans, and to convert the pronoias into timars was a simple matter. In time they also converted into timars large freehold estates owned by Christian lords and some lands belonging to monasteries. The timar system was from the earliest times a distinguishing characteristic of the Ottoman regime.

In the classical period of the empire the timar-holding sipâhîs in the provinces formed the greater part of the Ottoman army. The sipâhî was a typical mediaeval cavalryman, using conventional weapons; in the Ottoman army it was mostly the Janissaries who used firearms. According to one estimate,[1] in about 1475, when the kapĭkulu cavalry numbered three thousand and the Janissaries six thousand, there were twenty-two thousand timar-holding sipâhîs in Rumelia and seventeen thousand in Anatolia. A century later, during the reign of Süleymân I, it has been estimated that there were six thousand kapĭkulu cavalry, twelve thousand Janissaries and forty thousand provincial sipâhîs.

In order to establish the timar system and to maintain a continuous and centralized control, the government had to determine in detail all sources of revenue in the provinces and to make registers showing the distribution of these sources. Immediately after the conquest of a region, and subsequently every twenty or thirty years, when changes in tax yield became apparent, a commissioner called the *il yazĭcĭsĭ* was sent to an area to determine the sources of revenue. In a detailed register he recorded the name of every head of family in each village and the approximate amount of land he owned. Beneath each village he listed the total sum of money to be realized from the tithe, the *çift resmi* – a farm tax paid in cash, which Christians paid under the name of *ispence* – the other incidental taxes, such as fines or the marriage tax. He thus determined the amount of revenue due from each village. When the register was complete, the income from villages reserved for the sultan (that is, for the central state Treasury), viziers and beys, was deducted, and the remainder distributed among the sipâhîs as timars and *zeâmets*. A zeâmet was formally the fief of a subaşĭ, with an annual value of between twenty and one hundred thousand akçes. A fief with an annual value of more than one hundred thousand akçes was called *hâs*.

A second, summary register was then prepared, showing the distribution of revenues as hâs, zeâmet or timar, while a kânûnnâme at the beginning of the first, detailed register showed the rates and conditions according to which the sipâhîs of the sanjak would collect these revenues. The peasant paid his taxes in accordance with these regulations and could not change his status until a new cadastral survey. In case of dispute, these registers guided the kâdî in his decision. The timar was an indivisible and unalterable unit.

The central government retained a copy of each of these registers in the office of the nişancï who was the responsible official. The beylerbeyi of the province received the other copy.

Superficially, the timar system resembles medieaval European feudalism, but there are fundamental differences between the two. To implement the timar regime the state had to establish its own absolute control of the land, unimpeded by any private property rights. Following the example of earlier Muslim states, the Ottoman government announced that all rural agricultural land was *mîrî* – crown-land, belonging to the state. The only exceptions were *mülk* – freehold – and vakïf lands, which could remain or be revised at the sultan's discretion.

Under this system, agricultural land belonged to the state. The peasant who worked it had the status of an hereditary tenant, and in return for his labour he enjoyed a usufructuary right. The peasant's rights on the land passed from father to son, but he could not sell land, grant it as a gift, or transfer it without permission. Influential persons, however, continually sought to establish private property rights over the land. As in the Abbasid caliphate and the Byzantine Empire, in the Ottoman Empire too the struggle between the state and individuals to gain possession of the land was one of the most important problems of its social history. When the state was weak there would be a sudden increase in the area of land held as private property or as vakïfs; when a sovereign established a strong, central authority, he would abolish private property rights and vakïfs and re-establish state control. Bâyezîd 1 and, especially, Mehmed the Conqueror are famous for this type of reform.

When Mehmed the Conqueror reviewed all land holdings throughout the empire in about 1470, he established the principle that all vakïfs that had not received the sultan's sanction or whose buildings or purpose no longer existed should revert to the state. In this way over twenty thousand villages and farms became mîrî lands. Mehmed undertook this reform in order to increase the number of timar-holding cavalrymen. In Anatolia he left some of the land in the possession of landowners and dervishes from the former Islamic states, but required each of them to send a fully armed cavalryman to the army. In the reign of his successor, Bâyezîd ii, there was a reaction against Mehmed's reforms. Their opponents claimed that they did not conform to the şerîat and most private property and vakïfs reverted to their original owners. Selîm I and Süleymân I, whose vast military under-takings required more and more sipâhîs, returned to Mehmed's policy.

In 1528, about 87 per cent of the land was mîrî. With the growth in this period of the number of sipâhîs, the extent of mîrî land increased, at the expense of the old land-owning families and the ulema class. As more of the military class awaited timars the state appropriated more land, but from the end of the sixteenth century it again began to lose control of these mîrî lands, Ottoman writers considering this one of the principal reasons for the empire's decline.

The timar system was one of fragmented possession where the state, the sipâhî and the peasant had simultaneous rights over the land. The sipâhî, who held the timar, had some rights of control over the land, and was in this capacity termed 'land-owner'; but in fact what the sipâhî received from the state was not the land itself but the authority to collect a fixed amount of state revenue from the people in a defined area of land. The state granted him his rights over the land in order to guarantee his income.

The sipâhî exercised several rights. He enforced the state's land laws and he could rent vacant land on contract to interested peasants on receipt of a pre-paid rent. The peasant, for his part, undertook to work the land continuously and to pay the prescribed taxes. He could not alter the use of the land, whether arable, garden or meadow. If, with no reason, he left the land vacant for three years, the sipâhî could give it to another.

If anyone settled on vacant land within the boundaries of the timar, the sipâhî received from him the legally established taxes. In order to increase the area of productive land, the state rewarded any sipâhî who by settling peasants on his timar brought more land under cultivation.

For his own and his animals' needs, a sipâhî received one *çift* of land, a unit which varied according to place from 60 to 150 *dönüms*, or else a vineyard or orchard. Neither the sipâhî nor any of his relatives could take possession of land held by reâyâ, and in the second half of the sixteenth century sipâhî farms were to be given in their entirety to the peasants. Thus the timar-holding sipâhî held the position of a govern-ment official who enforced the state's land laws.

The head of a reâyâ family could hold a çift large enough to support a single family but could receive no more. On his death his sons worked this holding jointly but a çift could not be broken up. In addition to the tithe, the peasant holding a çift paid the sipâhî the çift resmi, an annual tax of twenty-two akçes. This tax, originally in lieu of services, was the equivalent of the hay, fodder, wood and services which the peasant had owed the fief-holder in Byzantine days. As we have seen, the Ottomans tried as far as possible to commute services for fixed cash payments.

THE REÂYÂ AND THE TIMAR

Again in order to guarantee his income, the state granted the sipâhî a number of rights over the reâyâ. In the widest sense of the word, the reâyâ were, whether Muslim or Christian, the productive, tax-paying subjects of the empire, as distinct from the military class. In a narrower sense the reâyâ were farmers, as distinct from urban dwellers and nomads, who had a different status.

The timar conferred on a sipâhî comprised both the land and the peasants. In the fifteenth century the reâyâ were the essential element in all agricultural undertakings, since there was more cultivatable land available than there was labour to work it. The sparseness of the village populations and the abundance of vacant land in the timars led to a continual battle among timar-holders to entice away each other's reâyâ. The sipâhî whose reâyâ fled lost his income, and for this reason the law forbade reâyâ to leave their settlements and go elsewhere. The sipâhî had fifteen years in which to compel a fugitive peasant to return to his land, but to do this he needed a kâdî's decree. If someone else, who paid the tithe, came and worked the deserted land, the sipâhî could not force the peasant to return but only claim from him the çift resmi. If the peasant entered a craft in a town he had to pay the sipâhî compensation known as the *çift bozan akçesi* – the farm-breaker's tax – amounting to slightly more than one gold ducat a year; but the sipâhî could not compel him to return.

In the sixteenth century these conditions appear to have changed. It seems that the population of the empire grew rapidly, causing an increase in the amount of land under cultivation. The land survey registers of Süleymân 1's reign show a significantly greater amount of cultivated land than the earlier registers. The value of land and land revenues increased. The laws against peasants who abandoned the land became less stringent, encouraging a flow of population from the villages to the towns. It seems that in this period the area of land under cultivation had reached the limits which the technology of the age allowed.

The state entrusted the sipâhî with other powers, making him also responsible for order in the village. Half of the money fines levied on the peasants for minor crimes belonged to the sipâhî and half to the sanjak beyi, but the authority to impose the fines rested only with the local kâdî. The sipâhî could arrest a wrong-doer but not set the fine. The sipâhî lived in the village which constituted his timar and performed his military duties but did not himself engage in agricultural production. To enable the sipâhî to live in the village, the Ottoman kânûn-nâmes imposed on the peasantry certain small labour services. They had to build a barn, but not a house, for the sipâhî; they had to carry the sipâhî's tithes to the barn or to the market, except where the market was more than a day's journey away. They had to help reap the sipâhî's meadow but not to carry the hay to his barn. If the sipâhî came to the village, the villager had to provide hospitality for three days, supporting both the sipâhî and his horse. The law also endorsed the custom of the peasants' giving the sipâhî gifts on festivals. In some district the custom remained of the peasants' working one to three days on the sipâhî's farm.

The kânûnnâme of each sanjak listed the taxes and services due from the peasants and the sipâhî could not impose any others. The government attached great importance to this, and in fact the main clauses in the kânûnnâmes were those regulating the relations between the sipâhî and the reâyâ. The sipâhî could lose his timar for acting contrary to the regulations. Thus the reâyâ were undoubtedly in a happier position than the serfs of medieval Europe, the main difference lying in the fact that the Ottoman peasant lived under the protection of a centralized state and its independent legal system. Nevertheless, sultans' decrees on the condition of the reâyâ from as early as the fifteenth century indicate that the sipâhîs and beys were abusing their privileges. The sipâhîs' attempts to continue former feudal customs was a main cause of the abuses. The peasants complained of illegal and excessive fines, and in particular petitioned against the habit of sanjak beyis and kâdîs staying in their houses on the pretext of maintaining order and pursuing suspects, and forcing them to feed them, their numerous followers and animals, free of charge. The peasants also complained that sipâhîs attempted to collect money from them through illegal imposts and attempted to collect the tithe in cash rather than in kind. Süleymân I issued a number of decrees forbidding these practices.

Most of the reâyâ in the Ottoman Empire were farmers tied to timar and hâs lands but there were social differences within the class. Ottoman, like Byzantine, law divided the peasantry according to whether they held one çift or half a çift, classifying the landless according to their marital status and imposing the reâyâ taxes accordingly. In the former Byzantine and Balkan lands the Ottomans found an unregistered landless group, known as elephteroi – free. In the Ottoman period, reâyâ who had fled the land or were unrecorded in the registers, sons who had left their father's home, and unregistered nomads, were similarly treated as a single class. These landless men worked as temporary agricultural labour or farmers on the timar lands, the timar-holders receiving from the latter the tithe and the reâyâ taxes, levied per dönüm of land. If they stayed for three years in the same place they became the reâyâ of that sipâhî. The state continually tried to settle landless men and nomads.[2]

Share-cropper slaves formed another class, whose situation closely resembled the serfs of western Europe. They were usually prisoners-of-war or purchased slaves whom the sultans and influential members of the governing class employed on their estates and vakîfs. Since those who came into possession of such lands were unable to employ reâyâ who had been recorded in the registers, they tried to attract unregistered reâyâ or to settle slaves on the land, as agricultural labourers. Most of the estates belonging to the ruling class were established in this way. This system was in operation from the earliest years of the Ottoman Empire but it was only after the end of the sixteenth century that it became widespread.[3]

The state, too, used share-croppers in rice cultivation and the other agricultural undertakings which provided for the needs of the Palace and the army. In order to revive the empty villages around Istanbul, Mehmed the Conqueror settled prisoners-of-war on them, giving them the status of share-croppers. They could not marry outside their own group and they gave the state half their harvest. In the sixteenth century, however, most share-croppers achieved reâyâ status.

In about 1634 an English traveller, H. Blount,[4] observed that the timar system aimed 'to awe the provinces wherein they live and cause them to be well cultivated.' One of the principal goals of this institution was, in fact, to ensure public order. A security system extending as far as the villages made it possible to protect the reâyâ against brigandage and to pursue and punish criminals. The subaşı and sanjak beyi were responsible for order in their district and periodically toured the sanjak, ridding it of bandits. It was the duty solely of the sanjak beyi to inflict the corporal punishments which the kâdî decreed.

THE TIMAR-HOLDING CAVALRY ARMY

Above all else the timar system was intended to provide troops for the sultan's army, by maintaining a large, centrally controlled cavalry force. The timar-holding sipâhî kept his own horse; he was armed with a bow, sword, shield, lance and mace, and if his timar income exceeded a certain sum he wore armour. For each three thousand akçes of timar income, a sipâhî had to provide one *cebelü* – a fully armed horseman; beys provided a cebelü for each five thousand akçes. Thus at the beginning of the sixteenth century a sipâhî with a timar yielding nine thousand akçes would wear armour and bring three cebelüs and a tent. Sanjak beyis built up large retinues of cebelüs in this way. The greater their retinue, the greater was the respect they earned. It is thus very difficult to determine the size of the sipâhî army, including all the cebelüs.

When the sultan ordered a campaign, the sipâhîs, under the command of the subaşıs, rallied to the sanjak beyi's standard. The sanjak beyis gathered beneath the beylerbeyi's standard, and each beylerbeyi then joined the sultan's army at the time and place commanded. The sultan, as a kind of inspection, then passed his army in review. The timar-holders were light cavalry, and in battle formation took their position on either wing, forming a crescent which allowed them rapidly to encircle the enemy. Since these troops received no pay from the central Treasury and their horses were tired by the end of summer, they sought to return home at the beginning of autumn. The campaigning season lasted from March to October and the Ottoman army was at its weakest towards autumn. Recognizing this fact, some European generals, like Hunyadi, would always attack at this time.

Timars were granted on the commanding officer's petition. The sultan would issue a decree in accordance with the petition, entitling the recipient to a timar of a certain value, and when a timar of that amount fell vacant in the sanjak the beylerbeyi gave the applicant a *tezkere* – certificate. The applicant approached the central government with his tezkere and received the sultan's diploma of appointment to a timar. This was the necessary procedure when receiving a timar for the first time, but afterwards the beylerbeyis could, with the authority of their own diplomas, assign timars worth up to 5,999 akçes in Rumelia and 2,999 akçes in Anatolia. In the fifteenth century, and especially in the frontier region, many sipâhîs held timars simply on the authority of the sanjak beyi's or even the subaşî's certificate. In the sixteenth century the central government tightened its control over the granting of timars. Neither could a timar-holder be dispossessed without the sultan's order. This strong centralized control distinguishes the Ottoman timar system from European feudalism; furthermore, there was no hierarchy or bond of vassalage on the European pattern.

To be eligible for a timar a man had to be from the military class; it was absolutely forbidden to grant timars to the reâyâ. A son inherited military status if his father were of military class or the kul of a sultan or bey. The Ottomans also accepted as military class the members of the equivalent caste in newly conquered states, and in this way many Christian fief-holders became timar-holding sipâhîs. In time, they or their sons accepted Islam. In the fifteenth and sixteenth centuries a large part of the timar-holding cavalry was, like the Janissary corps, composed of slaves. Only those Muslim Turks who had volunteered and performed outstanding services on campaign or on the frontier, or else the Turkish followers of frontier beys, could receive timars. Statistics from 1431, for the frontier district of Albania, show that 16 per cent of the sipâhîs were former Christian fief-holders, 30 per cent were Turks from Anatolia, and 50 per cent were slaves of the sultan and beys. Kâdîs, bishops and Palace favourites received the remaining 4 per cent of timars. Later, the proportion of sipâhîs of Turkish origin gradually diminished. Sons of deceased sipâhîs each received a timar in relation to the value of the timar held by their father. If, for example, the deceased had held a timar worth between ten and twenty thousand akçes the first son received a timar worth four thousand and the second received one worth three thousand akçes. If the original timar had been worth between twenty and fifty thousand akçes, the first three sons received timars worth respectively six, five, and four thousand akçes. Fathers could not, however, bequeath their fiefs to their sons as in western feudalism. If a sipâhî did not perform military service for a space of seven years he lost his sipâhî status and was registered with the reâyâ, becoming subject to taxation. There was thus no question of blood nobility in the timar system. If a dispossessed sipâhî went on campaign within seven years, he could on the commander's petition again receive a timar.

There were great distinctions within the timar class. The beys who received hâs and zeâmet holdings usually came from the Palace services. Beylerbeyis received from six hundred thousand to one million akçes per annum; sanjak beyis had hâs holdings worth from two hundred to six hundred thousand akçes; and subaşïs held hâs or zeâmets worth twenty to two hundred thousand akçes. In the fifteenth century timar-holding sipâhîs received, on average, two thousand akçes per annum. In the sixteenth century this rose to three thousand akçes.

In the 1500s a sanjak beyi's annual income was equalled from four to twelve thousand gold ducats, while in the same period the wealth of the richest money changers and merchants of Bursa rarely exceeded four thousand. The beys and zeâmet-holders formed the richest section of Ottoman society. In contrast, the yearly income of the average sipâhî in the fifteenth century was from thirty to forty gold ducats, a Janissary or master builder at the same period receiving about the same amount. For outstanding services a sipâhî could receive a 10 per cent increase in the value of his timar, and in this way bring his annual income up to four hundred gold ducats; but before he could receive a zeâmet he had to perform very exceptional services, since these holdings were reserved almost exclusively for slaves of the sultan or the children of beys.

Later, the beys were to abuse their authority, granting timars to unqualified people in return for bribes. Consequently, in the sixteenth century many persons originally of reâyâ status became sipâhîs. Süleymân I had no choice but to legalize this influx of outsiders but later took stringent measures to prevent those who were not sons of sipâhîs from receiving timars in future. The constant demand for timars was a vital factor in the internal affairs of the Ottoman Empire during the classical period. Dispossessed sipâhîs, kapïkulu troops and volunteers in the frontier districts exerted continual pressure for these holdings.

The need for land to distribute as timars constantly forced the state to undertake new conquests. The kapïkulu troops, moreover, desired war as a means of acquiring fiefs, since Janissaries who displayed valour in combat received timars and zeâmets. The need for timars was thus a motivating force in Ottoman expansion. There was also a great rivalry between the Anatolian volunteers and raiders on the frontiers, who awaited fiefs, and the sipâhîs in the hinterland, who already held them. This tension explains why in the first half of the fifteenth century the frontier forces in Rumelia often took an intransigent attitude towards the central authority.

The problem of timars again explains the antipathy between the old sipâhîs in the former Anatolian principalities and the newly established Ottoman regime. The Ottomans left some of the former sipâhîs in possession of their holdings, pensioning off those whom they mistrusted, but the enmity continued between the local sipâhîs and those whom the Ottoman sultan had appointed. In the Izmir and Saruhan revolts of 1416 and the Karaman uprisings of 1468–1511 these local sipâhîs acted as leaders

Similarly, during the revolts of the princes in Süleymân 1's reign poor or dispossessed timar-holders and others seeking timars or pensions gathered around the rebellious princes.

Only part of the state's income was allotted as timars. In 1528 state revenue had risen to 9,650,000 gold ducats, of which only 37 per cent was distributed as timars. About 50 per cent belonged directly to the sultan, that is to the state Treasury. A large percentage of this income came from the lands reserved as the sovereign's hâs; the remainder came from taxes levied on merchants in the cities, customs and mines. Only the central Treasury had the authority to collect the cizye – the poll-tax paid by non-Muslims – which amounted in 1528 to 750,000 gold ducats. The sultan distributed the greater part of the central Treasury's revenues to the Janissaries and kapïkulu cavalry as salaries paid in cash; the remainder he spent on the troops guarding fortresses, Palace expenses, and the construction and repair of public buildings.

Timars were granted not only to troops, but also to Palace and government officials, as a form of salary or pension. For example, çavuşes, müteferrikas, and secretaries in government offices could receive timars and zeâmets, and the sultan could even grant to his favourites timar and hâs incomes, under such names as 'shoe money' or 'money for fodder'. In the second half of the sixteenth century the assignment of timars for non-military purposes increased, and was an important factor in the break-up of the system.

THE ADMINISTRATION AND THE TIMAR SYSTEM

As an administrative organization the timar system, from beylerbeyi to sipâhî, represented the executive powers of the sultan in the provinces. The sipâhîs had several administrative tasks. They formed a sort of police force, charged with the protection of the reâyâ in the countryside, and had at the same time important duties in the collection of taxes and in the application of land laws. At the head of the provincial administration stood the beylerbeyi who represented the sultan's authority in the province. He heard and adjudicated suits concerning sipâhîs and executed the sultan's decrees. Beylerbeyis of important provinces, such as Egypt, held the rank of vizier and could use their authority in an absolute manner, dismissing kâdîs and imposing the death penalty.

Working under the beylerbeyi was the *timar defterdârî*, and the *defter kethüdâsî* who regulated matters relating to timars, and the *hazîne defterdârî*, who administered the sources of revenue belonging to the central Treasury. These officials each had their own offices. The officials and offices under the beylerbeyi were modelled on those of the capital, the beylerbeyi's council consisting of his *kethüdâ* – steward – who acted as his deputy, his tezkereci – secretary – who kept his correspondence, and the officials mentioned above, whom the sultan appointed. The beylerbeyi's council dealt mainly with timar matters, lawsuits involving sipâhîs and complaints of the people. When necessary, the kâdî of the city took part in the discussions.

Some beylerbeyiliks were financially autonomous. Under the supervision of the beylerbeyi, the hazîne defterdârî met all expenses out of the province's revenues, drawing up a balance sheet at the end of the year and sending the surplus to the central Treasury.[5]

From the beginning, the sanjak was the main administrative unit of the empire. A number of sanjaks composed a beylerbeyilik, or eyâlet, one of which was known as the 'pasha's sanjak' and was under the direct administration of the beylerbeyi. Several smaller units, known as *subaşîlîks*, made up a sanjak, the subaşîs themselves living in the towns and commanding the sipâhîs who resided in the villages in their district. In the larger villages of each subaşîlîk was an official known as the *çeribaşî*, who organized the sipâhîs for campaign and rallied them to the subaşî's standard.

The beylerbeyi's hâs holdings were dispersed throughout the sanjaks, those of the sanjak beyis throughout the subaşîlîks. Shares in several villages similarly made up the subaşîs' zeâmets and the sipâhîs' timars. This system aimed to widen the area of control and to prevent any one person dominating a district.

A second division of the provinces was according to *kâdîliks* – the administrative and judicial district of a kâdî. The kâdî himself lived in the town, sending his deputies to the various communities in the district and opening courts. He was first and foremost a judge administering the şeriât and kânûn, but at the same time he had the task of supervising the execution of the sultan's administrative and financial decrees. In this capacity, he was supervisor of financial affairs, immediately informing the government of any illegal actions by administrative officials. Acting on the sultan's orders, he would sometimes make a personal tour of inspection in the province.

The kâdîs formed the backbone of the Ottoman administration, and in the fifteenth century a kâdî could rise to become sanjak beyi or beylerbeyi. A number of kâdîs abused their wide powers. Since the number of kâdîs was limited there was great rivalry for the posts, just as there was for timars. Prospective kâdîs could wait for years on the applicants' rolls, and as soon as they received their appointment they sought to make money. Later, kâdîs were appointed for one year only. In the mid-sixteenth century so many students were studying to become kâdîs in the hundreds of Anatolian medreses that they became a heavy burden on the empire. They formed themselves into bands and began to disrupt life in the cities and plunder the villages.

The third pillar of the provincial administration was the hazîne defterdârî, who just as his counterpart in the central government represented the interests of the Treasury. He was, like the kâdî, independent. He could communicate directly with the capital and could lodge complaints against the beylerbeyi and other administrators. On the other hand, a beylerbeyi could dismiss a kâdî or hazîne defterdârî who abused their authority, but he had to inform the capital of this immediately. Thus there was a true system of checks and balances in the provinces. The centralization of government was intended to prevent pashas in the provinces becoming too powerful.

The Janissary garrisons established in important cities were another force preventing local authorities exercizing arbitrary power. These garrisons varied from three hundred to fifteen hundred men, according to the size of the city, and acted only on the sultan's orders. The beylerbeyis had no authority over the garrisons, which represented the sultan's authority against foreign and internal enemies. They prevented clashes between Muslims and Christians, escorted ambassadors on their journeys, and guarded caravans and money when it was transferred to the Treasury.

With the increasing provincial unrest after the second half of the sixteenth century, all towns, large or small, began to receive Janissary garrisons. In the seventeenth century, as central authority weakened, real power in the capitals of distant provinces, such as Algeria, Egypt or Baghdad, passed into their hands, opening the way for the formation of a new ruling class in the provinces.

Part III

ECONOMIC AND SOCIAL LIFE

CHAPTER XIV

THE OTTOMAN EMPIRE AND INTERNATIONAL TRADE

THE RISE OF BURSA AS A CENTRE OF INTERNATIONAL TRADE

With the establishment of the great Mongol Empire in the thirteenth century, Anatolia became the highway for east-west trade. Merchants from the Italian maritime states now met the caravans from the far east and Iran not only at Ayas in the south and Trebizond in the north, but also journeyed inland to Sivas and Konya. In Mongol times there was an imperial highway linking Tabriz to Konya through Erzurum, Erzincan and Sivas. Twenty-three magnificent caravanserais dating from the thirteenth century still stand on the road between Sivas and Konya. A branch of this imperial road from Sivas to Constantinople competed with the sea route to Constantinople from Trebizond. At this period the principal items of east-west trade were the fine cloths of Flanders and Florence, worn in the east mainly by the upper class, and Chinese and Persian silks.

In the thirteenth century Anatolia not only linked Europe with the east but was a crossing point for north-south trade between the Khanate of the Golden Horde in eastern Europe, and the Arab lands. Spices, sugar and various fabrics from the south were exchanged for furs and slaves from the north. Italian merchants transported these goods by sea, while Muslim traders also carried them overland from Antalya to Konya and Sivas or from Aleppo to Kayseri, Sivas, Sinop and Samsun. In this period the towns of central Anatolia – Sivas, Kayseri, Aksaray, Konya, Amasya and Ankara – became important commercial centres.

With the fall of the Ilkhanid Empire in Iran in the fourteenth century and the rise of the Ottomans in western Anatolia, the political and with it the commercial centre of gravity moved to western Anatolia, causing a change in the pattern of trade routes.[1] Bursa, which by the end of the fourteenth century was both the political and commercial centre of the Ottoman Empire, became the most important trading city of Anatolia and an entrepôt for east-west trade. By 1391 the old emporia of western Anatolia such as Palatia, Altoluogo (Ephesus) and Smyrna (Izmir) had already come under Ottoman control and were linked to Bursa.

121

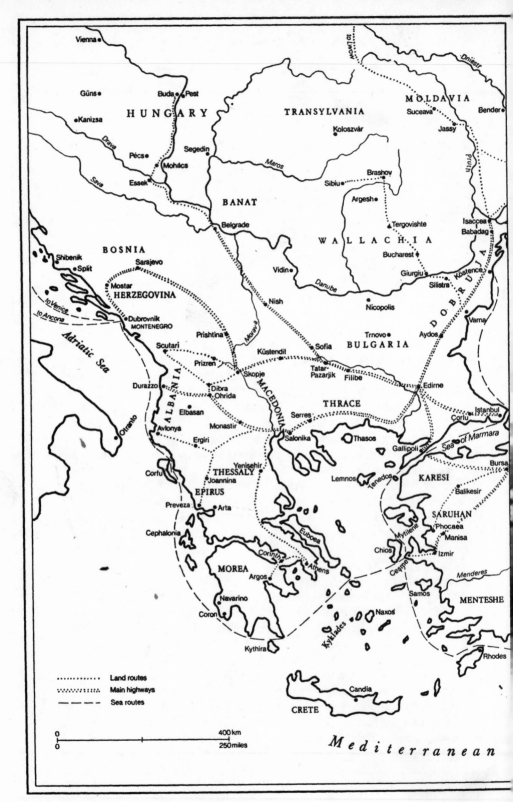

Trade Routes in the Ottoman Empire.

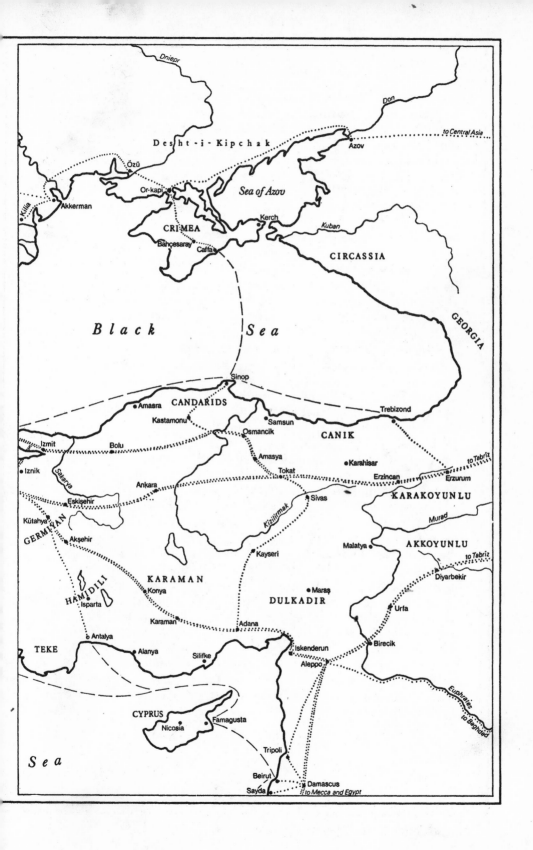

Caravans from Iran now reached there seaports through Bursa and, furthermore, by extending his dominions as far eastwards as Erzincan, through Amasya and Tokat, Bâyezîd I gained control of this caravan route. Persian silk caravans no longer followed the route through Trebizond, preferring to go overland to Bursa. In the fifteenth century the cities of Amasya and Tokat, situated on this route, became after Bursa the most important economic and cultural cities in Anatolia.

In 1399 Bâyezîd took Antalya and Alanya, the main ports of entry in southern Anatolia, for Indian and Arabian goods. This trade also followed the ancient overland route, cutting diagonally across Anatolia from Aleppo to Constantinople, through Adana and Konya. The Ottomans were able to gain complete control of this route connecting Bursa with the south only after the destruction of the Karamanids in 1468.

Muslim traders could now travel in security from Arabia and Iran to Bursa, and for European traders such as the Venetian, Genoese and Florentine merchants in Constantinople and Galata, the two most important centres of Levantine trade, Bursa was the closest market in which to purchase eastern goods and sell European woollens. Already in 1333 Ibn Baṭṭuṭa[2] could write that Orhan was the richest of the Turcoman sultans in Anatolia, and as early as 1352 the Genoese concluded a commercial agreement with the Ottomans. At the end of the fourteenth century Schiltberger[3] compared Bursa's silk trade and industry with that of Damascus and Caffa, noting that Persian silk was sent from Bursa to Venice and Lucca, then the centre of the European silk industry.

Trade in Persian silk was the mainstay of Bursa's development and prosperity. In the fifteenth century the European silk industry expanded greatly and Bursa became the international market place for the basic raw material of the industry, the extremely fine silk of Asterabad and Gilan in northern Iran. J.Maringhi,[4] the representative in Bursa of the Medicis and other Florentine houses, noted in 1501 that every year several silk caravans arrived in Bursa from Iran, and his letters reflect the impatience with which the Italian merchants awaited the arrival of the caravans, the rush to buy the goods and the fierce competition. The rewards were great, for in Italy each fardello – about 150 kg. – yielded a profit of seventy to eighty ducats. In Bursa about a thousand silk looms worked five fardelli of silk a day. The price of silk rose constantly from fifty akçes per fardello in 1467, to seventy in 1488, and eighty-two in 1494. An average caravan brought about two hundred fardelli of silk. Table 4 shows the value of customs receipts from silk in Bursa for various years, giving some idea of the volume of imports:

TABLE 4

Year	Receipts in gold ducats
1487	40,000
1508	33,000
1512	43,000
1521	13,000
1523	17,000
1557	24,000

The sudden decline in receipts after 1512 was a result of the Persian wars, and although an upward trend appears after the peace of 1555 they are far below their fifteenth-century level.[5]

Even after Istanbul had become the Ottoman capital, Bursa continued for another century as one of the empire's main commercial centres. Aleppo too had for a long time been an important centre of the silk trade and a rival of Bursa. Silk caravans from Iran came to Aleppo through Erzurum and along the Euphrates valley or, more often, from Tabriz through Van, Bitlis, Diyarbekir and Birecik. In 1516–17 the Ottomans captured Aleppo and gained control of these routes, so that all outlets for Persian silk open to Europeans were now in Ottoman hands. In the sixteenth century they even tried to bring the north Persian centres of silk production at Shirvan and Gilan directly under their rule.

Silk, however, was not the only item of trade in Bursa. Musk, rhubarb and Chinese porcelain formed an important part of the merchandise coming to Bursa from central Asia, Persian merchants taking back with them European woollens, precious Bursa brocades and velvets and, especially, gold and silver coins, which had a higher value in Iran.

The traveller Bertrandon de la Brocquière[6] has left a description of the land route from Damascus to Bursa in 1432. In Damascus he had joined a group of pilgrims and merchants returning from Mecca with a caravan of three thousand camels. The Turkish group in the caravan included many notables, over whom the sultan had appointed a merchant of Bursa. De la Brocquière, after a journey of some fifty days, reached Bursa, where he found Florentine merchants, as well as the Genoese from Pera, come to buy spices.

The merchandise carried on this caravan route consisted usually of lightweight, expensive goods, such as spices, dyestuffs, drugs and textiles. Towards 1487 annual customs receipts from saffron, gumlac and pepper imported into Bursa reached about two thousand gold ducats. This caravan trade was wholly in the hands of Muslim merchants, mostly from Aleppo and Damascus, many of whom had invested great sums. In 1500, for example, a wealthy merchant called Abû Bakr of Damascus sold in Bursa a shipment of spices worth four thousand gold ducats.

By 1480 Mahmud Gâwân, the powerful vizier of the Bahmanî kingdom in India, each year sent his commercial agents to Bursa with Indian merchandise. In 1481 some of these even crossed the Balkan to trade in Indian textiles and other goods.

In about 1470 a Florentine called Benedetto Dei could claim that he and his fellow merchants could buy spices in Bursa, as well as cotton and wax. The reports of Maringhi show that Bursa exported spices to Italy, however small the quantity. In 1501 he wrote to his associate in Florence that he had assigned him three sacks of pepper, and that if he wanted he could send more. As it turned out, however, the difference in price between Bursa and Florence was not large enough in comparison with the profits obtainable in the silk trade. In 1503 Maringhi wrote that the price of pepper might go up to twenty-seven gold ducats a *kantâr* – about 56 kg. – in Pera, if new supplies did not arrive. The official price in Edirne in 1501 was only eighteen gold ducats a kantâr, but at this date the Portuguese had already begun to transport spices to Europe directly from India.

THE OTTOMANS AND THE INDIAN TRADE ROUTE

In the sixteenth century the Portuguese failed, despite all their efforts, to sever the trade routes leading from India and Indonesia to the near east, through the Persian Gulf and the Red Sea. In the second half of the sixteenth century they even permitted the sale of spices to the near east in Hormuz.

When, in 1509, the Portuguese destroyed a Mamlûk fleet at Chaul and the Mamlûk ruler turned for assistance to the Ottoman sultan, the Ottomans immediately sent material and craftsman to Suez to build ships. In 1516–17 the Ottomans conquered Syria, Egypt and the Hejaz; at the same time the Portuguese entered the Red Sea, threatening to capture Mecca and Medina. In 1517, while still in Cairo, Selîm I ordered the construction of a fleet at Suez to drive the Portuguese out of the Indian Ocean, and in 1517 and 1525 the Ottoman admiral, Selmân, repulsed Portuguese attacks on Jidda, thence advancing on Yemen and Aden.

The Portuguese usually avoided open confrontation with the Turks, and seeing this the Ottomans passed to the offensive. In 1538 they sent a fleet of thirty ships to expel the Portuguese from Diu in northern India, but the expedition failed, largely because the Gujeratî sultan, the local Muslim ruler, refused to cooperate, fearing that the Ottomans had come not to assist him but to establish their own rule in the area.

At this date, however, the Ottomans successfully subjugated Yemen and Aden.[7]

The Ottoman Empire continued to receive spices directly from India and Indonesia throughout the century. Despite occasional shortages there was an active exchange of Indian goods with European merchants in the markets of Aleppo, Cairo, Istanbul and Bursa. In 1554 the Venetians alone bought six thousand quintals of spices in Alexandria, and their annual purchase of twelve thousand quintals between 1560 and 1564 was the same amount as before Vasco de Gama's discovery of the sea route to India. As a result the Lisbon market underwent periodic crises, and in 1564 a Portuguese spy in Egypt informed his government that thirty thousand quintals of spices had arrived in Alexandria.[8] Every year twenty ships, laden with spices, arrived at Jidda, the seaport of Mecca, and Ottoman pilgrims returned from Mecca carrying spices, dyes and Indian cloth.

In 1562 customs levied at Damascus, on spices which pilgrim caravans had brought, rose to 110,000 gold ducats. European merchants bought some of the spices at Damascus, exporting them through Beirut, while a large part of the cargo was forwarded to Bursa and Istanbul and thence to the Balkans and the north. The customs regulations of Bursa for 1545 show that European merchants were buying spices there, and by 1582 the customs receipts on spices in Bursa had reached 7,250 gold ducats, four times what it had been in 1487. Documents show that as late as 1590 the Venetians were bringing cloth to Istanbul and buying spices. In 1547 a Hungarian merchant brought kersey to Bursa and purchased 110 kantârs of spices, but by the mid-sixteenth century Hungary had begun to receive spices from the west.

Spices continued to arrive from India in the sixteenth century through the port of Basra as well as through the Red Sea. J. Eldred visited Basra in 1583 and wrote, 'To this port of Balsara (Basra) come monethly the diverse ships from Ormuz, laden with all sorts of Indian merchandise, as spices, drugs, indico and calico cloth.'

The sea routes from the ports of Syria and Egypt to Antalya, Alanya and Istanbul were no less important than the overland routes. Malipiero, writing in the 1470s, still considered Antalya an entrepôt for the spice-trade of Asia Minor. According to the customs register of Antalya for 1559, as many as fifty ships put in there in the course of a year, each ship accommodating from twenty to thirty merchants. Most of the ship-owners were Muslims. According to the customs registers for the fifteenth and sixteenth centuries, the chief exports from Asia Minor to Syria and Egypt were timber, iron and iron implements, Bursa silks, Ankara camlets, cotton textiles, carpets, rugs, opium, dried fruits, furs, wax and pitch. Ships from Syria and Egypt brought Indian spices and indigo, Egyptian linen, rice and sugar and Syrian soap. At this time, customs receipts in Antalya and dependent ports rose to seven thousand gold ducats a year.

Timber exports from the ports of southern Anatolia to Egypt had long been important. In the Taurus mountains a large group of Turcoman nomads, which came to be known as the *tahtacı* – woodmen – in place of their original tribal name, felled the timber, which was then sent from Antalya, Alanya, Finike and other ports. The export of timber was a government monopoly, customs receipts from timber and pitch reaching about 3,500 gold ducats a year in 1477.

Antalya was also a centre of the slave trade, exporting white slaves to the south and importing negro slaves, and a number of merchants from Bursa, active in the transit trade, lived there.[9] After the conquest of Egypt in 1516–17 a greater volume of goods followed the direct sea route to Istanbul and the road from Antalya to Bursa lost its former importance. In the seventeenth century Antalya was to become an insignificant local port.

Egypt and Syria were vital to the economy of Istanbul and the empire. Provisions for the sultan's Palace, such as rice, wheat, barley, spices or sugar, came by galleon from Egypt, and in the sixteenth century Syria annually sent 50,000 kg. of soap to the Palace. Sudanese gold came to Istanbul through Egypt; and the imperial Treasury in the capital took the surplus of the Egyptian budget, amounting to half a million gold ducats annually. The central government always insisted on receiving this sum as gold. There were other demands on the budget of Egypt. In 1532, for example, fourteen thousand gold ducats were sent as alms to the Holy Cities of Mecca and Medina; for the Palace 13,866 ducats were expended on sugar, spices and drugs and 12,053 on jewels and textiles. The rich provinces of Egypt and Syria were one of the main sources of the empire's wealth, providing in 1528 one-third of the budget income for the entire empire.

It is hardly surprising, therefore, that Christian corsairs, operating mainly from Rhodes, Cyprus and Crete, constantly menaced the sea route between Alexandria and Istanbul. In the fifteenth century the Catalans had been the most active pirates in the eastern Mediterranean; up until 1522 it was the Knights of St John on Rhodes who dominated the route between Istanbul and Alexandria. After the conquest of Egypt in 1517 the capture of Rhodes became an absolute necessity. In 1522 Süleymân I finally captured it after a long siege.

To protect themselves against corsairs, Ottoman ships on this route always travelled in convoy, accompanied by warships. In 1641 a Jew called Samuel described how a convoy of fifty ships left Istanbul, how twelve warships met them at the Dardanelles and the kapudan-i deryâ accompanied them into the Aegean.

THE OTTOMAN EMPIRE AND THE BLACK SEA TRADE

The Black Sea trade was one of the most important sections of the Ottoman economy and for a long time continued without foreign rivals. Since the Ottomans controlled the Dardanelles they were easily able to exclude the Italians from the Black Sea trade and develop the region as an integral part of the empire's economy, like Egypt or Syria. Foodstuffs to supply Istanbul and the Aegean region, such as wheat, fish, oil and salt, had since ancient times come from the northern Black Sea region. After capturing Istanbul and establishing a firm control over the straits, Mehmed II forbade the export of these foodstuffs to Italy, and Italian ships were closely inspected at Istanbul and Gallipoli. Since the Black Sea trade was largely in these commodities, this field of commercial activity was virtually closed to foreigners. In 1475 the Ottomans conquered the northern Black Sea ports of Caffa and Azov; Kilia and Akkerman fell to them in 1484. For military reasons they thereafter discouraged foreigners – meaning, at that time, Italians – from entering the region. The Italian ships on the Black Sea in the fifteenth and sixteenth centuries were either Venetian ships bringing wine from Crete or Chios or ships based on the Crimea belonging to Italians who had become Ottoman subjects. In the Black Sea ports, and also in Moldavia and Poland, Ottoman subjects – Armenians, particularly those from Caffa, Jews, Greeks and Muslim Turks – began to capture the Levant trade from the Italians.

In 1456, two years after the Prince of Moldavia, Aaron III, had accepted Ottoman suzerainty, the sultan granted a patent of privilege to Moldavian merchants, permitting them 'to come by sea in ships belonging to merchants in Akkerman, and to trade freely in Edirne, Bursa and Istanbul'. In the fifteenth century the trade of Akkerman and Kilia brought prosperity to the principality of Moldavia. The old trade route, from Caffa, Akkerman and Kilia into Poland passed through Moldavia, and Suceava in Moldavia and Lwow (Lemberg) in Poland developed as rich entrepôts. Poland's attempts to gain control of Moldavia, Akkerman and Kilia were unsuccessful. For the Ottomans, control of these two ports and of Caffa was as much an economic as a political necessity.

Ottoman customs registers for the years from 1490 to 1512 provide a detailed record of economic activity in Caffa, Akkerman and Kilia, the three great ports of entry for the trade of the northern lands with the Mediterranean.

According to the accounts for 1490, seventy-five vessels called at Caffa in four months. Of these, eight were Greek, seven Italian, and one Russian (Vasilan), and the remainder were under Muslim captains. Among the Muslim ship-owners were two Ottoman statesmen, Mesîh

Pasha and Sinân Bey. Most of the ships came from Istanbul and Galata, Trebizond, Azov, Sinop, and Izmit. They were usually small, accommodating on average the goods of three to five merchants.

One hundred and fifty seven merchants came with these vessels, of whom sixteen were Greek, four Italian, three Jewish, two Armenian, one Moldavian and one Russian. The remaining hundred and thirty were Muslims. Most of the goods which they brought were from Istanbul Bursa, the southern Black Sea region – Trebizond, Sinop, Kastamonu and Amasya – and central Anatolia – Ankara, Sivrihisar, Beyşehir, Uşak and Gördes.

Istanbul served these ports as a transit centre for European cloth, Bursa silks, Indian spices and dyestuffs, and in particular, cotton fabrics from western Anatolia. The Kastamonu region, with its port at Sinop, exported rice, iron, cotton fabrics and mohair, the town of Tosya being an important centre of mohair production. As well as exporting its own local products the region was a transit centre for Indian and Arabian goods such as silk, and henna and other dyes. Gold brocades and velvets, and silk fabrics woven in Amasya, a city on the silk route from Iran, were shipped through Sinop to Caffa. These goods were famous everywhere, creating a demand even within the Ottoman Palace. However, cotton goods were equally important in the export trade. Merzifon, near Amasya, became a centre of production, exporting thousands of bolts of cotton fabrics to the Crimea.

Caffa also received merchandise from the region of Trebizond, especially wine, arak, hazel-nuts and ships' masts. Cotton fabrics were the chief export of central Anatolia to Caffa and, after these, mohair and rice from Ankara, opium from Beyşehir, and the famous rugs of Uşak and Gördes. From the Aegean region, Caffa received olives, olive oil, beans, raisins and, especially, wine and vinegar. Merchants from Bursa brought silks, rugs and dyes.

Thus cotton fabrics and Mediterranean foodstuffs and wine were the main articles of export from Anatolia, through Caffa, to the Crimean khanate, Poland, the grand duchy of Moscow and the Tatars of the Desht-i Kipchak and the Volga. On the route from Istanbul to Caffa the principal items were European cloths and Arabian and Indian imports.

Caffa was the principal port for exports to the south. Wheat, flour, tallow, clarified butter, cheese and honey were shipped from the Crimea and the Kuban steppe through Caffa to Istanbul, and were essential food supplies for the city and Palace. In 1600 the Palace kitchens placed a single order for two thousand kantârs of clarified butter from Caffa. To increase the production of cereals to meet the demands of this market, the aristocracy of the Crimean khanate settled colonies of Russian prisoners on the steppe as agricultural labourers.

The semi-nomads of the northern Black Sea region also grew cereals for export.

Sturgeon fishing in the mouth of the Don and caviar production were also important in the economy of this region which supplied Istanbul and the south. The Venetians and Genoese had previously shipped flour, fish and caviar to Italy, but most of these now went to Istanbul. The state took 10 per cent of the fish catch, which it stored or shipped, salted in barrels. Before 1490 some hundred thousand sturgeon were caught annually. A continuous supply of fish, caviar and honey arrived at Caffa from the coasts of Circassia, through the ports of Kopa and Taman

Closely allied with the fish industry was salt production. The various mines in the Crimea, especially those at Sarukerman near Sevastopol, sent great quantities of salt to Istanbul and to Azov, where it was used to preserve fish. At the end of the sixteenth century the Khan of the Crimea shipped an annual average of a thousand to twelve hundred tons of salt, to be sold in Istanbul.

Caffa and the dependent ports of Azov, Kerch, Taman and Kopa were the principal market-places for the purchase of slaves, whom the Tatars had captured in raids on Russian and Polish territory. The captives were usually taken from Taman to Caffa, where they were exchanged for cloth, which Anatolian merchants had brought to the Crimea. The fact that in the mid-sixteenth century the state derived a yearly income of eighteen thousand gold ducats from the slave trade gives some idea of the size of the market. The tax on each slave was four gold ducats. Most of the slaves went to Istanbul, and some to Sinop and Inebolu. In pre-Ottoman times the Caffa slave trade had been in the hands of the Genoese.

The Turco-Tatar peoples sent southwards through Caffa, cattle, sheep and horses, harnesses, the famous Tatar bows and arrows and Morocco leather from Kazan.

The cultural affinities between the Ottomans and the Muslim inhabitants of the regions north of the Black Sea helped to promote commercial and economic ties, and in the fifteenth and sixteenth centuries the Ottoman Empire established commercial relations with Russia. Until the 1530s the good relations between the khanate of the Crimea, the Ottoman Empire and Muscovy encouraged Ottoman-Muscovite trade. Goods from Moscow reached Kilia and Akkerman through Chernigov and Kiev, and reached Azov and the Crimea through Kursk, Belgorod and Cherkassy. Furs and iron implements were the main Russian exports, but Russian flax, walrus tusks and mercury also became famous in the Ottoman markets. In 1497 the Muscovites, through the mediation of the Khan of the Crimea with whom they were allied, received the privilege to trade in the Ottoman

Empire, and Russian merchants began to come not only to Caffa, Akkerman and Kilia, but also to Bursa. Before the growth of European interest in the sixteenth century, Ottoman cities were the principal market for Russian sables and fox skins. In Ottoman court ceremonial the presentation of a costly fur was a mark of the highest favour and honour. In 1492 Bâyezîd II sent furs and silk fabrics to the pope as a gift.

When the rulers of Muscovy made the fur trade a monopoly, the Ottoman sultan appointed a special Palace merchant, with credentials for the tsar, to purchase furs. In 1577, for example, the sultan despatched to Moscow a certain Mustafa Çelebi, with four thousand gold ducats to buy furs. The tsar similarly sent his own representatives to Turkey to buy heavy gold brocades from Bursa. In 1512 a Russian merchant bought eight hundred gold ducats worth of silk and taffeta.[10]

Akkerman and Kilia were also ports of entry for the north-south trade, handling the same merchandise as Caffa. The fact that more than a hundred and twenty separate items, from drinking glasses and cotton thread to women's silk robes and slippers, were imported from Turkey indicates the close commercial ties between these ports and the regions to the south. Customs registers show that in four months of 1490 twenty-five ships called at Akkerman, of which fifteen were owned by Greeks, six by Muslims, three by Italians and one by an Armenian.

Kilia was an important transit centre for wines from the south. According to a customs entry, the casks of wine arriving in Kilia from the Morea, Crete and Terbizond 'are not sold in Kilia but after the payment of import duty are forwarded to the provinces of Poland and Moscow, where they are exchanged for local produce. Customs receipts from this transit trade in both directions have risen to six thousand gold ducats a year.' In the second half of the sixteenth century the Ottoman government granted the monopoly of this wine trade to the famous Levantine Jew, Joseph Nasi, who thereby accumulated great wealth and political power. Obtaining a concession from the King of Poland, Nasi's agents extended their business as far as Lwow where they aroused the envy of Polish merchants. Customs records show that the Venetians carried great quantities of wine from Crete, and when in 1592 the Ottomans closed the Black Sea to foreigners, Cretan wine merchants tried to send wine to Poland through Friuli.

Kilia and Akkerman were the outlets for the Moldavian trade. Most of the merchants in these two ports were native Moldavians, whether Rumanian, Armenian, Greek, Tatar or Jewish. They exported beeswax, honey, clarified butter, tallow and, above all, hides, also forwarding northwards goods which merchants had brought from the regions south of the Black Sea. Kilia also exported to the south, salted and in barrels, the cod and carp caught in the Danube estuary. In Akkerman, Russians traded in knives, furs and harnesses.

1 Portrait of Mehmed the Conqueror, by Gentile Bellini

Isles des Princes

Appartemens des femmes du Grand Se

Cuckana ou Remises des Barques du G

Sinan kiosc

Parti

2 The Topkapï Palace, seen from Galata

Chambre du Divan

Appartements des Officiers

Entrée du Serrail

Temple de S.te Sophie

ta

Le Blond ex

3 Plan of Seraglio Point

4 *Opposite:* The first court of the Topkapï Palace, between the Bâb-i Hümâyûn
(Imperial Gate) and the Orta Kapï (Middle Gate), then called Bâbussâde (Gate
of Felicity). On the left are depicted the Byzantine Church of St. Irene, then used
as an armoury, and the scales for weighing the Palace wood-supply. On the right is
the Palace sanatorium and, in the background behind the fountain, the office of the
kâğıt emîni, the supplier of paper to the Palace. Note also the *kapïcïs*, gate-keepers,
with staves in their hands

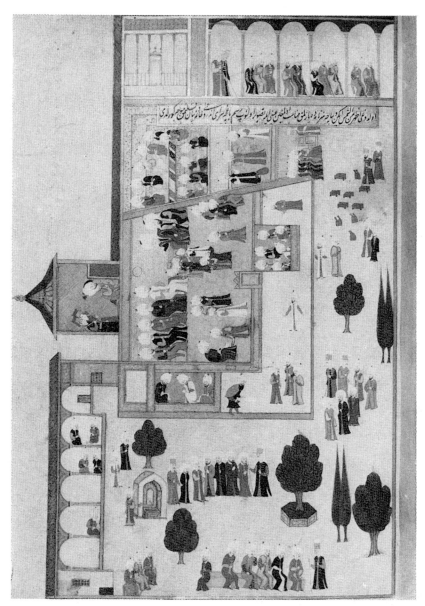

6 The west side of the second court, showing the imperial court in session for the payment of the Janissaries. The sultan is seated in the Adalet Kasri, the Mansion of Justice, attended by the *hâs oda başı*, Chief of the Privy Chamber, and the *silahdâr*, Sword-bearer. The grand vizier is seated below in the council chamber, with four viziers on his right and the two *kâdîaskers* on his left. On the left-hand side of the *nişancı*, the secretary to the council, is busy writing, while three *defterdârs*, heads of the Treasury, are seated on the right. The *çavuş başı*, head *çavuş*, and the *kapıcılar kethüdâsi*, the lieutenant of the gate keepers, are shown standing with staves in their hands. In the adjoining rooms on the right the secretaries are busy writing, while the Treasury clerks weigh the coins. The *kapıcıs*, doorkeepers, and *çavuşes* are on duty in the court

5 *Opposite:* The east side of the second court, between the Orta Kapı and the Bâbussaâde, then called the Bâb-i-Âlî (Sublime Porte). In the right-hand corner the *aga* of the Janissaries, with some of his men, awaits the money bags to pay his Corps. The *Kapı ağası*, the chief white eunuch, is shown inside the Bâbussaâde

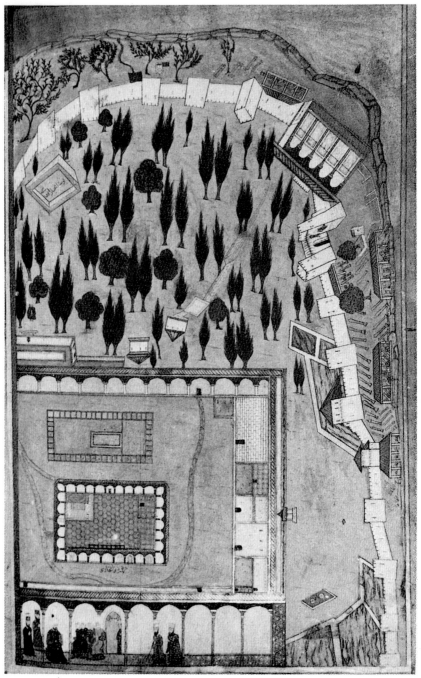

7 The east side of the third court and garden. The Arz Dîvânhânesi, the Reception Hall or
Throne Room, is seen just behind the Bâbussaâde. In the garden on the left is the
Bostancîlar Odasî, the Hall of the Gardeners, on the right the kiosk called Topkapĭ Sarayĭ,
the Palace of the Cannon Gate, which gave its name to the whole Palace. In the court on
the right are seen the Treasury rooms and the hall of the *seferli* pages

8 The west side of the third court and garden. On the right is seen the west side of the third court, with the apartments housing the Sacred Relics and Blessed Mantle of the Prophet, and the hall of the pages of the Privy Chamber. Adjoining them are the apartments of the Harem. In the garden outside the wall the sultan is shown being entertained by the pages. The kiosk on the shore is the Yalï Köşkü, Shore Kiosk

9 The Imperial Council
in session
10 Sultan Süleyman
hearing the complaint
of an old woman during
a hunting expedition

11 The accession of Mehmed II. On the left-hand side are the viziers and *kâdîaskers*,
on the right the agas of the pages, and the white eunuchs. In the foreground are the
military chiefs and ulema. The *çavuş başı* and the *kapîcîlar kethüdâsi* are seen with staves
in their hands. The aga of the Janissaries swears allegiance to the sultan

12 An ambassador of the Emperor in the presence of the sultan. Two doorkeepers hold him by the arms. Beside them stands the dragoman of the Porte

14 *Below: Acemî oğlans*, who are to become Janissaries, learning how to use muskets

13 *Acemî ağlans*, Christian children levied by the government, led to work in their white caps

15 *Çavuşes*

16 *Right:* The Janissaries
on parade

17 *Below:* Janissary
commanders

Fanmischarun

Beiutlchs haber der Janicharn

18 *Right:* The ağa of the
Janissaries

Janidschar aga

Spachi diemitt dem Türckischen Keysler
aufts getagt Reytten

19 *Sipâhîs* of the Porte on a hunting
trip with the sultan

Buchsen meyster

20 *Above:* Exercises at the Okmeyd:
in Istanbul

21 *Left:* Head-gunners

22 *Right:* The grand vizier, Sinan Pasha, and four other viziers precede the coffin in the funeral procession of an important man

23 *Below:* The doorkeepers of the deceased precede the coffin at a funeral

24 *Right:* Çavuşes carrying the coffin

25 Armed *sipâhîs*

26 Frontier raiders

Allso Reytt die Brautt vnderemem Himmel

27 Bride riding
beneath a baldachin

28 Bride's mother
riding with friends

Wie fie inn Feren Zimer fizen

29 *Above:* Turkish
ladies sitting in a
drawing-room

30 Turkish lady going
to the bath-house

31 *Above:* Passengers on board
ship

32 Boys to be circumcised led in
ceremony through the streets of
Istanbul

Wan man die kinder will beschneiden so Fuert
man sie in der statt Herumb mitt grossem Triumpht
Wan man sie beschmiden Hatt als dan Schneid man
innen die zopff auch ab

'Jungen So, Jern alcoran aus olesen
Haben samlen Alper damitt

33 Children carrying
the Koran, collecting
alms

34 Traders at an army
camp

35 Tailors in a procession on the occasion of the circumcision of Prince Mehmed in 1582

36 Glass-makers in the same procession

37 A model of a mill in
the same procession

38 A kebab-maker in the
same procession

39 *Above:* A view of the
Covered Bazar in the
nineteenth century

40 Peddlers at the foot of the
column of Arcadius at the
Avret-pazarĭ

41 Shopkeepers

42 Rest in a
caravanserai

43 A mill on a brook
in Bulgaria

44 Turks at the eating
table and Janissary
playing a lute

45 Offering a drink to
the people in the street
for God's sake

46 Feeding dogs in the
street for God's sake

47 Amusements for
old and young during
a festival

48 Exercise of the
cavalry, *cirid*, outside
the city walls of
Istanbul

56 Mosque of Sultan Ahmed I, also called Blue Mosque, built 1609–17

57 The Castle of Rumeli-Hisari, built in 1452.

In Kilia and Akkerman, as in Caffa, there were numerous merchants from Istanbul and Muslim traders from Anatolia dealing in cottons and silks. Many Muslim merchants came from the towns of Sofia, Provadiya, Plovdiv, Edirne, Nicopolis and Silistra in the Balkans to the ports of Caffa and, especially, Kilia, where most of them earned their living from the transit trade in spices, Bursa silks and Anatolian cottons and woollens. Kilia also received exports of shoes made in Edirne, the coarse woollens of the Tundzha valley in southern Bulgaria, and the woollens from Salonica and Dubrovnik. Kilia was thus an important centre both of Balkan commerce and the Black Sea transit trade, serving as a focal point for Giurgiu, Harsova, Tulčea, Isaccea, Mačin and Braila, the ports of the lower Danube.

Giurgiu was an entrepôt between Wallachia and the Ottoman domains. Here, Wallachian and Moldavian merchants exchanged cattle, hides, salt, horses, Wallachian knives, flax, honey and beeswax, for pepper, woollens, silks, cottons and Mediterranean foodstuffs. Tulčea was an important slave market. In the 1590s customs revenue and other dues for all ports dependent on Kilia, including Akkerman, rose to thirty thousand gold ducats. In about 1575 customs receipts for Caffa, excluding dues from the slave trade, were approximately forty-five thousand gold ducats.

As a result of this extensive trade these regions became an integral part of the Ottoman economy. It was easy and inexpensive to transport heavy goods from them to Istanbul, whose population was ever increasing.

Furthermore, the Black Sea had a military importance. During the Persian wars great quantities of grain were shipped to Trebizond from the ports on the Danube, and iron balls from Kigi near Erzurum were sent from Trebizond across the Black Sea and up the Danube to the Hungarian battlefields.

OTTOMAN TRADE WITH EUROPE

Until 1569 the Italian states, primarily Venice, handled Ottoman trade with the western Christian world, and so long as Venice was the main sea-power in the Mediterranean neither the other Christian states nor the Ottomans could change the situation.

Since Venice both dominated the trade of the Levant and possessed a colonial empire there, her relations with the Ottomans were extremely complex. The expansion of the Ottoman Empire against Byzantium meant that Venice lost a trading area which hitherto she had exploited at will, free of duties or control. Venice and Genoa had received commercial privileges from the local governments in most important points in the Levant, the area stretching from Azov to Alexandria. They then walled off their settlements, converting them into fortified bases under their own administration. The Ottomans, determined to bring the whole area under their own rule, wished to take control of these places.

With the expansion of the Ottoman Empire in the fourteenth and fifteenth centuries, Venice, to strengthen her position against this new power, also adopted an aggressive policy. She tried to take possession of any coastal regions which the Ottomans threatened, and thus in the fourteenth and fifteenth centuries gained control of the most important strategic points in Albania, the Morea and the Ionian Sea, and occupied the Aegean Islands and in 1489 Cyprus. Between 1423 and 1430 she held Salonica and even considered occupying Constantinople before the Ottomans did so. The Venetians sought at the same time to adapt themselves to the new conditions and benefit from Ottoman trade. So long as their vital interests were not threatened, they tried to avoid open war with the Ottomans

The Ottomans used many tactics against this great Mediterranean sea-power. When, during the reign of Bâyezîd I, the struggle had reached a height, they blockaded the Bosphorus by constructing a fortress, Anadolu Hisarı, at its narrowest point. Similarly, at Gallipoli they built a fortress and an inner harbour enclosed by a wall, where they moored a small raiding fleet. In 1416 the Venetians appeared before Gallipoli, burned the Ottoman fleet and tried to enter the inner harbour to destroy the naval base. It was Mehmed II who finally gained full control of the straits.

The Ottomans cooperated with Venice's rival, Genoa, granting the Genoese a capitulation as early as 1352 and giving them a long-term monopoly over alum production in Manisa, the main source of alum for the European textile industry. The Genoese colonies in western Anatolia – Foça and the island of Chios – became ports of entry for Anatolian trade. In return for this preferential treatment, Genoese ships assisted the Ottoman armies at crucial moments, notably in 1421 and 1444, when they transported troops across the Dardanelles, then under Venetian control. During the siege of Constantinople in 1453 the Genoese observed neutrality.

The Ottomans also used economic tactics against Venice. By renewing their commercial privileges and permitting them to trade in wheat, they persuaded the Venetians to make concessions and to relax their war effort. Since the wheat of Anatolia, Macedonia, Thrace and Thessaly was of vital importance not only to the city of Venice and the islands, but to the entire Po valley, Bâyezîd I was able skilfully to use the wheat trade as an instrument of policy. To appease the Venetians before the siege of Constantinople and to put them off their guard, Mehmed II granted them permission to export wheat. After the fall of the city he did not hesitate to grant Venice a capitulation, permitting a Venetian bailo to reside in Istanbul and Venetian merchants to trade freely in the empire, on condition that they pay customs duty, set at a mere 2 per cent.

Political tensions in the Morea and Albania finally led Mehmed the Conqueror into a long and dangerous war with Venice, lasting from 1463 to 1479, and forced him to take economic reprisals. He imprisoned all Venetian merchants and confiscated their goods. At the same time he sought to maintain trade with the west, by encouraging Florence and Ragusa (Dubrovnik) to take Venice's place. Up until this time Venice had usually bought Florentine cloth and sold it in the Levant, so that in the first half of the fifteenth century a doge of Venice could boast that he had bought sixteen thousand bolts of cloth in Florence and disposed of them in the Levant. In 1469 Mehmed the Conqueror granted new trade privileges to Florence. At that time there were some fifty Florentine houses trading in the empire, and Florentine merchants became increasingly active in the Bursa market. Bursa became an emporium for the sale of Florentine cloth to Anatolia and Iran, the Florentine traders buying Persian silk in return. Mehmed II kept on very good terms with the Florentines, condescending to attend their banquets in Galata, while Lorenzo de Medici (1469–92) attached particular importance to Mehmed's friendship, since the Ottoman market was an important source of Medici wealth. By annexing Bosnia and Herzegovina in 1463, Mehmed opened a new and direct trade route with Florence, through Ragusa. As trade with Florence expanded, the route between Ragusa and Bursa or Istanbul, through Foça, Novibazar, Edirne, and thence to Istanbul, or Bursa by way of Gallipoli, gradually gained importance. The Ottomans maintained strict security along this route. In 1501, for example, a load of silk belonging to some Florentines was stolen near Foça. The sultan immediately sent officers who found some of the load and made the local people pay for the remainder.[11] Goods from Ragusa passed to Ancona, a free port in papal territory, whence they were forwarded to Florence. The increasing number of Ottoman merchants – Greeks, Jews and Turks – who brought silks, spices and sugar along this route to the Italian fairs, began to cause Venice serious anxiety, even giving rise to rumours that Ancona was going to accept Ottoman protection. Settlements along this international trade route, such as Skopje, Foça or Mostar, grew to become typical Ottoman cities. While still a small town, Saraybosna (Sarajevo) established commercial links with the Dalmatian ports other than Ragusa, such as Split and Šibenik, and thus grew to become a great city and the centre of Bosnia. The famous Višegrad bridge across the River Drina and many caravanserais are among the masterpieces of sixteenth-century Ottoman architecture along this route.

Ragusa benefited the most from the opening of this Balkan land route. Although an Ottoman tributary in the time of Murâd II, this republic felt it necessary to remain on good terms with Venice and her nominal suzerain, the King of Hungary, even contributing ships to a crusading fleet against the Ottomans in 1444. At this period, Italy's trade with the Balkans, consisting largely of wheat and beeswax in exchange for gold or Florentine cloth, was largely sea-borne, passing through the port of Arta. After the extension of Ottoman rule over Bosnia and Herzegovina and the opening of the land route, Ragusa became completely dependent on the Ottoman Empire, and her annual tribute was increased to 12,500 gold ducats. As a tributary state, Ragusa paid less in customs than Venice, 2 per cent as against 4 or 5 per cent for Venice. She gradually enlarged her area of trade in the Ottoman Empire, exporting to the west wheat, beeswax, hides, raw silk and Bursa silk goods, and importing, like Venice, mainly woollens. This trade encouraged the growth of a wool industry in Ragusa, the first looms having been set up in the 1430s. Before the Ottomans opened the land-route in 1463, Venice sought to prevent the import of these woollen to the Balkans from the sea. In the second half of the fifteenth century the Ragusan woollen industry prospered and its products, although not of high quality, sold well in the markets of Istanbul, Bursa and Caffa. The cloth depot in Sofia became a Ragusan fondaco and colonies of Ragusan merchants established themselves in all important Balkan cities – Sofia, Belgrade, Sarajevo and Edirne – as well as in Istanbul and Bursa.

During the Ottoman-Venetian wars of 1463–79, 1499–1503, 1537–40 and 1570–73, Ragusa acted as an intermediary for trade between Venice and the Ottoman Empire. As a result, Ragusa's maritime trade prospered and her merchant fleet of twenty thousand tons at the beginning of the sixteenth century, had risen to sixty-five thousand tons by 1580. In the years 1537–40 Ragusa emerged as a serious rival to Venice in the spice trade between the Egyptian and Syrian ports and central Europe and Germany. The Fuggers and Ulstetters sent factors to Alexandria through Ragusa, and these transported the spices which they bought, in Ragusan ships. In 1531 in London the Ragusans loaded twenty-five thousand kerseys for the Ottoman market, having carried to London raisins and wine from Greece.

Ragusa was dependent on the economy of the Ottoman Empire. When the empire was economically linked to Italy in the west, Ragusa prospered under the sultan's protection. When, in the seventeenth century, the empire's economy became more dependent on the Atlantic states, Ragusa declined.

When there was no political or military dispute, the Ottomans unhesitatingly restored to the Venetians their commercial privileges. Venice always dominated the spice trade in the ports of Egypt and

Syria, and in 1546 the Ottomans granted Venice the monopoly of alum mining in return for a payment of twenty-five thousand gold ducats. Despite wars and conflicts, the Venetian economy in the sixteenth century continued in general to expand. Venetian ships sailed to the Levantine ports with woollens, her own silk brocades and satins, paper, glassware and mirrors, returning from Egypt and Syria with spices, drugs, dyestuffs, silk and cotton, and from Anatolia and Rumelia with wheat, hides, wool, cotton and silk.

In the sixteenth century the Levantine markets under Ottoman administration became richer and more attractive than before, and in the second half of the century France, England and Holland were actively participating in the trade, eventually confining Ragusan and Venetian commerce to the Adriatic.

Süleymân I made cooperation with France against the Habsburgs the cornerstone of his policy in the west. When Selîm I had occupied Egypt and Syria in 1517, the French had obtained from him a renewal of the capitulations which the Mamlûk sultans had granted. Süleymân I confirmed these at his accession to the throne. In February 1536 more extensive capitulations were negotiated between J. de la Forest and Ibrahîm Pasha, but these the sultan never confirmed, probably as a result of the execution of Ibrahîm in March. The first authentic Franco-Ottoman capitulations are those of 18 October 1569.[12] These capitulations for the first time extended to a western monarchy those commercial privileges, valid throughout the empire, previously granted to Venice. The French capitulations later served as a model for similar agreements with England, Holland and other European states.

France immediately began to compete with Venice. French consuls took up residence in Istanbul, Alexandria, Beirut and Tripoli in Lebanon. French ships bound for the near east carried Normandy textiles, paper and German hardware, bringing back wool, cotton, thread and cloth, cotton textiles and rugs from Anatolia, and silk, spices, perfume essences, drugs and mohair from Aleppo and Damascus. After the Ottoman–Venetian war of 1570–73 France began to displace Venice in the Levant. At the beginning of the seventeenth century there were about a thousand French vessels active in the commerce of the Levant, and the volume of trade rose to thirty million livres, half of France's total trade. Other European merchants, especially the English and the Dutch, traded under the French flag.

The Ottomans always tried to use these commercial privileges as a political weapon. For example they championed the Calvinists in France against the pro-Spanish Catholic League, and when Marseilles, the centre for the Levant trade, supported the league, the sultan abolished the commercial privileges and allowed the north African corsairs to attack the city. When Henry IV came to the throne in 1589 the Ottomans restored the privileges and French trade reached record heights.

Süleymân I had already in 1553 granted English merchants the right to trade freely in the Ottoman Empire, but they did not at first exploit this privilege. Hoping to obtain spices directly and more cheaply, they sought other routes, particularly the road from Moscow, through Iran to Hormuz. A Turkish embassy, sent to the shah in 1562, aimed at preventing this diversion. Finally, in 1578 the Ottomans invaded Azerbaijan and Shirvan and gained control of this route. At the same time, English merchants again approached the sultan. With Spain as a common enemy, the English and Ottoman governments clearly saw the advantage of a *rapprochement*, and despite the efforts by France and Venice to prevent it the sultan granted the English a capitulation in 1580 and a more extensive one in 1583. On 11 September 1581 the Turkey company which later, in 1492, united with Venice Co. to become the Levant Company was founded by royal charter. The Ottoman government lowered the customs rate for the English to 3 per cent, the French and other foreigners paying 5 per cent until 1673, when they succeeded in having it decreased also to 3 per cent. The Dutch traded under the English flag until 1612 when they received a similar capitulation.

The English competed fiercely with France and Venice, the former monopolists of the Levant trade. English pirates, sometimes in co-operation with the Algerian corsairs, began to raid the merchant fleets, Queen Elizabeth turning a deaf ear to all complaints. At the same time the English were selling fine quality woollens at low prices, and imports of English tin and steel were vitally important for the Ottoman arms industry. Venetian trade fell sharply, and in 1630 French trade declined by half, while the Levant Company dominated the Ottoman markets. English consuls settled in Istanbul, Izmir, Aleppo and Alexandretta. English attempts to break into the Indian Ocean after 1591 did not harm the Levant Company, since many people in London considered the Levant trade to be more important. In 1596 the English were buying spices from Egypt and Syria.

The mercantilist western states were eventually to change the character of the capitulations, gradually making the Ottoman economy a dependency of Europe. Ottoman statesmen considered it politic to encourage an ever-increasing flow of manufactured goods into the empire, in order to create abundance in the home market and to benefit the Treasury with increased customs revenue. The Levant thus became an open market for European commercialism. Nevertheless, since imports from Europe were limited to a few items, mainly woollens, minerals and paper, they did not greatly harm the native guild industries until the nineteenth century. It was only after the industrial revolution in Europe that the capitulations had disastrous consequences for the Ottoman economy.

In the early period, silver and silver coins were the most important items of trade with the west. To encourage its free import, the Ottomans removed all customs duties on silver, and from the 1580s, the cheap European silver which flooded the Levantine market caused a price revolution which shook the Ottoman economy and, with it, the traditional foundations of state and society.[13]

CHAPTER XV

THE OTTOMAN CITIES AND ROAD NETWORK, URBAN POPULATION, GUILDS AND MERCHANTS

THE IMÂRET SYSTEM, THE DEVELOPMENT OF ISTANBUL AND ITS RISE AS A COMMERCIAL CENTRE

In the traditional near-eastern empire the state undertook public works, such as the building and maintenance of canals, dikes, roads, bridges and caravanseries, since the promotion of trade and agriculture would enrich the ruler's Treasury. The Muslim historian, al-Tabarî (d. 923), noted that the Sassanids considered the establishment of towns, villages, roads and bridges as a fundamental duty of the sovereign. In the Islamic period the idea of public works as a pious or charitable act supplanted this tradition and thus, even when undertaken by a sovereign, they came to be regarded as independent institutions outside the realm of state activities.

Following the near-eastern tradition the Ottomans sought to transform their capitals – Bursa, Edirne and Istanbul – into great cities by increasing their population and encouraging their development as trading centres. The example of Istanbul best illustrates this.

Before the Ottoman conquest, the population of Istanbul had fallen to between thirty and forty thousand souls. After the conquest Mehmed could not, according to Islamic law, prevent his soldiers from pillaging the city, since it had not voluntarily surrendered; but he wished to take possession of his future capital as undamaged as possible. In the years following the conquest he took steps to transform Istanbul into the world's greatest capital.

First, he sought to induce the refugees to return by promising them the restoration of their property, freedom of worship and freedom of work. He released those prisoners who had fallen to him as his share of the spoils, and settled them in Fener, even for a time exempting them from taxation. Secondly, he ordered the provincial governors to send four thousand families from Rumelia and Anatolia to settle in Istanbul, announcing that he would grant the deserted houses in Istanbul to these new arrivals. They did not have to be Muslims but at least some of them had to be wealthy men, merchants or artisans. These orders were never fully executed. The Conqueror then selected and brought to Istanbul merchants, men of means and artisans from the important cities which he had conquered, in this way settling Christians from Amasra (1459), Old and New Phocaea (1460), Trebizond (1461), Corinth and Argos in the Morea (1458, 1463), Karaman (1470s), Euboea (1473) and Caffa (1475) in different quarters of Istanbul. According to a contemporary, J.M.Angiolello, 'within a short time, these new arrivals had constructed remarkable homes and churches.' Those who had been forcibly settled in the city could not leave but were exempted from a number of taxes and services.

Mehmed the Conqueror attempted to make Istanbul a universal metropolis by officially recognizing the spiritual leaders of the Greek Orthodox, Armenian and Jewish communities and establishing them in the city. After the conquest of Egypt, Selîm I was to abolish the office of the nagid to prevent his becoming a rival to the chief rabbi in Istanbul.

Throughout the fifteenth and sixteenth centuries the Ottomans encouraged the immigration of Jews from Europe, as an element bringing trade and wealth. During the reign of Mehmed the Conqueror, so many settled in Istanbul that by 1477 they formed the third largest section of the city's population after the Muslims and Greeks. To produce some of the food which the city and Palace required, Mehmed the Conqueror settled some thirty thousand peasants, captured during the Serbian and Morean campaigns, in thirty-five uninhabited villages near Istanbul. To prevent their abandoning the villages he held them in a servile status, not conforming to normal Ottoman practice.

A census of Istanbul and Galata taken in 1477 produced the results given in table 5.

TABLE 5

Community	Number of Families
Muslim	9,486
Greek Orthodox	3,743
Jewish	1,647
Armenian	434
Greeks from Karaman	384
Europeans, all in Galata	332
Non-Muslims from Caffa	267
Gypsy	31
	16,324

These totals probably do not include the military class. The total population of Istanbul must have been between eighty and one hundred thousand.

The construction of *imârets* – urban centres supported by vakîfs –

provided the city with public services and markets and played an important part in the growth of the city. The imâret was an old near-eastern institution which the Ottomans had adopted in the building of Bursa, Edirne and other cities. It was a complex of institutions – mosque, medrese, hospital, traveller's hostel, water installations, roads and bridges – founded with pious or charitable motives, and the institutions which provided revenue for their upkeep, such as an inn, market, caravanserai, bath house, mill, dyehouse, slaughterhouse or soup kitchen. The religious and charitable institutions were usually grouped around a mosque, while the commercial establishments stood nearby or in some suitably active place. These imârets were an essential part in the plans of all Ottoman towns, giving them their own peculiar character, and until recently they dominated the skyline of cities and towns in Anatolia and the Balkans.

Founders of imârets usually created them as vakîfs, the *vakfiye* – the deed of endowment – being drawn up before a kâdî, entered in his register and confirmed by the sultan. In fact, in Islamic society charitable institutions were nearly always established as vakîfs. This ensured the continued existence of the public service or institution, since a vakîf devoted in perpetuity the profits from any source to some charitable purpose, without impairing the capital. It was a legal fiction that from the time of its endowment only God had proprietary rights over a vakîf, so that even if governments or states should change the continuance of the public service was guaranteed. In the vakfiye recorded in the kâdî's register, the founder of a vakîf determined its purpose, conditions and forms of management, and appointed its *mütevellî* – chief trustee. In the Ottoman Empire, however, the state controlled and confirmed all vakîfs, since they had the character of freehold property.

A vakîf was a financially and administratively autonomous foundation. The endower appointed a mütevellî and, in large vakîfs, usually also a *nâzir* – superintendent. The mütevellî was responsible for all matters concerning the vakîf, taking measures for the collection and growth of its income and using these funds to fulfil the conditions of the endowment, to pay the foundation's employees and for maintenance and repair. The nâzir was an inspector, determining whether or not the conditions of endowment were being fulfilled and, once a year, the principal officers and employees of the vakîf would meet to discuss whether they had accomplished their duties as the vakfiye stipulated. This group could request the mütevellî's dismissal. The state, through the local kâdî or a specially appointed inspector, audited the accounts of each vakîf. The aim of all these precautions was to ensure that the institution continued to fulfil its proper function.

The system of vakîfs created the cultural and commercial complexes in Istanbul. Every important Ottoman city had a Great Mosque and a bedestan, and after the conquest, when Hagia Sophia became the Great Mosque of Istanbul, Mehmed the Conqueror ordered the construction of a bedestan as part of its endowment. With its stone domes and iron doors resisting fire and pillage, the bedestan was a monumental building, serving to protect not only valuable commercial goods but also the money and jewellery of the city's rich. Its doorkeepers, nightwatchmen and brokers were under government control. Shops were built around the outside of the central bedestan, and each group of shops, branching out and lining both sides of a road, formed a single market, occupied by members of a single craft or by merchants selling the same type of goods. These markets were usually roofed with stone vaults, as in the market at Istanbul, or else they stayed as lanes of open shops, shaded by trees.

There were 118 shops with store rooms in Mehmed the Conqueror's bedestan and 984 shops were erected in the surrounding markets. This was to become the main business centre of Istanbul, known today as the Covered Market. The construction of a bedestan, where merchants could congregate and valuable goods accumulate, usually played an important part in the growth of Ottoman cities. Orhan Gâzî had already in 1340 constructed a bedestan in Bursa, which to this day has remained as the commercial centre of the town. Trade centres grew up around bedestans in all large Ottoman towns in the Balkans, such as Tatar Pazarjik, Plovdiv, Sarajevo, Sofia, Skopje, Monastir, Serres and Salonica. In the seventeenth century the traveller Evliyâ Çelebi divided Ottoman cities into two categories, those with and those without bedestans.

In 1459 Mehmed the Conqueror assembled the empire's leading men and required each of them to create an imâret in any part of the city that he wished. The grand vizier, Mahmûd Pasha and, later, other viziers constructed fine imârets in the centre of the city and around the Golden Horn. Buildings devoted to the public good were erected around the mosque bearing the donor's name, and within a short time people settled near these imârets and founded new quarters. Istanbul thus took on its characteristic Turkish appearance.

Between 1463 and 1470 Mehmed the Conqueror built a Great Mosque and around it eight medreses, a school for children, a library, a hospital, two hostels for travellers and a refectory. To support these public institutions he built a large market of 318 shops nearby. Six hundred students studied in the medreses and each day the hostels accommodated 160 travellers. Travellers, students, servants of the vakîf and the neighbourhood poor received food from the kitchens. Two doctors, an eye specialist, a surgeon and a pharmacist served in the hospital, which a commissioner and his deputy administered. Two hospital cooks prepared the food under the doctor's supervision, and there were two hospital attendants whom the vakfiye enjoined to treat the patients kindly. The hospital accepted patients who could not afford to call a doctor to their home or to buy medicine. Two more hospitals, one for women and one for non-Muslims, were later added. Once a week the doctor visited poor patients at home and dispensed medicine. All the hospital's daily expenses, amounting to about five gold ducats, were met out of the endowment income.

Mehmed the Conqueror established other imârets in Istanbul. People from Bursa and other Anatolian towns settled around his foundation outside the city walls at Eyüp, which grew to become a large, separate town whose vakîfs included nine mosques and associated institutions. To meet the expenses of these foundations, Mehmed built in Istanbul markets (there were 260 shops in Galata and 783 in Istanbul, not including those in and around the bedestan), thirteen bath-houses, a number of dyehouses, bakehouses, warehouses, candleworks, oil-presses and fifty-four mills. Vakîfs with profits assigned to the up-keep of the Hagia Sophia mosque alone produced a yearly income of thirteen thousand gold ducats.

'Sultan Mehmed', in the words of the contemporary historian Neşrî, 'created Istanbul.'[1] His successors, Bâyezîd II and Süleymân I, and the royal women, statesmen, ulema, and merchants of the period, aided the city's rapid growth by founding imârets in other districts. According to an official survey of 1546, there were 2,517 vakîfs which non-royal persons had founded and to which 1,600 new vakîfs were added in the following half century.[2] The Ottoman sultans succeeded in developing Istanbul as a great imperial metropolis. With its population reaching four hundred thousand in the first half of the sixteenth century, Istanbul was the largest city in Europe, and it has been claimed that in the second half of the century its population rose to eight hundred thousand.[3]

To meet the city's food and water requirements became an enormous problem. The government, therefore, took measures to prevent the influx of new settlers, and in the seventeenth century the population did not change. At this time, 40 per cent of the population was non-Muslim, and Galata, where Europeans had received permission to reside, became a centre of international trade. In the mid-seventeenth century there were in Istanbul 152 Mosques, 126 medreses, a hundred caravanserais and about a thousand mansions which sultans, pashas and lesser persons had founded.[4] The necessity of maintaining a continuous food supply to the city, Palace and army, and supplying raw materials to the artisans, was a major factor determining the rigidly monopolistic character of the Ottoman economy with its strict governmental controls on the trade of necessities.

To prevent profiteering and inflation and the diversion of imports, the state regulated and controlled everything from the distant producer to the retailer in Istanbul. Food prices were fixed at the point of production; only state-authorized merchants bought the produce; and strict measures were taken to prevent smuggling. Provisions came to specified weigh-houses, whence they were distributed to representatives of the trade guilds. Large merchants and ship-owners had their goods or ships confiscated if they were caught smuggling or profiteering. Merchants who had received privileges to buy, in particular regions, sheep or wheat for Istanbul, undertook to deliver a specified amount of these items every year and appointed a guarantor.

The need to provide food for Istanbul linked the empire's various areas of production to a single centre and was a major factor in creating an integrated economy. The fact that in the mid-seventeenth century the city's ovens consumed 250 tons of wheat daily is an indication of the city's needs. Bulky foodstuffs, such as grain, oil, salt or sheep, could easily come to Istanbul by sea, and by the second half of the seventeenth century the number of food-carrying ships arriving each year in the docks of Istanbul had reached two thousand. Wheat, rice, sugar and spices from Egypt; livestock, cereals, edible fats, honey, fish and hides from the regions north of the Black Sea; cereals and hides from Thessaly and Macedonia; and wine and other Mediterranean products from the Morea and the Aegean islands, continually poured into Istanbul. Districts close to the capital were also dependent on the Istanbul market. From Tekirdağı came the wheat of Thrace, from Constanta and Mangalia the wheat of the Dobrudja. Timber was imported from Izmit. The Dobrudja, a no-man's land in the Middle Ages, became the granary of Istanbul, with the establishment there of hundreds of villages and the construction of state grain-storehouses at the ports. Rice from the Maritsa valley and western Thrace was an essential commodity for the Palace and army; from the plains of Bulgaria, Macedonia and eastern Thrace, dealers regularly sent sheep and cattle to the slaughterhouses of Istanbul.

As a transit and re-export centre, and as an exporter of manufactured goods, Istanbul provided an economic link between regions. The export of cottons from Merzifon, Tosya, Tire, Bergama, Denizli, Larende, Bor and Niğde in Anatolia, in return for foodstuffs for Istanbul from Rumelia and the north, appears to have stimulated the manufacture of cotton textiles in these places. At the same time, clothing, woollen and silk industries developed in Istanbul. In the trade triangle between the northern Black Sea region, Istanbul and Anatolia, a great deal of money came into and again left the capital. The state spent much of its revenue on the Palace and army in Istanbul, a large part of this money going to Anatolia and the Balkans.

THE EMPIRE'S ROAD NETWORK, CARAVANSERAIS AND HOSPICES

Istanbul was as much a terminus for caravan routes as it was for sea lanes. According to one account,[5] in the mid-seventeenth century six to ten caravans arrived each year from Iran, two from Basra, and three to four from Aleppo. Every three months, caravans left for Iran and central Asia. There was one caravan a year from Ragusa, one a month from Poland and one every eight days from Izmir.

There were three important highways connecting the Balkans to Istanbul; the ancient Via Egnatia from the ports of Albania through Ohrida, Monastir and Salonica; the great military road through Belgrade, Sofia and Plovdiv; and the road from the lower Danube region through the Tundza valley and Edirne. The caravan route from Iran and Anatolia reached Istanbul through Bolu, Izmit and Gebze, the road from Ankara joining it near Izmit. The pilgrim road from Arabia and Aleppo connected with the highway from Iran at Gebze, after crossing the Gulf of Izmit at Dil, beyond Iznik. In the fifteenth and sixteenth centuries the usual route from Istanbul to Bursa was by sea, through Mudanya, but it seems that in the seventeenth century the route from Gebze via Dil quay to Bursa became more important. Istanbul was thus connected through Bursa to Foça Çeşme, Chios and Izmir.[6]

Although Istanbul became the largest market in the empire, Edirne and Bursa did not decline; in fact they grew to become the largest cities and commercial centres of the Balkans and Anatolia.

Konstantin Jireček[7] wrote of Ottoman communications that 'not since the fall of the Roman Empire had any state in Europe devoted such care to its system of roads'. The Ottomans always kept in good repair the Roman road between Istanbul and Belgrade, improving it and repairing the broken sections as far as Belgrade with roughly hewn stones. They also built completely new routes along this track. Certain villages along the main routes had the task of constructing and maintaining roads, and in return for this service were exempted from extraordinary taxes. Waggons could travel along the road from Belgrade to Istanbul in one month. In 1566 Selîm II covered the same distance in fifteen days.

In Rumelia and the northern Black Sea region, heavy goods were carried by waggon; in mountainous areas mules were the normal means of transport. During the Belgrade campaign of 1521 the state hired thirty thousand camels from Anatolia and Arabia to transport the army's heavy baggage. About ten thousand waggons carried flour and barley from the Danubian regions. Both the state and individual merchants hired camels, horses and mules from nomads. Persian caravans consisted usually of three or four hundred animals, but some had one thousand or more, these animals normally being rented from and driven by Turcoman nomads. In the late fifteenth century a horse for the journey from Tabriz to Bursa and back could be rented for about nine gold ducats.

To ensure the ease and safety of travel on main roads, the sultans created establishments supported by vakîfs, and encouraged government and Palace officials, by granting them large estates, to do the same. Some of these were large establishments, like the imârets in the towns, only here the main buildings would be an inn, caravanserai and, perhaps, a bridge. Mosques and associated charitable institutions were less important. In 1443, for example, Murâd II constructed a great stone bridge, 392 metres long and with 174 arches, over the Ergene river near Edirne. At the head of the bridge he built a hostel to shelter and feed travellers, a mosque and a medrese, and met the expenses of the hostel and the cost of maintaining the bridge out of the income of a boza shop, bath-house and shops. He supplemented this income with the revenues from a caravanserai, bath-house and shops which he had built in Edirne. He settled people, mainly Turcoman nomads, nearby, to guard and maintain the bridge, in return for which they were exempted from taxation. On the other bank of the river he settled yayas – farmer-soldiers. In time, the population around this nucleus increased and the town of Uzunköprü came into being. In 1456 there were 431 families there. Another example is the imâret which Hersek Ahmed Pasha (d. 1517) established on the Istanbul-Damascus road, at the first station beyond the Gulf of Izmit. This later became the town of Hersek.

In the fourteenth and fifteenth centuries the frontier lords created similar foundations on the lands which they had conquered, and these nuclei were later to become Ottoman cultural and administrative centres. The city of Sarajevo grew up around the imâret which the frontier lord, Isâ Bey, had endowed, and the imâret which Minnet Bey had established on the Sofia-Edirne road became the nucleus of Tatar-Pazarjik, one of the most important commercial cities of Bulgaria. In this same town, on the military highway to central Europe, the grand vizier Ibrahîm Pasha constructed another great caravanserai which according to Evliyâ Çelebi dominated the city like a fortress. It contained two hundred rooms and eighty suites where important men could stay with their families. The rooms surrounded a courtyard shaded by a great tree, and an outer courtyard, with a pond in the centre, could accommodate five or six thousand horses. Day and night, servants received travellers, Muslim and non-Muslim. After sundown they brought each guest a bowl of soup, a loaf of bread and a candle, and each horse received a bag of oats. After evening prayer the caravanserai's band played and the gates were closed. Each morning, before the gates were opened again, the innkeeper asked the people who had spent the night there whether they had lost anything. If he opened the gates without doing this he was held responsible for any losses, for which he had to pay.

In 1555 the ambassador of the Holy Roman emperor, Busbecq, travelled to Istanbul in a horse-drawn carriage and has left a description of the caravanserai in Nish, where he complains that 'there is nothing done in secret; there all is open, and everybody may see what another does.' But he appreciated the suites in the hostel. 'They have several distinct apartments for lodging in them. There is no man to forbid the use of them, either Christian or Jew, rich or poor, they are open equally to all. Even Bashaws (Pashas) and Sanziacs (sanjak beyis), when they travel, make use of them. In these, I thought myself lodged as well as in the Palace of a prince.'

In his vakfiye, Mehmed the Conqueror required that all travellers staying at the hostel which he had endowed should be well treated and all their needs attended. Hostels offered three days free food and lodging, after which the traveller had to leave.

These foundations, constructed at regular intervals along the great highways, show the spread of Ottoman civilization. In the Ottoman period 232 inns, eighteen caravanserais, thirty-two hostels, ten bedestans and forty-two bridges were built in Bosnia and Herzegovina alone, the bridges including such architectural masterpieces as the Mostar bridge built in 1566, the Sarajevo Kozja bridge of about 1550, and the Trebinje bridge.

Buildings more modest than hostels, such as wells, fountains, places of prayer and small guest houses, were also constructed along the main road. Local benefactors usually built these, again as pious endowments. Thus travellers along the roads from Istanbul to Damascus, Erzurum and Belgrade had all their needs provided for, usually free of charge.

Some pashas were too zealous in founding such institutions. When the grand vizier, Mahmûd Pasha, was dismissed in 1637, he was accused of having built inns that were unnecessary and a burden on the people.

An important factor in the foundation of these vakîfs was the institution of *temlik* – the royal grant of property rights – according to which statesmen or Palace women could apply to the sultan with a project for a charitable undertaking and receive from him the freehold of a piece of land which in some cases included several villages. They then bequeathed these to the charitable enterprise which they had founded, thus assuring not only their own salvation in the next world but a continuous and secure livelihood for their own families and descendants by appointing them mütevellîs of the pious endowments. The second and third generation descendants of Ottoman notables frequently enjoyed a comfortable retirement as mütevellîs of vakıfs, forming a kind of a class of absentee landlords.

Caravanserais and bedestans were strongly fortified against brigands. Busbecq did not take the land route between Buda and Belgrade for fear of bandits, called 'hayduks', and there are many instances where highwaymen stole money belonging to the state. In the sixteenth century the situation was better than the seventeenth, where government troops were often ineffective against large bands of robbers armed with guns. In about 1647 a brigand called Kara Haydaroğlu operated in the mountainous region near Eskişehir, raiding caravans bound for Istanbul from Iran, Damascus and Izmir. He was overcome only with difficulty. Again in the mid-seventeenth century a Christian bandit with five hundred men made a night raid on the bedestan in Monastir and met with no resistance.

The government, therefore, took measures to maintain security on the roads, establishing zâviyes and posting *derbendcis* – guardians of a pass – near mountain passes, fords and bridges. Often, the entire population of a village was responsible for public security and the maintenance of a particular road or bridge, for which they received a number of tax exemptions. If the derbendcis deserted their posts they were brought back by force. In the mid-sixteenth century the state appointed 2,288 village families in Anatolia, and 1,906 in the eastern Balkans, as derbendcis. Zâviyes were institutions concerned especially with the security of travellers on the road.

Zâviyes played an important role in the Ottoman Empire, especially in the very early period, and were a prototype for the imâret. A zâviye was a pious foundation which a şeyh or dervish had founded to accommodate travellers in cities or, more frequently, along distant and lonely roads and passes. The şeyh or dervish who founded the zâviye would receive from the ruler a small parcel of land as freehold property, which he would bequeath to his foundation. He, and the dervishes who had gathered round him, would work the land, guaranteeing themselves a living and meeting the expenses of the zâviye, of which the şeyh and his descendants, like the mütevellîs of other pious foundations, were the hereditary administrators.

In the early Ottoman period, zâviyes played an essential role in settling Turkish immigrants on the frontier and in areas which the Ottomans had conquered. Dervishes, or poor immigrants posing as dervishes, came from Anatolia to a newly conquered zone, selected a plot of land and organized a zâviye, securing from the sultan a document which confirmed that this land was a vakıf for the zâviye. Since members of the zâviye received tax exemptions, new immigrants flocked to its lands, which became the nucleus of a new Turkish village. This was the origin of most of the Turkish villages established in the fourteenth century in western Anatolia and the Balkans. These hospices served at the same time as shelters for newly arrived immigrants and even for the gâzîs.

The şeyhs who established the zâviyes belonged to various religious orders, but many bore the title of 'ahî'. In the newly conquered land of Thrace, ahîs founded hundreds of zâviyes.[8] Ahî-ism was a less religious order than a social organization, of which Ibn Battûta, who visited Anatolia in 1333, has left us a vivid description:[9]

They exist in all the lands of the Turkmens of al-Rûm, in every district, city and village. Nowhere in the world are there to be found any to compare with them in solicitude for strangers, and in ardour to serve food and satisfy wants, to restrain the hands of the tyrannous, and to kill the agents of police and those ruffians who join with them. An ahî, in their idiom, is a man whom the assembled members of his trade, together with others of the young unmarried men and those who had adopted the celibate life, choose to be their leader. The ahî builds a hospice and furnishes it with rugs, lamps and what other equipment it requires. His associates work during the day to gain their livelihood, and after the afternoon prayer they bring him their collective earnings, and with this they buy fruit, food and other things needed for consumption in the hospice. If during the day a traveller alights at the town, they give him lodging with them.[10]

As the Ottoman Empire developed as a strong, centralized state, the government abolished most of the zâviyes, since by the sixteenth century many of them had lost their true functions while still enjoying tax exemptions, and so long as they remained as vakîfs the state could not use their lands for financial and military purposes. The state, therefore, abolished those zâviyes which were not situated on roads and performed no service for travellers, and those which did not expend their income on the charities for which they had been founded. The state would abolish the vakîfs and aquire the land. In the mid-sixteenth century there were eleven hundred hospices in Asia Minor. To revive villages destroyed in the Persian wars, Süleymân I permitted the establishment of zâviyes on the Erzurum road.

URBAN POPULATION, GUILDS AND MERCHANTS

The traditional near-eastern concept of society recognized farmers, merchants and craftsmen as the three productive classes. The last two groups formed the urban population, with the craftsmen on the lower rung of the social ladder. The sultan ordered the members of each class to wear clothes indicative of their station in life, forbidding craftsmen and shop-keepers to wear the luxurious garments of the upper classes.

The urban population of the empire, like the village populations, was divided into the two categories of Muslim and non-Muslim, but this was a classification which the şerîat imposed, and did not correspond to the real social and economic divisions in society. Muslim and non-Muslim merchants and craftsmen, in fact, belonged to the same class and enjoyed the same rights, while rich Jewish, Greek and Armenian merchant dressed and acted like Muslims. From time to time the sultans sought to fulfil the provisions of the şerîat by issuing laws forbidding non-Muslims to wear the same clothes as Muslims, to own slaves or to ride horses, but these decrees were ineffective. The guilds, too, sometimes tried to discriminate against non-Muslims in accordance with the şerîat but this was usually from motives of economic rivalry.

Away from work, however, the members of different faiths lived apart in separate quarters of the city, under the headship of their own religious leaders. Ottoman cities always had separate Muslim, Christian and Jewish quarters, the gypsies too having their own district, regardless of their religion. In each Muslim ward there was an imam, as religious head of the community, and a kethüdâ as its secular representative. Priests and rabbis performed the same functions in non-Muslim quarters representing the community before the government. This situation did not hinder the good relations between Muslims and non-Muslims. Muslim men often married non-Muslim women without the woman having to change her religion. The children, however, had to be Muslim.

In Ottoman cities the craft guilds were the mainspring of economic life, and guild members made up a great part of the population. The origins of guilds in the Islamic world remain obscure,[11] but there seems to be a close similarity between the Islamic and the mediaeval European guild systems. The commonly held theory maintains that the corporations of the Graeco-Roman world continued under Islamic administration, but that by the tenth century they had assumed a wholly Islamic character. In this century, the Karmatians, who emerged as the representatives of a religious, social and political movement opposing the government of the Abbasid caliphs, organized the guilds in this struggle. The Islamic guilds thus became Karmatian fraternities as much as professional organizations. After the Mongol invasions of the thirteenth century the Sufi orders and, especially, *futuwwa* ethics exercised a great influence over the guilds. The futuwwa societies, which young, unmarried workers organized in the larger cities, recall the fraternities of the Roman Empire. According to futuwwa ethics the perfect person is one who is generous, self-sacrificing, self-disciplined, obedient to his superiors and sober. Admission to such an organization entailed a symbolic ceremony, after which futuwwa ethics were inculcated in the entrant. During the thirteenth and fourteenth centuries this movement, under the name of ahî-ism, was the prevailing element in Anatolian society. In the cities, each group of craftsmen was organized, according to futuwwa principles, under the leadership of an ahî whom they chose from their own ranks. Since there was no strongly centralized authority in Anatolia during this period, the ahîs performed a number of public functions and became a political force in the cities. In fact from their inception the Islamic guilds had represented the popular opposition to the ruling military and administrative class.

In the early period the ahîs played an important role in Ottoman state and society, but with the growth of absolutism and centralism the state brought them more and more under its own control. In the cities, ahî-ism became simply a guild organization but the futuwwa ethics, nevertheless, continued within the crafts-guild.

It is an exaggeration to say that the state created and controlled the Ottoman guilds, or that they formed a socially undifferentiated community.[12] In near-eastern society, groups with common ideals and interests had since ancient times organized themselves according to a definite pattern, the same pattern and usually the same terminology being found in the Palace, army, medreses, religious orders and guilds. The most important member of a group thus organized was usually the man who represented it to the outside world and directed its external affairs. He was called kethüdâ by the Ottomans, sheikh by the Arabs and ahî in thirteenth-century Anatolia. In the guilds the master craftsmen selected as kethüdâ one of their own number who could execute the guild regulations and successfully petition the government on their behalf. This election was of paramount importance, since a guild without a kethüdâ was not considered independent. When a group of craftsmen within a guild wished to establish themselves as a separate body, they elected a kethüdâ and went before the local kâdî who registered them as an independent guild. The master craftsmen could, if they wished, remove a kethüdâ, and they always resisted government interference in the election of a new one. There are a number of documents concerning the guilds' rejecting kethüdâs whom the governor or kâdî wished to impose on them, and in fact the central government usually felt constrained to respect the autonomy of the guilds.

In this mediaeval society, these communities sought a religious and moral justification for their existence and for their regulations, and thus at the head of each craft-guild was a şeyh, representing this moral and religious authority. Although in the Arab lands the şeyh became the chief administrator of the guild, in the Ottoman heartland of Rumelia and Anatolia he remained in the position of a spiritual leader. The şeyh played an important role in the guilds, presiding at the apprenticeship and mastership ceremonies, and communicating and administering the penalties within the guild. He was elected from the experienced masters of the guild, who were well-versed in futuwwa ethics. Associated with the şeyh was an official who conducted the ceremonies. The government

communicated with the guilds through the kethüdâs, who also collected
and delivered to the government the taxes which the guilds owed.

Above the guild kethüdâs was a town kethüdâ, who was consulted on
matters common to all the guilds, and who together with other notables
represented the town to the government. Another important guild
member was the *yiğitbaşi*, the officer directing the guild's internal affairs.
He, too, was chosen from among the old and experienced masters, and
when the kethüdâ was absent from his duties the yiğitbaşi took his place.
He bought the raw materials in the market and distributed them to the
masters, checked whether the finished goods conformed to guild speci-
fications and delivered them to the other guilds or shops. It was also his
duty to notify the şeyh if anyone violated guild regulations and to inform
him and the kethüdâ of any person who sought promotion to a mastership. In some guilds the yiğitbaşi's assistant sometimes performed the
same tasks. Each guild also elected one or two *ehl-i hibre*, experts selected
from among the masters and thoroughly schooled in the intricacies of
the craft. They gave their opinions on the quality of the goods, settled
price disputes, helped in fixing the market price and chose the workers.
The selection of these experts was particularly important in delicate
crafts such as silk-weaving. In some guilds the ehl-i hibre also performed
some of the duties of the kethüdâ and yiğitbaşi.

In the larger and more developed guilds, these six people formed a
committee called 'the Six', but in many guilds only the şeyh and the
kethüdâ or yiğitbaşi are mentioned. These officers rose from among the
masters but the method of selection is not clearly known. It appears that
a consensus of opinion named the candidates for these positions and that
after the election, if there was no opposition to the candidate, all the
masters appeared before the kâdî to record the election in his official
register.

Ottoman guilds conformed to fixed rules and regulations. General
laws, principles and ceremonies had grown up over the centuries, many
of them being set down in manuals of futuwwa, guild certificates and
fermâns. Members of the guild discussed and decided on any new
regulations, entering them in the kâdî's records. After registration, they
were considered legally valid. To these one should add the *ihtisâb* regulations, fixing prices and quality, which were concluded in discussions
between the guild masters and representatives of the government, and
which the sultan confirmed. The state intervened in the guild organizations mainly to guarantee tax revenues from this source and to ensure
the application of the ihtisâb laws.

Ihtisâb was an old Islamic institution. The near-eastern state
regarded as its most important duties the protection of the people from
injustice and the remedying of their complaints. The Koran commanded that for the good of the Islamic community the authority should

actively support generally accepted social standards and prohibitions. These became part of the Religious Law, gathered under the heading of *hisba* or ihtisâb, and to implement them was one of the caliph's duties. In practice, hisba regulations mainly concerned trade and aimed at preventing fraud and profiteering, fixing fair prices in the markets and controlling weights and the quality of merchandise. In this way, methods of price control and inspection of weights and measures, which had already been in force in the ancient near-eastern states, were included in the framework of the şerîat, under the name of hisba.

The Ottoman state punctiliously applied the ihtisâb regulations, reviewing ihtisâb laws to which the guilds were subject on the accession of each new sultan. It inspected all weight and measures and the *muhtesib* – the officer enforcing ihtisâb regulations – constantly patrolled the markets to ensure the enforcement of these laws, bringing those who violated them before the local kâdî, and flogging or fining them according to the kâdî's decision. He stamped certain materials, such as timber, tile or cloth, according to their standard and prohibited the sale of unstamped materials. The local kâdî and the muhtesib had the authority to adjust market prices, which were fixed according to an established procedure. Prominent members of the community and the ehl-i hibre from the guilds would meet in the presence of the kâdî. They established the amount and quality of raw materials, added labour costs and fixed a market price giving a profit of about 10 per cent, or, if highly skilled labour had been employed, 20 per cent at the most. Sometimes the sultan himself inspected the registers of Istanbul market prices.

In order to control prices, prevent profiteering and collect dues, the state laid down a number of conditions for the sale of raw materials and finished goods in the markets. Merchandise for the city market had to enter the city through particular gates, whence it was carried through certain streets to specified markets or caravanserais, where it was sold under the supervision of officials on duty. Valuable goods had absolutely to be sold through special brokers under government control. After the goods had been weighed in the presence of guild representatives and taxed according to quantity, permission was given for their sale. The guild representatives – the kethüdâ and the yiğitbaşı – bought their goods or raw materials there, distributing them among the guild masters. The state collected from the guild masters a tax levied on each shop and another tax on some manufactured goods. There was also a sales tax, paid by weight or by the piece, on goods sold in the market place. Separate kânûnnâmes fixed the rate of these taxes for the cities and markets of each province. The concentration of the guilds in certain markets, and the sale of their goods at particular times, helped the state to collect these dues. If craftsmen dispersed in order to avoid paying them the state would forcibly bring them back to a particular market place.

The government interfered in the guild organizations only to protect the interests of the Treasury or the general public and did not intervene in their internal affairs. The guild regulations, however, recognized the higher authority of the state. The kâdî recorded all the elections and decisions of a guild and if they could not settle disputes among themselves or punish offenders against guild regulations, they referred the case to the state authorities, consulting first the local kâdî and then appearing before the imperial council in the capital.

The state usually attached importance to the preservation of the traditional guild regulations. Before the centralized Ottoman Empire had come into being, the guilds were much freer and much stronger. At the end of the thirteenth and beginning of the fourteenth centuries there was no strong government in Anatolia and, as Ibn Baṭṭuṭa observed, the ahîs at the head of influential guilds in the large cities possessed great power and influence. At this time, guild members carried weapons and punished troublemakers. Also a guild was not simply an economic organization but one bound by strong social bonds, permeated with the religious and mystical atmosphere of the futuwwa and revering a patron saint with whom it connected its traditions. In the Ottoman period, when the kethüdâ took the ahî's place, the guild's religious character weakened. To preserve their own authority, the officers of the guild began to invite the state to take a more and more active part in guild affairs. It became customary for them, on their election, to receive a diploma from the governor or the sultan, thus strengthening their own authority within the guild, and with the support of the state they succeeded in stemming the new currents which threatened the guild system, on which their own material interests usually depended.

The Ottomans, like the Mamlûks, almost always supported the senior masters of the guilds and sought to preserve the traditional guild structure. This conservative policy stemmed from the idea that any innovation would plunge society into disorder and anarchy, and that as a result the state Treasury could lose its sources of revenue. The guild masters, whenever they wished the state to act on their behalf, were always careful to make these points in their communications. Finally, administrative and military interests required stability in the price and quality of goods. This conservative policy continued until the nineteenth century, when reforming Ottoman statesmen adopted European liberal ideas. It was this conservatism that prevented the near-eastern economy breaking away from the restrictions of the guild system and hindered the growth of a strong Ottoman bourgeoisie.

In the nineteenth century the import of European manufactured goods limited the field of guild activity, and after 1840, in the face of European industrial capitalism, the guilds were economically destroyed.

In economic terms the guild structure was an attempt to satisfy the law of supply and demand in the face of certain difficulties. Guild representatives bought raw materials in the market at a fixed wholesale price and distributed them to the masters, because until the modern period the primitive system of communications meant that these materials were available only in limited quantities. Raw materials had to reach the guild concerned at a fair price, without falling into the hands of other parties or profiteers, and they had to be distributed among the guild-masters in a way which left none of them unemployed. This was a main reason necessitating guild organization. Scarcity of raw materials frequently caused high prices and unemployment in Ottoman towns and constituted a serious economic problem. These shortages could arise from hoarding and profiteering, from the attempts by some artisans to buy excessive raw materials, from the interest of another guild in the same material or from its purchase by merchants from another region or country, who offered higher prices. The guilds sought government controls to prevent the first and last of these situations, and the sultan issued decrees penalizing profiteering and permitting foreign merchants to buy goods from the market only after local people had made their purchases. Sometimes the state completely forbade the export of certain important raw materials. To prevent the second and third of these situations, which arose from competition among themselves, the guilds could only organize themselves to buy the raw materials wholesale and distribute them justly. A guild would obtain a decree from the sultan to prevent raw material from falling into the hands of outsiders and to give it a monopoly on production.

With only a limited amount of raw materials available, it was necessary to restrict the number of shops and workshops. Since there was a similar shortage of workmen, especially of highly skilled craftsmen, the guild officers also controlled the distribution of manpower. In Bursa, for example, the velvet weavers would, on a particular day of the week, gather in a particular spot where the guild's ehl-i hibre would assign them to the various masters, the aim of this system being to find qualified workers and to prevent competition among the masters for workers.

A second economic factor determining the guild structure was the limitation of the market. The rudimentary economic system and primitive communications meant that most of the urban guilds worked only for the limited local market, consisting of the town and surrounding villages. Furthermore, in the fifteenth century most Ottoman towns were very small.

It was necessary to regulate production according to the limited market, and this too determined a number of the guilds' characteristic aspects. First, the necessary limitations on production led to a restriction on the number of shops and workshops belonging to a guild, and secondly, it was necessary to protect the market from outsiders. The state, therefore, granted each guild a monopoly within a town or within a clearly defined area, and, furthermore, since each guild master had to be able to sell his own manufactures within this limited area, there could be no competition within the guild. To prevent competition, manufactured goods had to conform to well-defined standards. Methods of production, types of raw material, tools and particular features of the workshops were regulated; the ehl-i hibre and the yiğitbaşï continually inspected production; and finished products were again carefully inspected before going onto the market. They could then be sold only in certain market-places or shops, and in some guilds the yigitbaşï or kethüdâ sold the finished goods wholesale.

To preserve the balance between production and the market, only qualified masters had the right to open their own shops, a situation maintained partly by guild traditions and partly by the self-interest of established masters. To become a master and, above all, to open an independent shop, was extremely difficult. A candidate could attain mastership after a three- to five-year period spent gaining experience and skill, after which he underwent an examination and a ceremony in which the şeyh girded him with an apron, the symbol of mastership. His apprenticeship was a period of strict discipline and abstinence, surrounded by the obscure symbols and rhetoric of the futuwwa. Futuwwa ethics inculcated in the apprentice absolute obedience, modesty and disdain for wealth and taught him to regard greed and competition as the ugliest moral defects. A newly admitted master received tools, and a workshop under the control of the senior masters. Many new masters in the guilds, lacking the capital to open a shop, would work for the older members as kalfas – salaried foremen – or else go into partnerships.

However, despite this rigid structure, already in the fifteenth century, there were social and economic distinctions in the Ottoman guilds. Among the velvet-weavers of Bursa, for example, there was a distinction between those who owned the looms and shops and those whom they employed. Some of the workshop owners had fifty looms, representing a capital investment of 2,500 to 3,000 gold ducats. The velvet-weavers, however, formed a developed guild, producing valuable textiles for the external market. In the more traditional guilds, such as the tanners, if a master became sufficiently rich and independent he had to leave the guild and was considered a merchant.

In many of the guilds in large Ottoman cities, such as Istanbul,

Bursa, Salonica or Edirne, and especially in those producing for the outside market, there was a growing social and economic distinction between guild members who became capitalist entrepreneurs and those whom they employed. In those cities, guild production increased rapidly. In Istanbul, for example, the number of brocade workshops, officially fixed at a hundred, had risen to 318 in 1564, and even decrees from the sultans could not lower this to the official figure. In the sixteenth century there was an average increase of 80 per cent in the urban population of the Ottoman Empire and, consequently, the market for guild products expanded. This created a situation favourable to the wage-earning masters and kalfas in the guild, encouraging them to embark on independent enterprises. Many of them opened independent shops in different quarters of the town and began production. The heads of the guilds were unable to combat them successfully, as they had done in the past, and the rebels thus not only shared the increased profits of the guild masters but at the same time undermined the guilds' regulations and controls. They changed the traditional standards of productions, lowered quality and sold more cheaply; they introduced new fashions and stimulated demand. In an attempt to preserve their monopoly in the expanding market, the old masters urged the government to take action against their competitors, insisting that they were unskilled novices who had neither learned their craft fully nor received master's certificates, and that by lowering quality and raising prices they harmed the people and undermined the state's ihtisâb laws. When their competitors introduced a popular but expensive pointed-toe style, the shoemakers' guild of Istanbul accused them before the government of leading the people along the path of frivolity and immorality. The old masters struggled to the end to close the shops of any who introduced technical innovations. The Ottoman government's strong support of the traditional guild structure prevented the development of separate organizations for workers and foremen, and for capitalist masters, as in Europe.

The government's conservative policy strengthened the monopoly of the old masters in the guilds. Masters who possessed workshops began to leave these as family heirlooms to their sons, sons-in-law or relatives, and in time the titles of master, kethüdâ and yiğitbaşı became hereditary, passing from father to son or, very occasionally, to an old foreman. Finally, by the eighteenth century these possessions and titles lost all connection with craft or craftsemanship, becoming simply matters of legal ownership.

The entrance of kapïkulu troops into the town guilds was another factor in the decline of the Ottoman guild system. Their military privileges freed them from the control of the muhtesib and kâdî, enabling them to alter the guild structure to their own advantage.

They frequently ignored the officially fixed market price, lowered quality, and opened shops wherever they wished, without first receiving a master's certificate. They frequently forced established masters to take them into partnership and divide the profits and, worst of all, their large-scale profiteering in raw materials went unpunished. All these factors played a major part in the deterioration of the traditional guild structure and the decline of Ottoman crafts in general.

In prosperous towns, new guilds were formed as offshoots of the old ones, to produce new types of goods or to undertake particular stages of production. For example, tanners who worked leather in different colours formed separate guilds, as did the silk twisters and weavers in the textile industry. In large cities, men working in the same craft but in two different markets were able to form separate guilds. If a group working in a specialized branch of a craft became sufficiently large, they chose a kethüdâ and appeared before the kâdî to inform him that they wished to become a guild. The main guilds often opposed this, refusing to recognize the elected kethüdâ and claiming the new guild's masters to be unqualified. In such a case the government's approval was essential for the establishment of the guild. The government would confirm the guild's existence if it did not consider this to be contrary to hisba regulations or harmful to the interests of the people.

Associated guilds frequently struggled among themselves, while guilds in the position of entrepreneurs were able to reduce others to a dependent status, these subject guilds being known as *yamaks*. For example, in the highly developed silk industry of Bursa, the silk merchants dealing in raw silk formed a guild which acted as entrepreneur. They bought imported raw silk in the bedestan, giving it to the twister's guild to work into thread and to the dyers' guild to colour, finally selling the prepared skeins to the weavers. The yamaks sometimes sought to overthrow the domination of the larger guilds by refusing to work, but since such actions resulted in unemployment and a drop in tax revenues, the government usually supported the main guilds. The formation of new groups, however, was a dynamic aspect of the guild system and their number varied according to the size and prosperity of the town. In Istanbul there were about one hundred and fifty important guilds. There were about sixty in Bursa in the fifteenth century, and about fifty in seventeenth-century Manisa. (It has been estimated that there were one hundred and fifty guilds in ancient Rome and two hundred and ten in mediaeval Cairo.)

The Ottoman guilds varied in their stages of development according to the prosperity of the cities and the demands of the external market, but there was a general tendency towards an unrestricted system of production in big cities. Domestic industries grew up outside the guild system. In Anatolia, for example, the cottage weaving industry supplying the merchants with cotton cloth spread from the towns to the villages, much of its production being destined for the foreign market. In industries regularly supplying the state with materials in bulk, there are indications of capitalistic production. For example, the wool industry in Salonica, which each year supplied thousands of bolts of coarse woollen cloth to the Palace and the Janissaries, developed under state control and employed about a thousand Jewish families. It produced woollens for the entire empire and for the foreign market. In 1664 it was agreed to concentrate in one place all the workshops making broadcloth for the state.

To meet its own need for firearms and powder the state created, in Istanbul, factories employing hundreds of labourers, financed by state capital and directed by government-appointed commissioners. During the Cyprus campaign of 1571 the Kağïthane gunpowder factory in Istanbul produced seventeen tons of gunpowder a month. Private individuals, however, did not imitate this model. Although there were, in Istanbul and Bursa, a number of places where many workers were employed together, Ottoman industry in general never developed beyond the putting-out system.

Apprentices, workmen on wages and slaves made up the main work force of the guilds. In the Bursa weaving industry, slaves trained in the craft were the main source of labour, securing their freedom when they had woven an agreed amount of cloth. The free labourers who hired themselves out were usually kalfas with no capital and were usually employed on a weekly basis. Apprentices were normally children or youths whom their parents had placed with a master to learn a trade. According to the contract, the master promised to teach an apprentice the trade within a certain length of time, usually 1,001 days. The parent hired out the child, receiving a lump sum from the master during the course of the contract. After this, the apprentice received either no wages or perhaps a small weekly sum, and in accordance with guild ethics he owed the master complete obedience. The master, for his part, had to treat him like a son. The masters' greatest worry was that the hired help might leave in the middle of the week, or that the apprentices might change masters, and to prevent this they sought the intervention of the government.

Some guilds employed women. In Ottoman towns, silk-winding and cotton-spinning were usually left to women and children, and in this way poor urban women could earn a living. Cotton-weaving guilds from time to time tried to make the government prevent merchants buying up cotton in the markets, leaving the women unemployed.

In near-eastern society artisans played a more important part in politics than has often been thought. The *Mirror for Princes* literature taught that the ruler who did not defend the urban merchants and artisans against the injustices of government officials, would eventually fall, and events bore out this view. Any government which had lost the support of the urban population saw its authority weakened, and at times of foreign invasion saw its urban subjects desert to the enemy. The ruling military class was, therefore, careful to win the favour of local notables who were the spokesmen for their districts. In the towns, the ulema, rich merchants and guild officials took it upon themselves to represent the townspeople. It was they, for example, who would appear before the kâdî to complain of a government official or to demand the abolition of an illegal tax, and it was they who would send a committee to the imperial council in Istanbul. The government usually considered it expedient to accept their requests. Before the reign of Mehmed II, and from the end of the sixteenth century when the central government was weak, these notables, who collectively re-presented the interests of the city, became extremely influential. They could force any governor whom they disliked to depart, and no admini-strator could perform his functions without their approval and media-tion. Some cities, such as Kayseri and Sarajevo, obtained important privileges, including exemption from some taxes and a prohibition on troops' entering the city. These privileges were so wide that some modern writers have regarded these towns as free cities and even as city-republics.

The most effective means by which artisans could resist the govern-ment was to close their shops and suspend production, the equivalent of peasants' fleeing the land. Typical of this was the artisans' uprising in Istanbul in 1651. When the government tried to force the artisans to buy some confiscated goods at too high a price and to call in gold at one-third of the current rate, a vast crowd of artisans went to the imperial council to demand justice from the grand vizier. They were driven away, and on the next day they closed their shops and assembled under their banners. According to an eyewitness,[13] some 150,000 men assembled, many of them carrying weapons, eventually forcing the sultan to dismiss the grand vizier. This was the first event to challenge the power of the Janissary junta which at that time tyrannized the state.

As in other near-eastern states, the lower strata of urban artisans always opposed the ruling military class. During military uprisings the sultan would look for support to the guilds, while the Janissaries, seeking revenge, would plunder and burn the shops in Istanbul. At the end of the sixteenth century, however, this situation changed. More Janissaries began to enter the guilds and military insurrections assumed a more popular character.

In Ottoman towns, and throughout the whole near east, traders as well as craftsmen organized guilds. There were, however, two classes of trader, those who handled local and guild produce having an inferior status to those who handled the caravans and overseas trade. The first category were known as *esnâf*, a term used for shopkeepers and artisans alike, and the second usually as *tüccâr* or *bazirgân* – merchants. The esnâf shopkeepers were subject to the ihtisâb regulations and organized according to the traditional guild structure, while the ihtisâb laws did not affect the large merchants. These were the real capitalists of near-eastern society. There was nothing to stop them undertaking any kind of enterprise and increasing their wealth to an unlimited extent. In fact the state encouraged their enterprises. The upper administrative class – pashas, beys, Palace officials and rich pious foundations – who were able to amass fortunes in coin, invested their money through these merchants. The institution of *mudâraba*, a form of commercial cooperation where an investor placed his money in a trading venture by caravan or ship, was widespread in the Ottoman Empire.

Luxury goods, such as jewels, expensive textiles, spices, dyes and perfumes, made up most of the overseas trade. Large merchants, therefore, dealt mainly in these goods, most of them conducting their business in the bedestan. This class of wealthy merchants provided the state with its tax farmers and formed an influential group in the towns. Some were extremely rich, like the two Bursa merchants who in 1480, in partnership, invested eleven thousand gold ducats in the Egyptian trade. For comparison, the Italian merchant Andrea Barbarigo had in the 1450s a total capital of only fifteen thousand gold ducats.

The kâdîs' registers record the wealth of people who died in the great Ottoman city of Bursa in the second half of the fifteenth century. They show that 26 per cent of the deceased had possessed less than twenty gold ducats; 58 per cent had possessed twenty to two hundred; and 16 per cent had had over two hundred. Thus one-sixth of the population were well-off, the very rich, with more than two thousand gold ducats, representing 1.3 per cent of the total. These were the merchants, money-changers, jewellers and silk weavers. Money, property, male and female slaves, silk and other fine textiles constituted their wealth, the main sources of which were the silk trade and industry and credit operations.[14]

After the second half of the sixteenth century the families descended from kapïkulu officers gained control of tax-farming and began to dominate the towns, both socially and politically, a development running parallel with the decline of near-eastern international trade and the weakening of the merchant class.

Part IV

RELIGION AND CULTURE IN THE
OTTOMAN EMPIRE

CHAPTER XVI

LEARNING, THE MEDRESE AND THE ULEMA

Taşköprülüzâde's* concept of knowledge and his division of the sciences provides a starting point for a study of learning and medrese education in the Ottoman Empire.

Taşköprülüzâde recognizes four stages of knowledge – spiritual, intellectual, oral and written – parallel with the theory of creation in Islamic mysticism.† The spiritual sciences he divides into two branches, practical and theoretical. These he further subdivides into those based on reason alone and those based on the Islamic religion. Thus all the sciences fall into one of these seven categories.:

A. The calligraphic sciences: writing implements, styles of writing, etc.

B. The oral sciences: the Arabic language and phonetics, lexicography, etymology, grammar and syntax, rhetoric, prosody, poetry, composition, history and the other literary sciences.

C. The intellectual sciences: logic, dialectics.

D. The spitiual sciences.

The spiritual sciences he divides into:

1. The theoretical rational sciences: general theology, natural sciences, mathematics.

2. The practical rational sciences: ethics, political science.

3. The theoretical religious sciences: the Koran and traditions of the Prophet, and the sciences devoted to their interpretation – Koranic exegesis, the study of prophetic traditions, Islamic theology and the principles of Islamic law and jurisprudence.

4. The practical religious sciences: practical ethics, etiquette, ihtisâb, and all subjects relating to Muslim life and worship.

The goal of all knowledge and, in particular, of the spiritual sciences, is knowledge of God.

* Taşköprülüzâde Ahmed (1495–1561); Ottoman encyclopaedist and medrese teacher best known for his *Shakâik al-nu'mâniya*, a biography in Arabic of 522 Ottoman şeyhs and ulema, and *Mawdû'ât al-'ulûm*, an encyclopaedia of the sciences.

† A sufi doctrine according to which God manifested himself in stages, as the universal spirit, the intellect, nature and man.

Among the hierarchy of the sciences there is another category, where they are arranged according to their utility and where the useful sciences such as politics, are referred to as *fen*. The sciences are similarly divided into good and bad. Those which aid religion are good; sciences like astrology are bad.

In his religious views Taşköprülüzâde inclines to mysticism. Following al-Ghazâlî*, he maintains that contemplation is a necessary complement to the spiritual sciences. This contemplation is the subject of the mystical sciences, whose goal is divine gnosis, a mystic knowledge which a man may attain when through asceticism and meditation he divorces himself from worldly interests. The scholar who studies only the exoteric religious sciences is a poor man, excluded from the greater realities.

A student, according to Taşköprülüzâde, must study all the sciences, since they complement each other in forming a single word. A man who devotes his life to a single branch of knowledge is far removed from divine truth.

The essential element in an Islamic education was the *müderris*, a man of recognized authority in the religious and spiritual sciences. He could also be a specialist in a particular field; but every student had, before anything else, to undergo a thorough education in the religious sciences. Similarly, he received a grounding in all aspects of Arabic, the language, of the sciences. If a student required a specialist training, he would travel to wherever there was a well-known scholar in the field and seek from him a diploma of competence in this science. It was thus the müderris himself who was important and not the institution.

The first Ottoman medrese was created in Iznik in 1331, when a converted church building was assigned as a medrese to a famous scholar, Dâvûd of Kayseri. In later years, when an Ottoman sultan wished to establish a new medrese, he would invite scholars from the old Anatolian cultural centres, such as Konya, Kayseri or Aksaray, or from elsewhere in the Islamic world, from Persia, Turkestan Egypt or Syria. In the reign of Murâd II, Alâ al-Dîn of Tus (d. 1482) and Fakhr al-Dîn,† who had been brought from Persia, enhanced the reputation of the rapidly developing Ottoman medrese. During the formative period of Ottoman culture in the fourteenth and fifteenth centuries, Ottoman ulema travelled to Egypt, Persia or Turkestan to complete their education under the great scholars of those lands. For the study of Koranic exegesis and jurisprudence they went primarily

* Al-Ghazâlî (1058–1111); a great Muslim theologian, jurist and mystic, whose doctrine reconciles the orthodox teachings of the şerîat with the mysticism of the sufis. His influence on Islam has been compared to that of St Augustine on Christianity.

† Fakhr al-Dîn; Persian scholar. He studied in Iran and Turkey and settled in Edirne as müderris and müfti under Mehmed I and Murâd II.

to Egypt and Persia; Mehmed al-Fanarî,* Alî al-Fanarî,† Şeyh Bedreddîn and others travelled to these countries. In the fifteenth century, scholars such as Sa'd al-Dîn al-Taftazânî‡ and Sayyid Sharîf al-Jurjânî,§ famous in the religious sciences, flourished in the territories ruled by the dynasty of Timur, and more and more students went there to study under them. For the study of mathematics the Ottoman ulema went usually to Samarkand.

Mehmed the Conqueror lamented that although he had established a great empire, his realms contained no ulema comparable with those of other lands. Among the native ulema he could take pride only in Molla Hüsrev‖ and Hocazâde. After the conquest of Istanbul he converted eight churches into medreses for eight famous scholars; and when, between 1463 and 1470, he built the Conqueror's Mosque, he established around it the eight famous medreses known as the *Sahn-i semân* or the *Semâniye*, and again assigned each one to a scholar. These stone medreses, fine examples of the Ottoman architecture of this period, were built on either side of the mosque; there were eight higher medreses, for specialized studies, and eight lower medreses, which prepared students for these. The daily pay of the müderris in charge of each one was fifty akçes, equal to about one gold ducat. Each medrese had nineteen rooms and one classroom. Fifteen of these rooms were allocated to specialist students, known as *dânişmends*, whom the müderris selected from among the students who had completed a course in a lower medrese. These students each received two akçes daily from the endowment income and food from the hospice. Each medrese had an endowed library and there was a separate general library. The müderris selected one of the dânişmends as an assistant, who repeated lessons and supervised student discipline. He received five akçes daily. Students were required to devote their whole time to study.

At this period, the Semâniye medreses were the highest ranking educational institutes in the empire. Below them came the Dârülhadîs medrese which Murâd II had founded in Edirne, and below this the medreses which the earlier sultans had established in Bursa. Beneath these royal foundations were those endowed by great men of state in

---

* Mehmed al-Fanarî (1350–1431); traditionally regarded as the first şeyhülislâm of the empire. He studied in Anatolia and Egypt.

† Alî al-Fanarî (d. 1497); grandson of Mehmed al-Fanarî, müderris and kâdîasker.

‡ Sa'd al-Dîn al-Taftazânî (1322–89 or 1390); writer on Islamic law, theology, metaphysics and other subjects. Born in Khorasan, he moved eventually to Timur's court at Samarkand.

§ Sayyid Sharîf al-Jurjânî (1340–1413); theologian, grammarian and logician. He taught first at Shiraz and then, after Timur's conquest of that city, moved to Samarkand. He died in Shiraz.

‖ Molla Hüsrev (d. 1480); Ottoman scholar and jurist. He became müderris, kâdîasker and şeyhülislâm under Murâd II and Mehmed II. His works on jurisprudence became standard textbooks in Ottoman medreses.

these three towns or in the provinces. The most famous of these were the medreses of Alî Pasha in Edirne, Şihâbeddîn Pasha in Filibe (Plovdiv), Mahmûd Pasha in Istanbul, Eski Alî Pasha in Bursa and Ishâk Bey in Üsküp (Skopje). Ranking with these were the old medreses which had been founded in Anatolia before the Ottomans.

Ottoman medreses fell into two major categories. The first category, known as *hâriç* – exterior – medreses, gave preparatory instruction in the 'Fundamentals of Knowledge', that is in Arabic and the intellectual sciences. The second category, called *dâhil* – interior – gave instruction in 'Higher Knowledge', that is in the religious sciences. These, too, were divided according to their degree:

THE HÂRIÇ MEDRESES

(a) The lower medreses, known as *ibtidâ-yi hâriç*, taught the rudiments of Arabic grammar and syntax, logic, scholastic theology, astronomy, geometry and rhetoric. These medreses were called 'Tajrîd medreses', after Sayyid Sharîf's commentary on the 'Tajrîd' of Nasîr al-Dîn of Tus,* a theological work which was the main textbook in their course. They were known also as 'medreses of twenty', since the müderris received twenty akçes daily.

(b) Next in rank came the medreses called either the 'medreses of thirty', or the 'Miftâh medreses', after their chief textbook, the *Miftâh*, al-Sakkâkî's† work on rhetoric. They gave instruction in rhetoric and the literary sciences.

Most of the 'medreses of twenty and thirty' were in the provinces.

(c) Above these came the 'medreses of forty' and the 'medreses of fifty', which princes, ladies of the royal family, or viziers, had founded in Istanbul, Edirne and Bursa. They gave an elementary course in the interpretation of the *Miftâh*, an intermediate course in scholastic theology, based on 'Adûd al-Dîn's *Mawâkif*,‡ and a higher course in jurisprudence, based on al-Marghînânî's *Hidâya*.§

THE DÂHIL MEDRESES

(a) Dâhil 'medreses of fifty', known as the *ibtidâ-yi dâhil*, founded by

* Nasîr al-Dîn of Tus (1201–74); a leading Muslim mathematician and astronomer who distinguished himself also in philosophical and ethical subjects.

† Al-Sakkâkî (1160–1229); scholar, born in Transoxiana, remembered for his *Miftâh al-'ulûm*, a work on rhetoric, known as the most complete of its kind.

‡ 'Adûd al-Dîn (after 1280–1355); honorific title of the theologian al-Ijî. Born in Shiraz, he is remembered for his *al-Mawâkif ftilm al-kelâm*, a comprehensive work on Islamic theology.

§ Al-Marghînânî (d. 1197); a hanafite legist, active in Ferghana. The *Hidâya*, which summarises his own legal compendia, is considered the most comprehensive work on Islamic jurisprudence.

sultan's daughters, princes or viziers. At an elementary level they taught the *Hidâya*; at an intermediate level they taught the principles of jurisprudence from al-Taftazânî's *Talwîh*; at an advanced level they taught Koranic exegesis from al-Zamakhsharî's *Kashshâf*.*

(b) Above these came Mehmed the Conqueror's eight preparatory medreses, known as *tetimme* or *mûsile-yi sahn*.

(c) At the highest level were the Semâniye medreses, where students studied a group of three subjects – Islamic jurisprudence, Koranic exegesis or scholastic theology, rhetoric, and related studies – and received specialized training.

Süleymân I made an important change in the hierarchy of Ottoman medreses. Around the mosque which he founded in Istanbul between 1550 and 1556, he established four general medreses, and two more for specialized studies, the one devoted to the science of *hadîth* – the traditions of the Prophet – and the other to medicine. To these he gave the highest rank, thus establishing the hierarchy of medreses which was to continue until the end of the empire. All the hundreds of medreses throughout the empire were categorized according to these eleven grades.

Medreses were concentrated in certain large cities. In 1529 there were fourteen in Edirne. In the seventeenth century there were as many as ninety-five in Istanbul alone; by the nineteenth century their number had risen to 170. Forty-nine of these medreses had been founded by pashas, thirty-five by other members of the ruling class, thirty-five by ulema, twenty-six by sultans and the rest by others.

The medrese, both in the pre-Ottoman and the Ottoman period, was an institution supported by a vakîf, and was usually one component in a complex of mosque, hospice and other charitable institutions. The mütevellî of this complex entrusted to the müderris the funds allotted to the medrese; the müderris was responsible for selecting students, for disbursing these funds to students and servants, and for the general administration of the medrese. Thus a medrese was a self-governing unit within a vakîf, itself an autonomous institution. The müderris was appointed by royal warrant.

The ulema were recruited from the medreses. Islam does not, in principle, accept as an intermediary between God and man any priestly class representing a compulsory religious authority. Nevertheless, the ulema, a religious group similar to the priestly class in the old near-eastern civilizations, did eventually emerge in Islam and came to play an important part in every aspect of social and political life.

The ulema had the dual role of interpreters and executors of Islamic

* Al-Zamakhsharî (1074–1144); a philologist and one of the most famous Koran commentators, active in Khwarezm.

Table 6

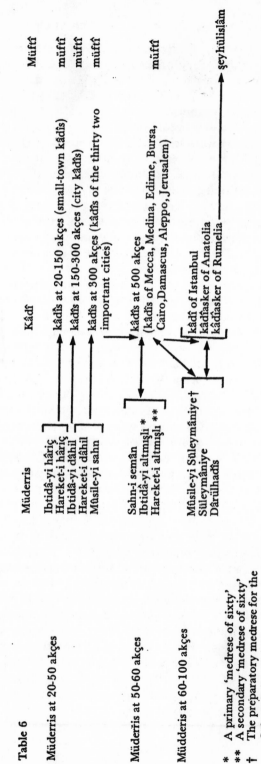

Müderris	Kâdî	Müftî
Ibtidâ-yi hâriç Hareket-i hâriç Ibtidâ-yi dâhil Hareket-i dâhil Mûsile-yi sahn	kâdîs at 20-150 akçes (small-town kâdîs) kâdîs at 150-300 akçes (city kâdîs) kâdîs at 300 akçes (kâdîs of the thirty two important cities)	müftî müftî müftî
	kâdîs at 500 akçes (kâdîs of Mecca, Medina, Edirne, Bursa, Cairo, Damascus, Aleppo, Jerusalem)	
Sahn-ı semân Ibtidâ-yi altmışlı * Hareket-i altmışlı **		müftî
Mûsile-yi Süleymâniye† Süleymâniye Dârülhadîs	kâdî of Istanbul kâdîasker of Anatolia kâdîasker of Rumelia	şeyhülislâm

Müderris at 20-50 akçes

Müderris at 50-60 akçes

Müderris at 60-100 akçes

*   A primary 'medrese of sixty'
** A secondary 'medrese of sixty'
†   The preparatory medrese for the Süleymâniye

law, the *müftîs* performing the first of these duties and the kâdîs the second. They were responsible for the application of the şerîat in the state. The political authority, founded on physical strength, was in practice the dominant element of state, but according to Muslim theory political authority was merely a means for the application of the şerîat: 'The state is subordinate to religion.' For this reason the ulema class regarded the secular authority as its subordinate and strove to put this theory into practice.

The ulema attributed their sole authority in the şerîat to their competence in science. To enter their ranks a candidate had first to study science, that is to acquire the knowledge necessary for a true understanding of the Koran. One of the ulema had then to certify their competence. This act of certification was a link in a chain stretching back to the Companions of the Prophet Muhammed: 'The ulema are heirs to the knowledge of the Prophets.'

In the Ottoman Empire there was a rigid hierarchy of ulema – müderrises, müftîs and kâdîs – and a strict system of promotions. Table 6 shows the outlines of this system.

The müderrises of hâriç medreses or graduates of the Semâniye medreses could become kâdîs of small towns, earning between 50 and 150 akçes daily. The senior kâdîships, at three hundred akçes or more, reach the most elevated posts in the religious and legal professions and were known as *mollas*. For example, a kâdî earning three hundred akçes or more could become defterdâr of the imperial dîvân. A müderris at the Semâniye or at a higher medrese could become a molla earning five hundred akçes, with a possibility of promotion to become kâdî of Istanbul and, later, kâdîasker. A kâdî earning five hundred akçes could become nişancı of the imperial dîvân. Thus the highest ranks in the bureaucracy and not only the religious and legal professions were open to them; many became viziers and attained positions of political power.

The kâdîaskers of Rumelia and Anatolia, the kâdî of Istanbul and the kâdîs of the eight most important cities were the highest-ranking ulema. It was they, with the şeyhülislâm at their head, whose oath of allegiance confirmed the sovereignty of each new sultan to ascend the throne. When a sultan was deposed it was this group of ulema who confirmed and legalized the deposition. However, it should not be forgotten that the religious head of the Islamic community was always the sultan-caliph, and that the ulema at all times exercised religious authority in his name. In the Ottoman Empire the power of appointing and deposing the ulema always remained in the hands of the sultan and his grand vizier, representing the secular authority. The şeyhülislâm, however, occupied a special position.

The şeyhülislâm was the head of the ulema, appointed by royal warrant and chosen until the sixteenth century from among the müderrises distinguished for their learning. His duty was to issue fetvâs, that is to give written answers, based on standard religious authorities, to any problem falling within the scope of the şerîat. He received, on principle, no fee for performing this duty. Anyone else of recognized religious authority could issue fetvâs and every important town or city in the empire had its müftî to perform this task. These men formed a separate class under the şeyhülislâm.

In the attempt to characterize the importance of the şeyhülislâm, western observers have compared him with the pope. The Kânnûnâme of Mehmed the Conqueror placed his rank on a level with that of the grand vizier, and protocol required that he should receive the greater respect. Until the second half of the sixteenth century the şeyhülislâms were not customarily deposed. As representatives of the şerîat they tried to act independently of the political authority. During the course of the sixteenth century, as the şerîat became increasingly dominant in affairs of state, the influence of the şeyhülislâms increased accordingly; but at the same time, and in the same proportion, they became more dependent on the political authority. The şeyhülislâm's first taste of secular power came when he received control of the kâdîships, an arm of the executive firmly attached to the political authority. From this time onwards the power to appoint kâdîs earning more than forty akçes daily, and kâdîs with the rank of molla, passed from the kâdîaskers to the şeyhülislâm.

CHAPTER XVII

OTTOMAN SCHOLARSHIP

Ottoman scholarship was bounded by traditional Islamic concept which saw religious learning as the only true science, whose sole aim was the understanding of God's word. The Koran and the traditions of the Prophet formed the basis of this learning; reason was only an auxiliary in the service of religion. The method of the religious sciences was to seek proof for an argument first in the Koran, then in the traditions of the Prophet, then in recorded precedent, and only as a last resort in personal reasoning. Tradition fettered Islamic thought and it became almost impossible for later Muslim thinkers to make any innovations. By the Ottoman period, precedent was the guiding principle not only in the religious law but in every aspect of Muslim scholarship. After the great imams of the eighth and ninth centuries, who had completed and perfected tradition with reasoned analogies, innovations in the religious sciences were considered possible only in accessories and not in essentials. Résumé, compilation, annotation and commentary became the essential forms of Muslim scholarship, and the works of the Ottoman ulema were of this kind.

There has so far been no serious attempt to establish the position of Ottoman learning within the whole field of Muslim scholarship, and so it is difficult to assess its contribution to the Islamic sciences. We can record only Mehmed al-Fanarî, Şeyh Bedreddîn, Molla Gurânî,* Molla Hüsrev, Hocazâde Mustafa, Ibn Kemâl and Ebûssüûd as scholars who are still famous in the Islamic world. Some have classed Şeyh Bedreddîn as an authority inferior only to the great imams of the ninth century, because in his work on jurisprudence he exercised his independent opinion on certain questions of detail; but others have regarded his opinion as false, contrary to the basic sources and old authorities.

Most Ottoman scholarly writers held the rank of kâdî, müftî or müderris. They came from various backgrounds. Some were from the

* Molla Gurânî (1416–88); Ottoman scholar and legist. Mehmed II appointed him kâdîasker and şeyhülislâm.

173

distant towns of Rumelia, such as Sofia or Sarajevo; some had grown up in the old Seljuk centres, such as Konya or Kastamonu; the more distinguished of them settled in the great cities of the empire, such as Istanbul, Bursa or Edirne. Some were from humble families and some even of slave parentage. Many of them had sufficient command of Arabic and Persian to write in these languages, Arabic being the language of religious works.

It is worth noting that in religious works they often discussed topics of public interest or questions of state politics. For example, many of Ibn Kemâl's works are concerned with shiism, at that time a question of vital importance in the Ottoman Empire. He attempted to use religious arguments to prove the legality of a Holy War against the shîa. At another time, to refute Molla Kâbiz's claim that Jesus was superior to Muhammad, he wrote a treatise proving Muhammad's superiority over all other Prophets. The Ottoman ulema were particularly distinguished in jurisprudence, which was a matter of practical importance. The collections of Turkish and Arabic fetvâs, which the şeyhülislâms had issued, are perhaps the most important Ottoman contribution to the religious and legal sciences.

Ottoman scholars were also important as encyclopaedists; Mehmed al-Fanarî, and later Molla Lutfî, Taşköprülüzâde and others created a sort of encyclopaedia of the Islamic sciences designed to meet practical needs. A great encyclopaedic work was Kâtip Çelebi's* bibliographic *Kashf al-Zunûn*, which to this day remains a standard reference book.

The library had an important place in Ottoman society. The Ottomans founded libraries in mosques, hospitals and *tekkes* and collected private libraries in their own residences. Many of these private book collections found their way to vakîf libraries, since it was considered meritorious to leave books to a pious foundation. The library was a single unit in a vakîf complex, established usually in a stone room or separate building. The vakfiye stipulated how the books were to be preserved and used and appointed a librarian paid from vakîf funds. These libraries still preserve more than two hundred thousand manuscripts, from all lands and epochs of the Islamic world, and forming the richest source for the history and culture of Islam.

The Ottoman attitude towards printing is particularly interesting. In about 1590 a decree of Murâd III permitted the sale of non-religious books, printed in Italy in the Arabic alphabet. The Ottomans recognized the advantages of printing, but as early as 1555 Busbecq reported that the Turks esteemed it a sin to print religious books. By 1494 immigrant Jews had already established a non-Muslim press in Istanbul printing their own publications.

---

* Kâtip Çelebi (1609–58); one of the greatest Ottoman scholars and encyclopaedists, known to the west as Hajji Khalifa.

Ottoman writers used Arabic in their religious and legal works, but by the fourteenth century they had already begun to make translations into Turkish. At first they were usually translations of useful or instructive works on such subjects as history, politics and morals, etiquette, astrology, natural history or gemmology, made for the sultans or influential men of state. Side by side with these were many general works on Islam and popular books on medicine, either written in Turkish or translated. Two popular books, dating from 1449, are still among the most widely read Turkish works; these are the poem, the *Muhammediye* (The Book of Muhammed) and the prose work *Envâr al-Âşikîn* (The Lights of the Lovers) of the Yazïcïzâde brothers.* The Yazïcïzâdes belonged to the *Bayramî* sect, and at the conclusion of the first work, where they describe the life of the Prophet and the other world, they explain the meaning of gnosticism.

In Islam, the intellectual sciences were undoubtedly the field where originality was most possible. In pre-Ottoman Islamic societies new developments had occurred in the intellectual sciences which gave a new direction to all Islamic thought, including the religious and legal sciences. The most recent and most powerful movement was mysticism. The peripatetism which had reached its climax with Ibn Sînâ† and Ibn Rushd‡ gave way before the increasingly influential currents of mysticism which with al-Ghazâlî penetrated sunnî Islam.

By the Ottoman period, al-Ghazâlî's thought dominated sunnî Islam. In the diplomas which the Ottoman ulema issued, the tradition of knowledge was traced back, through Sayyid Sharîf al-Jurjânî, Nasîr al-Dîn of Tus and al-Râzî,§ to al-Ghazâlî. Al-Râzî, by the fusion of mysticism with the intellectual sciences, had established a more philosophical concept of Islam. The Ottoman ulema recognized him as their master. Sirâj al-Dîn of Urmiye had first established al-Razî's reputation in Turkey during the Seljuk period and, later, one of al-Râzî's descendants, Jamâl al-Dîn, settled in Aksaray; the influential Mehmed al-Fanarî, the founder of the Ottoman medrese tradition, was of his school. The Ottoman ulema equally respected Sa'd al-Dîn al-Taftazânî from Iran and Sayyid Sharîf al-Jurjânî from Turkestan,

* The Yazïcïzâde brothers,; Yazïcïzâde Mehmed (d.c. 1453), the author of the *Muhammediye*, and Yazïcïzâde Ahmed (d. after 1453), author of *Envâr al-Âşikîn*, both works based on the former's *Maghârib al-Ƶamân* in Arabic.

† Ibn Sînâ (980–1037); philosopher, known in the west as Avicenna. Apart from his philosophical works in the neoplatonic tradition, he is known for his medical and scientific treatises.

‡ Ibn Rushd (1126–98); philosopher, known in the west as Averroes. His work reconciles philosophy with revealed religions. Of the Muslim philosophers he is the purest Aristotelian.

§ Al-Râzî (1149–1209); theologian. His theological work *Al-Muhassal* shows the influence of philosophy on Islamic theology. He is also famous for his commentary on the Koran, *Mafâtîh al-ghayb*.

both of whom followed the traditions of al-Râzî and whose works formed the basis of Ottoman medrese education.

The Ottoman medreses thus followed the most broad-minded traditions of sunnî Islam. There had always been some fanatical ulema who regarded intellectual sciences such as logic, mathematics or astronomy as contrary to religion, but in general the ulema of the Ottoman medreses held al-Ghazâlî's view that hostility to logic and mathematics was futile since these contained the essential elements for all the sciences. They accustomed the mind to correct thinking and thus helped to reveal divine truths. The result of this was the early adoption of the intellectual sciences into the curricula of Ottoman medreses. In the fifteenth century, under the patronage of Mehmed II who attached great importance to these sciences, the Ottomans achieved a real distinction in mathematics and astronomy within the Islamic world. Mehmed al-Fanarî specialized in the intellectual sciences; his work on logic was an essential part of medrese courses until the last days of the empire.

The Ottoman mathematical genius was Mûsâ Pasha, called Kâdîzâde, whose commentaries on Euclid and al-Chaghmînî* formed part of the medrese courses until the latest period and were also printed. Kâdîzâde went to the court of Timur's grandson, Ulugh Beg,† and became director of the Samarkand observatory where he worked on the *Astronomical Tables of Ulugh Beg*, considered the last word in Islamic astronomy. His student, Ali Kuşçu (d. 1474), succeeded him at the observatory and cooperated with Ulugh Beg in completing the *Astronomical Tables*. Later, Mehmed II granted him special favours, inviting him to Istanbul and inaugurating a brilliant era in Ottoman mathematics. Kuşçu wrote his classic works on arithmetic and astronomy in Istanbul and at the same time trained such first-class mathematicians as Molla Lutfî (d. 1494) and Mirim Çelebi (d. 1525).

Again following al-Ghazâlî, the Ottoman ulema maintained that the study of philosophy was permissible only as a preparation for the study of scholastic theology, which aimed to confirm the dogmas of Islam by rational argument; it was not permissible to study philosophical problems which could not be reconciled with the Koran. Certain theses of the philosophers – that God has no knowledge of particular things, that the resurrection of the body is impossible, and that the universe is eternal and not created – were clearly blasphemous. Nevertheless, certain of the Ottoman ulema, Şeyh Bedreddîn in particular, accepted these tenets. The Ottoman government, however, tended

* Al-Chaghmînî (d.c. 1345); astronomer, known for his astronomical work *Al-Mulakhkhas fî hay'a*.

† Ulugh Beg (1393–1449); the grandson of Timur, ruled in Samarkand from 1408. He built his famous observatory to correct Ptolemy's astronomical tables, setting down the results in the *Zîj* [astronomical tables] *of Ulugh Beg*.

to ignore them so long as they did not split public opinion by propagating their views.

Scholastic theology flourished in the first two Ottoman centuries. The broad-minded Mehmed the Conqueror reopened the famous controversy between al-Ghazâlî and Ibn Rushd over the relationship between religion and philosophy, and invited the two great theologians of the period, Alâ al-Dîn of Tus and Hocazâde of Bursa (d. 1488), each to write a treatise on the subject. The ulema of the day judged Hocazâde's the superior work and Alâ al-Dîn, feeling himself slighted, returned to his native Iran. Ibn Rushd had maintained, against al-Ghazâlî, that philosophy and religion could be reconciled and that rational inference was necessary in acquiring a complete knowledge of God. Hocazâde maintained that while reason was an impeccable instrument in the mathematical sciences its use in theological problems led to delusions and errors. He also claimed that in certain respects he had improved on al-Ghazâlî's occasionally faulty methodology. Hocazâde declared openly that his aim was to defend the şerîat against the claims of philosophy. Thus while averroism – the philosophy of Ibn Rushd – was studied in Italy and became a major factor in Renaissance thought, a thoroughgoing scholasticism established itself in Ottoman medreses. Hocazâde's work has maintained its reputation in the Islamic world until the present day, and in the nineteenth century was printed together with the works of Ibn Rushd and al-Ghazâlî.

It should be noted that the basic texts in Ottoman medrese courses were not the translations of the Greek philosophers, made in the Abbasid period, or even the works of Ibn Sînâ and al-Farâbî,* but the summaries and commentaries of the later scholastic school, such as Adûd al-Dîn's *al-Mawâkif*, Nasîr al-Dîn of Tus' *al-Tajrîd*, or al-Baydâwî's† *al-Tawâlî*. The only new works were commentaries on or annotations of these.

Mehmed II gave an impetus to the study of mathematics and theology, which firmly established them in Ottoman medrese circles as closely related subjects. It is worth noting that the free-thinking ulema were those who specialized in the rational sciences. Such was Alî Kuşçu's pupil, Molla Lutfî. Lutfî was a müderris of Bâyezîd II's reign, distinguished as a mathematician and theologian, who with his free thought and open mockery of superstition angered conservative ulema. They opened a propaganda campaign against him, accusing him of heresy and nicknaming him 'the mad'. As rumours and suspicions grew, the sultan commanded that a committee of ulema be set up to

* Al-Farâbî (875–950); son of a Turkish commander in Transoxiana, he is considered the greatest Muslim philosopher. He was known as 'the second teacher', the first having been Aristotle.

† Al-Baydâwî (d. 1286?); compiler and annotator, remembered chiefly for his commentary on the Koran.

discuss the case and to establish whether or not these claims were true. This was the normal procedure when trying ulema. His rivals accused him of heresy; hundreds of witnesses gave evidence and the people followed the case with great interest. Lutfî constantly stressed that he had never been guilty of polytheism, but the ulema informed the sultan that the evidence against him required his execution. Bâyezîd hesitated, but on the insistence of these ulema condemned him to death. In 1494 Molla Lutfî was beheaded on the Atmeydanı (Hippodrome Square) in Istanbul, before great crowds. Nevertheless, some of the ulema regarded the whole incident as a result of rumour and slander and public opinion came to regard Lutfî as a martyr to truth.

Despite Molla Lutfî's tragic end, the rational sciences, although naturally within the narrow bounds of Islamic learning, were for some time longer to maintain their importance in the Ottoman Empire. The mathematician Mirim Çelebi served many years as a müderris, and the great scholar Ibn Kemâl (1468–1534), also known as Kemâl Paşazâde, flourished at this period, gaining fame throughout the Islamic world. Ibn Kemâl was a typical broad-ranging Muslim scholar. He had studied theology under Molla Lutfî; he wrote a commentary on Hocazâde's treatise; he composed over a hundred religious treatises; and he left a monumental ten-volume history of the Ottoman Empire.

CHAPTER XVIII

THE TRIUMPH OF FANATICISM

As early as the 1540s Taşköprülüzâde was lamenting that scholastic theology and mathematics had lost their old popularity among the ulema in the medreses and that the general level of scholarship had fallen. He complained that books on the theoretical sciences were no longer sought after and that the ulema considered themselves scholars after reading only simple handbooks. They attached importance not to sciences such as theology and Koranic exegesis but only to the worldly aspects of Islamic law or to 'frivolities' like poetry, composition or anecdotes. In fact, these useful arts and sciences were of value in acquiring worldly positions.

The fate of the observatory, established in 1577 in Galata, is an event which demonstrates the clear victory of religious fanaticism over the rational sciences. The observatory was founded for the purpose of correcting Ulugh Beg's *Tables* and was at the time the only observatory in the Islamic world. The sultan's chief astronomer, Takiyyüddîn Mehmed (1520–78) founded this observatory, and to increase the accuracy of his observations built some new instruments, in particular an astronomical clock. The observatory was no less advanced than Tycho Brahe's, then the most modern in Europe; in fact there was a striking similarity between the instruments which these two astronomers used. Takiyyüddîn has left an account of how he examined clocks imported from Europe and how he used these as models when he made instruments.

Now it seems that Murâd III built his observatory for astrological rather than astronomical purposes. The sultan's favourites approved of this, but their rivals, a group of ulema, including the şeyhülislâm, regarded an interest in astronomy and astrology as irreligious and ill-omened, like magic and fortune-telling. The şeyhülislâm used the outbreak of plague as a pretext for petitioning the sultan to the effect that these bold efforts to penetrate God's secrets had caused the plague. In 1580 a group of Janissaries razed the observatory to the ground.

It is known that among the five specialist assistants in this observatory there was a Salonica Jew. It was not deemed an offence against religion to employ non-Muslims in astronomy, which was considered as a non-religious, practical science. Since the fifteenth century the Ottomans had been adopting and imitating European geography, military technology and, especially, medicine, without anyone raising religious objections. The practice of adopting the useful aspects of foreign cultures is much older than the so-called 'westernization' of the eighteenth century, since these had no influence on the fundamental values of Islam. At this time such borrowings were of vital importance.

The ulema and medrese circles came to take a firm stand against novelties both in the practical and in the rational sciences. For example, when in 1716 Alî Pasha's* books were confiscated, the şeyhülislâm issued a fetvâ forbidding books from the collection, on philosophy, astronomy or history, to be bequeathed to libraries.

These conditions made it extremely difficult for the Islamic world to benefit from scientific developments in the west, even in the realm of the practical sciences. A few individuals from the bureaucratic class and a few physicians, converts to Islam, had the courage to translate works on geography and medicine from western languages, but their efforts were confined to these subjects of practical everyday importance.

The Ottomans began early to adopt European geography. Pîrî reîs† made use of Christopher Columbus's[1] map and the latest Portuguese portolanos. There is a translation dating from 1580 of a Spanish work on America, whose introduction draws attention to the danger to Islam of European overseas expansion. In the second half of the seventeenth century a knowledge of world geography, and in particular the geography of Europe, became increasingly necessary for political and strategic intelligence. This led to the translation, with the help of renegades, of two important geographical works written in Latin, Mercator and Hondius's *Atlas Minor* of 1621 and Joan Blaeu's *Atlas Major* of 1662. Kâtip Çelebi, who had instigated the translation of *Atlas Minor*, recognized the superiority of western geography, and to increase his knowledge of Europe also had Carion's *Chronicle* translated. This translation convinced Kâtip Çelebi that the world is round and he attempted to prove from Islamic sources that this view was not contrary to religion. In 1685 Abû Bakr of Damascus patronized the translation of *Atlas Major*, which acquainted the Ottomans for the first time with the Copernican system.

Medicine was an indispensable practical science. Islamic rulers

* Çorlulu Alî Pasha (d. 1711), grand vizier 1706–10.

† Pîrî reîs (1465–1554); Turkish admiral and cartographer. His *Kitâb-i Bahriye* (Book of the Sea), written in 1521 and enlarged in 1525, is a *portolano* giving sailing instructions and maps of the Mediterranean coastline. A map of America, part of his world map, is copied from Christopher Columbus's map of 1498.

from the earliest times had employed foreign physicians, but new European advances in medicine and pharmacology became known only in the seventeenth century, through translation which renegades had made from western languages into Turkish or Arabic. Hayâtîzâde Feyzî (d. 1691), famous for his medical works written in Turkish but based on western sources, was a Jewish convert to Islam and head physician at the Palace. However, these borrowings never brought with them the fundamental principles of western scientific thought but merely made a few additions to traditional knowledge. Even Kâtip Çelebi in any kind of scientific investigation always sought his first proofs in the Koran.

It has been claimed that in an earlier period Mehmed the Conqueror had taken an interest in Italian Renaissance culture but that after him this movement was halted. He was certainly the most broad-minded of the Ottoman sultans. In order to learn the principles of the Christian religion from a qualified person he ordered the patriarch Gennadius to write a treatise on Christianity; in his Palace he gathered Greek and Italian scholars such as Amirutzes of Trebizond, Critoboulos of Imbros and Ciriaco of Ancona. He ordered a map of the world from Amirutzes, had Ptolemy's geography translated, and created a Palace library of classical Latin and Greek works. He showered favours on Gentile Bellini, whom he brought from Venice to decorate the Palace walls with frescos in the Italian style and to paint his portrait. Berlinghieri intended to present his *Geographia* to Mehmed, and Roberto Valturio his work entitled *De re militari*. Giovanni-Maria Filelfo wrote his poem *Amyris*, eulogizing the Conqueror. This has led some people to regard him as a true Renaissance sovereign, a view which is far from the truth. His interest in the Christian world sprang only from a desire to become its conqueror and ruler. Culturally he was a Muslim; he had a profound admiration for Hocazâde and believed implicitly in his şeyh, Akşemseddîn's visions of the unknown. His epoch's admiration for the European style in art and a few superficial borrowings in the practical sciences did not constitute a new cultural direction.

The Ottomans were hanafites. Of the four schools of sunnî Islam, the hanafite gave the greatest scope to *icmâ* – consensus of opinion – as a basis for legal inferences and was thus the most tolerant and flexible. All Turkish states had been hanafite since the Karakhanids of the tenth to twelfth centuries, the first Islamic Turkish khanate of central Asia. The reason for this policy must have been the desire of the Turkish rulers to retain as much freedom as possible in their political and executive authority, and it was at the same time one of the main factors giving Turkish societies a distinctive social and cultural character within the Islamic world. The Ottoman Empire, of all Islamic societies, was the one most open to foreign cultural influences; but from the beginning of the sixteenth century the forces of religious fanaticism became increasingly powerful. As we have tried to explain above, the diminishing influence of the frontier traditions and the growing consciousness of the empire's status as a classical Islamic caliphate must have had their effect on this development. The Kızılbaş movement, a deadly weapon of Safavid Iran against the Ottoman Empire, may also have been a contributory cause. In the intellectual life of the empire religious fanaticism displayed itself in the increasingly powerful opposition to the intellectual sciences, scholastic theology and mysticism. In everyday life it became apparent in coarse acts of fanaticism carried out in the name of the şerîat.

The same tendencies were apparent in affairs of state. Süleymân I took his title 'Caliph on Earth' with the greatest seriousness. He personally studied Islamic jurisprudence and entrusted Ebussüûd (1490–1574) with the task of bringing the secular laws of state into conformity with the şerîat. During each clash with Iran the strict measures taken against heretics resulted in a rising tide of fanaticism against all innovations.

The trial of Molla Kâbiz (d. 1527) is interesting in this respect. Molla Kâbiz was one of the ulema who in 1527, during the revolt of the Kızılbaş Kalender Çelebi in Anatolia, defended the view that Jesus was superior to Muhammad. In his first trial in the imperial council the kâdîaskers were unable to bring sufficient religious evidence against him to secure his execution. The sultan, following the trial, was furious that 'this unbeliever, who belittled the glory of the Prophet, should be allowed to go free', and he received a second trial in the presence of the şeyhülislâm, Kemâl Paşazâde, and the kâdî of Istanbul. There was a verbal debate between the Molla and the şeyhülislâm. The şeyhülislâm produced proofs designed to silence him; but the Molla did not retract his views and the kâdî ordered his execution.

In 1537 all governors in the empire received a command that anyone who doubted the words of the Prophet should be deemed an unbeliever and executed. Another command required them to have a mosque built in each village and to join the congregations in the Friday prayer. This was a measure against heretics who did not wish to worship in a sunnî congregation.

In Ottoman society there was always a class of fanatical ulema who regarded the intellectual sciences, mysticism, music, dancing and poetry as impious; against these was a class which defended them as coming within the scope of religion. The fanatics were usually the popular şeyhs and ulema who preached and taught in the mosques, while the ulema in higher medreses or in government service formed the second group. Taşköprülüzâde was one of these. He complained bitterly of those ulema who exploited the people's ignorance to lead them astray: 'God preserve us from those who show fanaticism in religion.' He believed that each man is free to choose his own religious school and that to regard one's own school as indisputably correct and the others as false, and to attribute unbelief to any Muslim, is contrary to true religion. Only God can recognize true faith. He thus regarded fanaticism in the accessories of jurisprudence as futile since no one can claim infallibility in these matters.

With other high-ranking ulema, Taşköprülüzâde accepted al-Ghazâlî's moderate views, believing that, like religious fanatics, *bâtinites* and philosophers were in error. The bâtinites sought to destroy the şerîat, while the philosophers worked from principles unacceptable to Islam.

From the earliest times the ulema in Ottoman medreses went a step further in their mystical beliefs than al-Ghazâlî, and followed the traditions of Ibn al-'Arabî* and al-Suhrawardî.† Taşköprülüzâde accepted that mysticism was the only road to divine gnosis and held that it could be criticized only in the light of its own terminology. For example, not to interpret the mystic's utterance 'I am the Truth'‡ in its mystic sense was to commit an injustice against him. We learn from Taşköprülüzâde that in the early years of Süleymân's reign fanatical ulema incited the people against mysticism.

Taşköprülüzâde did not regard music and dancing in the ceremonies of mystic orders as contrary to religion, since they awakened in the soul a love of God and divine esctasy; the relationship between music and the spirit is a divine secret and the soul aroused by dancing achieves divine gnosis. Music and dancing were to be forbidden only when used to arouse worldly desires. Nevertheless, the traditional ulema regarded musical recitation and dancing as blasphemous, and at the same time attacked such things as the decoration of mosques, melodic incantation of the Koran and the payment of religious instructors. As much as they attacked mysticism they attacked the intellectual sciences and scholastic theology as undermining religious faith.

These movements of fanaticism were soon to take forms which endangered public order and alarmed the government. There had for centuries been a small group of preachers who had branded as 'impious innovations', and incited the people against, beliefs and practices which although they were outside the scope of the Koran and the traditions of the Prophet, the Islamic community had adopted. One of these ulema was Mehmed of Birgi (1522–73) who flourished between the years 1558 and 1565 when the persecution of the Kızılbaş was at its

---

* Ibn al-'Arabî (1164–1240); a leading Islamic mystic philosopher.
† Sihâb al-Dîn al-Suhravardî (1145–1234); mystic philosopher and founder of the Suhrawardiya order.
‡ 'I am the Truth'; the mystic's utterance indicating his total absorption in the deity for which al-Hallâj (d. 922) and his imitators were put to death.

height. He was under the patronage of the sultan's teacher, Atâullâh efendi. When he said 'It is incumbent on me to defend the people with my pen and with my tongue from what God has prohibited, and it is a sin for me to be silent', he was, on the one hand, attacking the scholastic theologians and the mystics and, on the other, the high-ranking ulema in the service of the state. This Muslim puritan regarded such practices as holding ceremonies to commemorate the dead or visiting tombs and mausolea to seek aid from the deceased as contrary to the spirit of Islam. He rejected such established practices as shaking hands, bowing in greeting and kissing the hand or garment as being contrary to the sunna, since they had not existed in the Prophet's day. His attack on a number of the fundamental institutions of Ottoman society, such as the payment of those in the service of religion and the bequest of money and movable goods as vakîf, was a threat to the established order, and Ebûssuûd felt it necessary to issue a fetvâ confirming the legality of these institutions. Mehmed of Birgi did not hesitate to attack the şeyhülislâm directly, claiming that his fetvâs were in error. At the same time his writings against incantation and dancing in religious ceremonies were disquieting members of the religious orders.

Mehmed of Birgi's student, Kâdizâde (d. 1635), and the group of preachers attached to him and known as *fakîs*, continued the argument. Their propaganda campaign from the pulpits of Istanbul mosques led to a great social upheaval, splitting the people into two groups. The fakîs condemned all practices introduced since the time of the Prophet as 'innovation', and those who practised them as unbelievers. They announced that tobacco and coffee, and any kind of song and dance, were contrary to the religious law, and demanded the abolition of mathematics and the intellectual sciences from the medreses. In his desire to re-establish the royal authority, Murâd IV tried to gain the support of the fakîs by appearing as a champion of Islam. He issued laws such as those prohibiting tobacco and alcohol and showed no mercy towards those who disobeyed them.

The fakî demagogues did not, however, appeal only to popular religious fanaticism, but at the same time attacked the luxury and extravagance of the ruling classes and railed against the injustices and lax morals of the age. When in 1656 they intended, with an attack on all the tekkes in Istanbul and a general massacre, to strike religious heresy at its roots, they found most of their support among the poor medrese students and humble tradesmen. Aware of their influence on the mass of the people, some Palace officials took the fakîs' side and made them the instrument of a number of conspiracies. The high ulema holding official posts, and the bureaucratic class in general, were opposed to the fakîs, claiming that they undermined state and society and sowed dissent among the people. The new grand vizier, Köprülü Mehmed

(d. 1661), was able to quieten the situation and prevent civil war only by exiling the inflammatory fakïs from Istanbul.

The theoretical basis of this dissent was the question of 'innovation' in Islam, a problem which affected all Ottoman culture and society. Kâtip Çelebi summarized the general opinion of the higher ulema when he wrote that customary practices and innovations, which the greater part of Islamic society had adopted, could not and should not be abolished by force. An innovation might not conform to the şeriat, but then man, the slave of God, is helpless and imperfect, while God is all-forgiving. Islam prefers tolerance to force, and in any case the use of force is wrong since it produces resistance which in turn produces unrest and divisions in state and society. Finally, laws change with time. The Prophet made laws for certain reasons and when these reasons no longer existed the laws had no more force. At the same time, Kâtip Çelebi defended the mystics, and Ibn al-'Arabî in particular. He saw the cure for fanaticism in the study of the intellectual sciences, as in Mehmed ıı's day, claiming that Mehmed of Birgi had not understood the social role of customary law and usage because he had not studied history and philosophy. Debate, he believed, was always profitable; however, only the ulema, and not the people, should discuss religious questions.

Among Ottoman official circles, the general view of 'innovation' was based on the tolerant hanafite concept of icmâ as a basis for religious and legal opinions. Against this, Mehmed of Birgi and the fakïs adopted the strict traditionalism of the *hanbalites*. These regarded as contrary to Islam any innovation which an objective interpretation of the Koran and the sunna could not admit. They opposed mysticism and any esoteric interpretation of the principles of religion. In our own day the modernization of Islamic societies has again caused a collision of these two opposing views.

CHAPTER XX

POPULAR CULTURE AND THE TARÎKATS – MYSTIC ORDERS

During the Seljuk period, educated circles in the cities of central Anatolia had adopted high Persian culture, while on the frontiers the Turkish popular culture of the gâzîs and dervishes, with its currents of mysticism and chivalry, was predominant. The dervishes on the frontier, usually named *baba*, *abdal* or ahî, and in close relationship with the first Ottoman beys, had been coming to Anatolia since the eleventh century with the waves of migrating Turcomans. They were the social and spiritual centres of the Turcoman tribes, like the old Turco-Mongol shamans.

Arabic sources describe with amazement the hundred or so dervishes who came to Syria with Barak Baba in 1307, and we could use the same description to apply to the heretical dervishes on the frontiers:

They hung bells and knucklebones around their necks, shaved their beards and let their moustaches grow. In their hands they carried wooden swords, or cudgels crooked at the end. Drums and pipes accompanied them, and when these sounded they danced with vigorous movements. The objects round their necks made such a noise that the spectators went out of their mind. They attached no importance to prayer and fasting. Barak Baba distributed the alms he collected to his dervishes and to the poor.

Barak Baba believed himself to be in direct contact with God, and like the old shamans had great influence over the Mongol khans of Iran. In the following centuries Ottoman sources and European accounts of travels in the Ottoman Empire were to leave similar accounts of the groups of dervishes who wandered from town to town.

In the mountains and high summer pastures of Anatolia, and especially in the frontier regions, it was difficult to compel the semi-nomadic Turcomans to observe the orthodox forms of Muslim life and worship. The abdals and babas inculcated heretical forms of Islam derived from shamanist beliefs and conforming to a tribal social structure. At the same time, the government attempted to protect its true source of revenue – the peasantry and the cultivated lands – by taking strong measures against the nomads, who therefore became bitterly opposed to the central administration and its policy of religious orthodoxy. They became fanatically devoted to the babas, who represented the ideals of their own forms of society and culture. Within these groups a Turkish culture, in particular a literature derived from the traditions of Turkish central Asia, continued to flourish and was quite distinct from the cosmopolitan culture and literature of the towns and the Palace. The Turkish nationalists of the twentieth century were to turn to this as a source for the creation of a new national literature.

It is hardly surprising that popular uprisings in Anatolia, whose fundamental causes were social and political, nearly always took the form of heretical religious movements. In central Anatolia in 1241, two years before the Mongol invasion, a dervish called Baba Ishâk led the first great Turcoman revolt of which there are historical records. The uprising was suppressed after a bitter struggle, and many of the heretical Turcoman dervishes, known as *babaîs*, fled to the western marches, where Turcomans formed the majority of the population and where the Turcoman beys received them well.

One of these babaî şeyhs was Sarï Saltuk. In 1261 he was forced to take refuge in Byzantine territory with about forty Turcoman clans. He was settled in the Dobrudja, whence he entered the service of the powerful Muslim Mongol emir, Nogai, who ruled the steppes to the north of the Black Sea. Sarï Saltuk became the hero of an epic, as a dervish and gâzî spreading Islam into Europe. In 1473–80, the Ottoman prince Cem had the popular stories about the heroic exploits of Sarï Saltuk, and about the wars of the Ottoman Turks in Rumelia, gathered together under the title *Saltuknâme* (The Book of Saltuk). He is portrayed as exhorting the Turks of Anatolia to leave their internecine quarrels and to fight the infidel in Europe: he extols Holy War as the highest form of worship. His propaganda among the Christians usually leads to war and ends in victory. Dressed as a Christian monk he preaches Islam in the churches, and massacres with his wooden sword the priests who come against him. Like St George, he slays a dragon which is terrorizing the people, and in thanks to him the Christians accept Islam. The Dobrudja and the Crimea are the centre for his activity in the Balkans, Poland and Russia; he flies across the seas. He declares that the continuous advance of Islam and the retreat of Christianity is the greatest of all miracles, proving that Islam is the true religion. In 1354 the Ottoman teachers in Iznik had said exactly the same thing to the Archbishop of Salonica, Palamas, declaring that the spread of Islam was a miracle and the will of God.

At this time, enthusiasm for the ideal of spreading God's word by conquest animated all Ottoman society. This is apparent in the first Ottoman anonymous histories, which have some of the qualities of heroic epics like the *Saltuknâme*. These legendary exploits represented the ideals of frontier society and its ideal types, the gâzî and the dervish. In the extraordinary deeds of a Sarı Saltuk who could fly through the air, popular imagination found its own ideal hero. Naturally enough these popular legends of heroism include old Turkish epic motifs and many elements drawn from native Anatolian and Balkan folklore and from Christian and pagan tradition. It is sometimes difficult to distinguish Sarı Saltuk from a Christian saint. Sarı Saltuk's base in the Dobrudja was, throughout the Ottoman period, a centre where Turcoman tribes, gâzîs and heretical dervishes thrived and where their uprisings were most frequent.

The reign of Bâyezîd I was a period when orthodox Islam and classical Islamic culture, aided by a policy of centralization, became increasingly strong; but the rout at Ankara in 1402 initiated an era of social and political upheaval and reaction, with heretical religious movements spreading throughout Ottoman territory, and great religious and political uprisings. The revolt of Şeyh Bedreddîn (d. 1416), the foundation of the Bayramî order of dervishes, and the spread of the Hurûfî movement in the Ottoman Empire, were signs of this unrest.

Şeyh Bedreddîn's movement is as significant from its social and political as it is from its cultural aspects. Bedreddîn Mahmûd's mother was Greek; his father was an Ottoman gâzî who fought on the most forward frontier and had been one of the first to cross into Rumelia. In his youth he had been kâdî to the warriors on the marches. During Prince Mûsâ's sultanate in the Balkans he had held the title of kâdîasker and, with the bey of the frontier warriors, Mihaloğlu, had been a chief supporter of the new revolutionary regime. By having timars in the hinterland given to the unpaid gâzîs on the frontiers he became the chief protagonist in the old struggle of the frontiers against the central state. When Mehmed I defeated Mûsâ Çelebi in 1413 he exiled Bedreddîn to Iznik and dispossessed his followers of their timars; but when in 1416 Mehmed was in a critical situation, Bedreddîn raised the standard of revolt on the Dobrudja march. Bedreddîn claimed a relationship with the Seljuk royal house and undoubtedly nursed some political ambition, probably to rule in the place of the Ottoman dynasty.

Bedreddîn was a great religious scholar, mystic and saint, and his revolutionary is a good example of how, in the Islamic world, mystic thought is interpreted in social and political action. who at his signal rose in revolt in the regions of Izmir, the Dobrudja, were Turcomans, as the babaîs before The rest of his followers were malcontents of various frontier gâzîs, sipâhîs who had been dispossessed of their students or Christian peasants. The şeyh's latitudinarian and esoteric interpretation of Islam allowed him to form a single society from these diverse elements.

Şeyh Bedreddîn was not a simple dervish. For his works on the religious sciences and, in particular, on Islamic law, he has been classed among the great scholars; but as a mystic he found the 'exoteric sciences' unsatisfying, entered a tarîkat and became a şeyh. He abandoned exoteric for esoteric knowledge.

Bedreddîn derived his mysticism mainly from Ibn al-'Arabî, and we know that he wrote a commentary on Ibn al-'Arabî's *Fusûs al-hikam* (The Quintessence of Wisdom). In the book *Vâridât* (Divine Inspirations), compiled from his discourses and reflecting his own form of mysticism, Bedreddîn explains the philosophy of monism in these words: 'Although God's essence is in itself the Whole and is itself the Whole, it is freed from the Whole.' Its manifestation is a necessity of its being. This world of manifestations, 'with its absolute types, species and persons is ancient', without beginning and without end; it was not created in time. If the physical world were to disappear, the spiritual and incorporeal world would also disappear. 'Creation and destruction is an eternal process.' 'This world and the next, in their entirety, are imaginary fantasies; heaven and hell are no more than the spiritual manifestations, sweet and bitter, of good and evil actions.' He did not believe in the Day of Judgement or in the resurrection of the body. He believed that Jesus died in his elemental body but that in his spirit he is eternal. He interpreted all the tenets of orthodox Islam as the esoteric theologians before him had done, and orthodox ulema have been unanimous in regarding him as an extreme bâtinite who completely ignored the şeriat. He has left his own sincere account of his mystic experiences:

Ecstasy came to me, and I remained in wonderment at God's presence. I was lost in emotion . . . One day I saw my body as God in His entirety . . . The mystic who has perceived God loses his feelings. He spreads to the whole universe; he is one with the mountains and streams. There is no here or hereafter; everything is a single moment.

Writing in the late fifteenth century, the sunnî historian Idrîs of Bitlis (d. 1520) gave this description of the şeyh's beliefs and plans:

He thought himself the Mahdi, believing that at a signal from the unseen world, at the head of his disciples, he would distribute the lands among his followers. Then the secrets of God's unity would prevail in the world of reality, and the sect of imitators [meaning those who professed the şeriat] would fall from power. His own latitudinarian sect would make many forbidden things lawful.

According to Idrîs, with these promises he gathered thousands of ignorant and simple-minded people around him by appealing to their animal instincts. As in the *Bektaşî* order, the şeyh permitted wine and music and ignored religious differences.

Bedreddîn's disciple, Börklüce Mustafa, instigated the first revolt among the Turcomans in the mountainous region of Karaburun near Izmir. The contemporary Byzantine historian Ducas[1] gives an interesting account of the uprising. Börklüce preached that all things, except for women, were common property. He ignored the differences between Christians and Muslims; the Muslim who called a Christian an infidel was himself an infidel. Börklüce's disciples were said to have treated Christians as though they were angels. Börklüce invited the priests of Chios to join his sect, and we know that his Christian followers joined the rebellion; but most of the rebels, whose numbers have been estimated at six thousand, were Turkish nomads. The revolt was suppressed only with the greatest difficulty. Börklüce was captured and crucified, and the captive dervishes did not accept a 'renewal of faith' but resigned themselves to death. Idrîs states that two thousand men were executed and that at the same time, in Manisa, four thousand followers of Torlak Kemâl, another of the şeyh's disciples, were put to the sword.

Bedreddîn's sect in the Dobrudja and Deliorman, known as the *Simavnîs* or the *Bedreddînlüs*, continued for centuries after his death, and the Ottoman government always looked on it with the greatest suspicion. In the sixteenth century they were regarded as identical with the Kızılbaş. At the time of Süleymân I their leader was a descendant of Bedreddîn, a certain Çelebi Halîfe, whose followers and missionaries propagated his cause throughout the empire. At the beginning of the seventeenth century a sunnî şeyh, Hüdâyî Mahmûd, recommended the government to stamp out this movement and to execute one of their şeyhs as a warning to others. He advised that the government should close all Kızılbaş lodges and appoint to each village a sunnî imam, entrusted with the education of the children.

Bedreddîn's revolt clearly shows the relationship between religious mysticism and popular movements. Since the thirteenth century Anatolia had been a home of mystical doctrines and religious orders. Among intellectual circles in the cities, mysticism took theosophical forms, while among the people it became the basis of popular religious orders whose beliefs were a compound of shiism and other esoteric doctrines and a source for the popular religious-social movements.

It is thus possible to divide the religious orders in the Ottoman Empire into two main groups. The first group consisted of the established orders, with lodges supported by the income from vakîfs which sultans or great men had founded, with a clearly defined organization and fixed rites and ceremonies. The most famous of these orders were the *Nakşbendîs*, the *Mevlevîs*, the Halvetîs, and their various branches.

They usually settled in the cities and drew their novices from the upper ranks of society. Each order had its own standard and head-dress and its own form of recitation and ceremony. Each one, according to the inclination of its beliefs, recognized a famous sufi, saint or companion of the Prophet as its patron, and established his family tree. The secret orders, known usually as the *Melâmîs* or *Melâmetîs*, comprised the second group. In the eyes of the people they sought not fame and respect but blame and censure, hence their name.* They avoided all forms of ostentation, all external organization and symbols, and their forms of worship were secret and esoteric. They established no links with the state and were more or less opposed to authority. They were accustomed to live off the fruits of their own labour, accepting no bequest or alms from the state or from individuals. Among this group were the wandering dervishes, known as *kalenderîs*, *haydarîs*, abdals or babaîs, and the *hamzavîs*, those Melâmîs who lived as though secretly insinuated among the guild members in the towns. These were the tarîkats which particular social groups, opposed to the political order, adopted. In fact, shiite and esoteric religious movements in the Islamic world had always given the tarîkats a sectarian and militant character, and supported the various religious-political movements. Shiism itself had originated as a militant political movement, recognizing the Prophet's cousin and son-in-law Alî, and his descendants as heads of the Islamic community. It later absorbed many and various social and religious movements, all of which were opposed to the sunnî ruling classes. In many Islamic states, among them the Ottoman Empire, it came to represent the opposition to the existing order, to the power of the absolute state and the sunnî Islam which it represented. The supernatural qualities attributed to Alî and his descendants were interpreted according to the theories of the mystics, and many believed that the Divine Light, which was supposed to have inspired Alî, passed to his descendants who were thus able to interpret the esoteric meaning of the Koran. These beliefs were more or less the common property of the tarîkats in the Ottoman Empire, taking an extreme form in the Kızılbaş movements. In the sixteenth century, with the rise in Iran of the Safavid dynasty which represented these beliefs, the movement became a major problem for the Ottoman Empire. But, first, we shall examine the Bayramî, Hurûfî and Bektaşî orders, tarîkats which had been established in the Ottoman Empire in the fifteenth century.

Like Şeyh Bedreddîn's movement, the Bayramî order was a religious-social movement born of the period of upheaval and reaction after 1402. Its founder was Haccî Bayram (d. 1430), a peasant from near Ankara, and a Melâmî dervish in the broadest sense. He wanted his disciples to subsist on the fruits of their labour and he and his followers

* These words are derived from the Arabic *malâm*, *malâmat:* 'blame, censure'.

tilled the fields together and together disposed of the produce. In
Ankara and its villages there were many cloth-workers, producing
for the outside market, and most of these became his followers. He
collected money in the market of Ankara and distributed it to the poor.
The account of his life relates that as the number of his disciples
increased he aroused the suspicions of the government. He was seized
and brought before Murâd II. The sultan, however, pardoned him and
even granted his disciples certain tax exemptions, thus helping the
rapid spread of the movement. Murâd II was sympathetic towards the
dervishes and shared something of their temperament, but there can
be no doubt that his support for this new tarîkat was partly a deliberate
attempt to spread his own influence among the people. The Bayramî
movement later split into two. One group accepted sunnî Islam and
the protection of the state. Hajji Bayram's follower, Akşemseddîn,
became şeyh to the conqueror of Istanbul and played an important
part in the conquest. The other group was faithful to the traditions of
the Melâmîs, remaining a secret sect, extremist in its beliefs and in-
clined towards monism and shiism. This group had links with the
guilds in the towns, organizations which had always regarded the
political authorities with suspicion. The first *kutb* of this group was a
cutler in Bursa, a disciple of Hajji Bayram. The melâmîs formed a
close-knit group around a *kutb* – pole – that is, a spiritual leader who
according to mystic beliefs was the centre of the universe, cognizant
of divine secrets. The kutb was everything and demanded absolute
obedience. They organized secret meetings, and tried the accused in
their own courts, throwing those whom they found guilty into their own
prisons. They had no wish to establish links with the state but rather
required their members to work at a trade and earn an honest living.
They condemned idleness and adopted the principle that 'he who earns
money honestly is beloved of God'.

The Melâmîs were like those sects which had always existed in the
old Islamic cities, outside the control of the state, drawing their members from the guilds and always treated with suspicion by governments.
In the sixteenth century, when the Melâmîs, like the Kïzïlbaş in the
villages, began to show Safavid leanings, the government pursued them
ruthlessly. In 1529 the kutb of the Melâmîs, Ismâîl Maşûkî, was
captured and with his twelve disciples executed on the Atmeydanï, in
accordance with the şeyhülislâm's fetvâ. After his death some came to
revere him as a saint and it became necessary to issue a new fetvâ
condemning these and approving the execution. In 1561 a fetvâ of the
şeyhülislâm, Ebûssüûd, condemned to death another Melâmî, Hamza
Bâlî of Bosnia, declaring him a heretic and an atheist. He had never
hesitated to declare the belief of monism openly before the people,
and is reputed to have gathered a few thousand disciples around him

in his homeland in Saraybosna. His execution had a deep effect on the minds of the people, who were divided between his supporters and his detractors. Hamza became a patron saint of the Melâmîs, who henceforth were often known as Hamzavîs. In the seventeenth century the Hamzavîs concentrated in Bosnia were mercilessly persecuted. Nevertheless, Melâmî-ism began to spread in the great cities of the empire, such as Istanbul and Edirne, and later even to the ruling classes.

The Hurûfîs were another sect which the government persecuted. A certain Fadlullâh (d. 1394) had founded this sect, which can virtually be regarded as a new religion, in Astarabad in Iran. Fadlullâh declared himself to be the manifestation of God, the Mahdi whom Muslims, Christians and Jews awaited, announcing that he brought the final word which was to unite all three religions. He interpreted the Koran according to an ultra-esoteric system based on the cabalistic interpretation of its letters and, like Şeyh Bedreddîn, he maintained that 'the world is eternal and creation is a continual process'. He did not believe in the hereafter. Like the Melâmîs, he insisted on manual work as the only rightful source of profit. Fadlullâh was himself a maker of skull-caps and his tarîkat spread first among guild members in towns. Hurûfî-ism, persecuted in Iran, began from the early fifteenth century to spread rapidly in the Ottoman towns in Rumelia and Anatolia, where Christians and Muslims lived and worked together in the same guilds. In Anatolia the great Azerî Turkish poet Nesîmî, who in 1408 was flayed alive for his beliefs, belonged to this sect. The Hurûfî propagandists sought to convert the rulers of the age to the new religion and organized plots against those who opposed them. It is certain that in 1444 the Hurûfîs formed a fairly numerous sect in the Ottoman capital, Edirne, and that a Persian missionary had influence in the Palace.

The Hurûfîs' views on Jesus and Christianity gave rise in the west to rumours that they were Christian propagandists. At this time, fear of a Christian crusade prevailed in Edirne. The people were stirred and the sunnî ulema reacted sharply. The Persian missionary was burned and many of his followers had their tongues cut out. A contemporary account puts their number at 2,007,[2] but this must be an exaggeration. The violent persecution of the Hurûfîs, who were considered atheists, continued into the fifteenth and sixteenth centuries, increasing in strength after the plot against Bâyezîd II. The movement united with the Bedreddînlüs and the kızılbaş-Bektaşîs, and a strong Hurûfî influence is apparent in Bektaşî thought. Ottoman documents show that as late as 1576 there was a general massacre of a Hurûfî group in the villages near Filibe in Bulgaria.

In time the Bektaşî order was to become the most important popular tarîkat and one which gradually absorbed various other tarîkats and the groups of dervishes, known as abdal, kalenderî or haydarî, who had been preaching to the people since the fourteenth century.

The founder and patron saint of the order was Hacci Bektaş, a disciple of the Baba Ishâk who had led the rebellion of 1241. Hacci Bektaş was active in the second half of the thirteenth century in Seljuk Anatolia, on the important Ankara-Kayseri trade route, situated on the western border of the high summer pastures, an area with a dense population of Turcoman tribes. In the villages of the same region there was an old Christian population. The Ottomans acquired this region during the reign of Murâd 1. In the Ottoman Empire, Bektasî-ism first became important when it spread among the Turcoman tribes and then when it became the tarîkat of the Janissary corps.

Bektaşî dervishes appeared on the Ottoman frontiers in Rumelia from the middle of the fourteenth century, and adopted as their own Sarĭ Saltuk, who had become the patron saint of the Ottoman gâzîs in Rumelia. By the fifteenth century, Bektaşî-ism had established itself in the Janissary corps. Some have sought to explain this by the fact that the majority of the Janissaries had originally been Christian children from the devşirme, or else prisoners of war. However this may be, these devşirme children, who had been sent to live in Turkish villages in Anatolia in order to learn the Turkish language and the Islamic religion, tended towards the popular forms of religion rather than to sunnî Islam. From the end of the sixteenth century Hacci Bektaş was officially recognized as the patron saint of the Janissaries, and a Bektaşî father permanently resided with the corps. The Bektaşî order and the Janissary corps became so inseparable that when a new *dede* was chosen as head of the order he came to the Janissary barracks in Istanbul to be crowned by the ağa of the Janissaries.

Bektaşî-ism was particularly strong among the Turcoman nomads and in the villages which they had established, and among them came to take the place of babaî-ism. The influence of Bektaşî-ism was very strong among Turcoman groups in Anatolia, especially in the region between the Kĭzĭlĭrmak and Erzurum (at the beginning of the twentieth century F.Grenard put their number at one million) and in the Taurus mountains in the south (principally the Tahtacĭ and Varsak tribes). It spread to the yürük Turcomans between Vize and the Danube in the Balkans; in the Dobrudja and Deliorman in eastern Bulgaria; and in the Rhodope mountains, in southern Macedonia and Thessaly. In the fifteenth and sixteenth centuries many of these nomads settled and founded villages.[3]

During the second half of the fifteenth century these Turcomans came under the influence of a new heretical tarîkat which had arisen in the east. This was the extreme shiite sect of Safiyy al-Dîn of Ardabil.*

---

* Safiyy al-Dîn of Ardabil (1252–1331); the ancestor of the Safavid dynasty.

Henceforth the Turcomans accepted this creed and became known as Kïzïlbaş – 'red head' – from the red head-dress which they wore. The Kïzïlbaş movement was as much social and political as it was religious, and from the fifteenth century it became an expression of the strong Turcoman opposition to the Ottoman administration. In the fifteenth century, as subjects of the Karamanids and the Akkoyunlus, states which retained a tribal structure, these Turcomans fought bitterly against the Ottomans, whose policy of centralization was incompatible with their way of life. When the Safavid dynasty replaced the Akkoyunlus in Iran, its founder, Shah Ismaîl, intensified his propaganda with his own Turkish religious poems and by sending his disciples and propagandists among these warlike Turcomans in Rumelia and Anatolia, thus conquering the Ottoman Empire from within. In 1511 the Kïzïlbaş, under the command of one of Shah Ismaîl's followers, Şah Kulu, raised a terrible rebellion in south-west Anatolia, burning and destroying everything which stood in their way, and advancing as far as Kütahya. The rebellion shook Ottoman rule in Anatolia to its foundations and was put down only with the greatest difficulty. Selîm I's merciless repression of the Kïzïlbaş and his victory over Shah Ismaîl at Çaldïran in 1514 only temporarily halted the movement.

The beliefs and ceremonies of the Kïzïlbaş were not fundamentally different from those of the Bektaşîs, but the Turcomans were fanatical shiites, and by mixing their own tribal customs and shamanist beliefs with Bektaşî-ism they created their own peculiar form of the sect. At the same time, the hereditary chiefs of the tribes gained the position of religious heads and were usually known as şeyhs. The Turcomans attached great importance to the hereditary principle and were distinguished from the other Bektaşî groups by the fact that they recognized as heads of the tarîkat, the Çelebis, who it was claimed were descendants of Hacci Bektaş. In 1527 a descendant of Hacci Bektaş, called Kalender, led the great Turcoman revolt in central Anatolia. Turcoman tribesmen made up the greater part of the rebel forces, and among them were many abdal and kalenderî dervishes. The suppression of the revolt required the presence of the grand vizier himself, with a force of Janissaries. In 1511 sipâhîs from the old Beylik of Karaman, and in 1527 sipâhîs from the old Beylik of Dulkadir, led the revolt, and the most prominent among these were again the old tribal chiefs. This strongly emphasizes the social and political nature of the movement.

During the Ottoman-Safavid wars of 1534–5, the kïzïlbaş-Bektaşî poet, Pîr Sultan Abdal, expressed in verse the feelings and political ambitions of this group.

In these poems he laments the injustice of the persecutions:

> I gave my heart, I declared my faith to Alî,
> I shall stand firm if they cut me to pieces.
> They called me a heretic and hanged me –
> Strange, for where is my sin?

Sometimes he turns to the Shah of Iran, whom he regards as a Mahdi from the line of Alî:

> My holy Mahdi must come,
> He must set up his high council,
> He must destroy the unjust,
> And one day take revenge for me.

He imagines the shah leading the Kızılbaş, conquering Anatolia and coming to the throne in Istanbul:

> He marched on the land of Rûm,
> The great Imam from the stem of Alî is coming.
>
> Let the breasts of dissenters be burned,
> Let the Lord of the Age's word be law,
> Let it be known who is the sultan.
>
> In Istanbul the Glorious Lord
> Must walk with the crown of state.

When at last there was no more hope of victory, he longed to take refuge with the Shah of Iran:

> O black earth, so long as I am above you,
> I too shall go from these pastures to the shah.
>
> If you kill those who name the shah,
> I too shall go from these pastures to the shah.

The Kızılbaş groups who from 1511 took refuge in Iran constituted an important part of the Safavid armies; but these nomads, with their extremist heretical beliefs recognizing the shah as Mahdi, could not fit into Persian society and there too they were persecuted as heretics.

The Kızılbaş always maintained close contacts with Iran, acting as though they were Safavid subjects. The shah appointed his representatives among them, and to each of these sent a warrant, cloak, sword and money. For their part, the Kızılbaş in Anatolia regularly sent the shah a kind of tax known as 'Şah hakkı' ('the shah's due') or 'nezir' ('the offering'). The Kızılbaş did not go to Mecca for pilgrimage, but to Ardabil in Iran where Safiyy al-Dîn was buried. There are Ottoman documents showing that the government held searches for forbidden books and tracts coming from Iran. The government also sent spies to the Kĭzĭlbaş, who found out who had contacts with Iran and punished offenders with execution or banishment. The Ottoman archives show that from time to time throughout the sixteenth century the government made close investigations of the various heterodox groups and searched the dervish lodges. For example, it forbade the Işĭk group, the old abdals and kalenderîs 'who raised standards, played on the pipe and drum, and acted contrary to religion in all things' from travelling from town to town and village to village. In the sixteenth century the long and bitter struggle with the Kĭzĭlbaş strengthened the position of narrow sunnî Islam in the Ottoman Empire. Among the Kĭzĭlbaş, repression led to secrecy, and more than ever before they lived as a closed group opposed to the sunnî state and society.

Bektaşî-ism was a major factor in spreading Islam among the native Christian populations of Rumelia. The eclectic nature and peculiar features of this popular tarîkat made Islam easily acceptable to many Balkan peasants. For example, it looked tolerantly on all religions, it attached importance to the esoteric and not to externals, it did not compel the observance of Islamic rites such as ritual prayer and fasting, it permitted wine-drinking, and allowed women to go unveiled in public and to mix socially with men. The effective propaganda of the Bektaşî fathers attracted these Christians to this mysterious and democratic sect, which did not seem to them so different from Christianity. But this type of Bektaşî-ism was distinct from the Bektaşî-ism of the Kĭzĭlbaş. The Bektaşî dervishes in lodges which were under state control and supported by vakĭfs were usually faithful to the government. They did not accept the hereditary principle in choosing their fathers and dedes; their intellectual level was higher and mystical thought was dominant.

Bektaşî-ism was a sect with beliefs composed of various elements of popular religion and drawn from a multitude of sources, from shamanism to the religious beliefs of the Balkan peoples. It was essentially a continuation of babaî-ism and clearly shows relics of old Turkish folklore and customs, in particular relics of shamanism. Shamanist influence is particularly clear in the ecstatic dances, and the exact equivalent of the miraculous powers attributed to Bektaşî saints is found among the Buddhist Turks in Chinese Turkestan. The ancient Turkish tradition of the ritual meal, and remnants of the shamanist stone and tree cults, continued in the Bektaşî rites. Women retained the position of freedom and equality with men which they had enjoyed in pre-Islamic Turkish society. Scholars like Jakob and Hasluck have also drawn attention to the influence on Bektaşî-ism of the paganism and Christianity native to the Balkans, maintaining that certain Bektaşî beliefs and rites seem to be derived from Christianity. For example the concept of the Trinity is reflected in the Bektaşî belief that God, Muhammad and Alî are one; bread, wine and cheese were offered to the novice in the ritual admitting him to the orders; disciples confessed their sins to the şeyh. From the sixteenth century celibacy was incumbent on dervishes living in tekkes, and in many other respects Bektaşî lodges resembled Christian monasteries. These native influences displayed themselves in many forms, such as the choice of places accounted holy by Christians as sites for tekkes or as shrines for pilgrims, and the adoption of the old Christian or pagan legends attached to these places and attributing them to Bektaşî saints.

At the same time, Bektaşî-ism derived a number of its beliefs from the mysticism of the Muslim cultural elite. The *Makâlât* (Discourses), attributed to Hacci Bektaş, outlined the foundations of these beliefs. As in the traditions of the sufis, the novice passes through four doors. The first door is the 'şerîat', the orthodox Islamic law; the second door is the 'tarîkat', the teachings of the religious order; the third door is 'marifet' – the mystic knowledge of God; and the fourth door is 'hakîkat' – the immediate experience of the essence of Reality. Parallel with this the Koran has four meanings: for the people, the external text; for the wise, the refinements of this text; for saints, its esoteric meaning; and for prophets, the absolute truth. Bektaşî rites and traditions did not differ a great deal in their general outlines from those of other tarîkats. They established themselves gradually under the dedes who followed Hacci Bektaş, taking their final form with a number of innovations which Balîm Sultan* introduced at the end of the fifteenth century.

The arrangement of the order was hierarchical, with the *pîr* or dede at the head, below him the *halîfes* or fathers, then the şeyhs, and then the *mürîds* or *muhibs* – friend. The dede lived in the tekke built near to Hacci Bektaş's tomb. He chose, from among his dervishes, the fathers to head each individual tekke, granting them a warrant like the sultan's. The man or woman who was a candidate for the order was called an *âşik* – lover – and, after an initiation ceremony called the 'ceremony of confession of faith', became a muhib. Most of the adherents of the Bektaşî order were muhibs but it was possible to attain full membership by becoming a Bektaşî dervish. In a ceremony known as 'the dedication of his existence' the muhib who was to become a dervish put on the Bektaşî crown. He then began a long period of fasting and initiation as the father in the tekke gradually disclosed to him the secrets of the order. The father, in his capacity as *mürşîd* – spiritual guide – required total obedience and, one by one, according to his ability, revealed

* Balîm Sultan (d. 1516), of whose life there is no authentic account, assumed the headship of the order *c.* 1500.

these secrets to the dervish. The muhibs and dervishes formed an exclusive society around the tekke. The father was responsible for many matters arising in the Bektaşî community. He conducted marriage and funeral services, listened to confessions, and new-born children were brought to him for blessing. Anyone with a sick relative came to the father, visited the tomb of the tekke's patron saint and made vows. Mutual support among the Bektaşîs was very strong; if any one of them fell into distress the father collected aid for him from the community.

Bektaşî-ism had a profound influence on Turkish social and cultural life. With its democratic and national character it did not remain confined to the nomads and peasants but in time came to include members of all social classes. In the mid-seventeenth century Evliya Çelebi* wrote that there were seven hundred Bektaşî tekkes in the Ottoman Empire – which may be an exaggeration – and at the beginning of the nineteenth century it was recorded that one-fifth of the population of Istanbul were Bektaşîs and that they had fourteen tekkes. The town Bektaşîs distinguished themselves from the Kïzïlbaş, whom they regarded as followers of baseless legends and evil practices. In Turkish folklore the Bektaşî represented a particular type, someone who did not head the follies of the world, gently ridiculed religious fanaticism and treated all things with tolerance in the belief that they are transitory and relative. The Bektaşîs have even included among their patron saints the immortal philosopher and jester of Turkish folklore, Nasreddîn Hoca.

From earliest times mysticism was a main element in the thought of the Ottoman intellectual elite and was not confined to the popular beliefs of the tarîkats. This tradition goes back to the Seljuk period. The Seljuk sultans welcomed in their lands the famous scholars and mystics from Turkestan and Iran, fleeing before the Mongol invasion. Thus the Seljuk cities such as Konya, Kayseri, Aksaray or Sivas became the most brilliant centres of mystical thought in the Islamic world. The illuminism of al-Suhrawardî which reconciled the Platonic and old Iranian philosophies, and the mystical thought and philosophy of Nasîr al-Dîn of Tus, found favour here; at the same time the system of Ibn al-'Arabî, one of the greatest mystical theorists in the Islamic world, was prevalent in intellectual circles. Like al-Suhrawardî, Ibn al-'Arabî was personally invited to the Seljuk lands and honoured by the sultan. By interpreting and disseminating his works his stepson, Sadr al-Dîn of Konya (d. 1273), played a major part in establishing Ibn al-'Arabî as a dominant influence in Turkish thought. Mystical belief thus became a well established tradition among the sunnî ulema. The great scholar and founder of the Ottoman medrese tradition

* Evliya Çelebi (1611-after 1684); Turkish traveller. He left an account of his travels in his monumental *Seyahâtnâme*.

Mehmed al-Fanarî, as a follower of the Konya school clearly betrays the influence of Ibn al-'Arabî, and for this reason he was censured by the Arab ulema in Egypt. It is true that since al-Ghazâlî sunnî ulema had recognized mysticism next to the şeriat as a more advanced and more profound form of the religious life, but Ibn al-'Arabî was sufficiently extreme in his esoteric thought to be regarded as heretical by many leading ulema, among them Ibn Khaldûn,* and even as an infidel by Ibn Taymiyya.† From time to time, Ottoman ulema who shared this opinion wrote polemics against Ibn al'Arabî, but in general his influence on Ottoman Turkish though was great. The şeyhülislâm, Kemâl Paşazâde, issued a fetvâ approving all his works, and in Syria in 1517 Selîm I showed his respect for this great sufi by building a mausoleum on his tomb and next to it a mosque. Ottoman scholars made many Turkish translations of his works and he has many Ottoman commentators; Dâvûd of Kayseri, Kutbeddîn of Iznik and Yazîcîzâde Mehmed of Gallipoli in the fourteenth and fifteenth centuries, and Bâlî of Sofya (d. 1533) and Abdullâh of Bosnia (d. 1660) in the sixteenth and seventeenth.

The patron saint of the Mevlevî order of dervishes was Maulânâ Jalâl al-Dîn Rûmî (1207–73), one of the world's greatest mystical writers. He grew up in Konya, the Seljuk capital, where Ibn al-'Arabî's thought prevailed. He first achieved fame as a scholar and preacher, thoroughly trained in the religious sciences, but at a certain stage in his life he became a saint, devoting his whole existence to mystic love. His lyrical verse tells how in a mystical ecstasy he saw all differences of race, religion and creed disappear and how he was exalted above the principles of the şeriat. In his assemblies he swept his listeners to a state of divine rapture. In his person he united the traditions of the dancing babaî dervishes and the profound mysticism of the Melâmîs, exalted above all religious laws. Even in his own lifetime the cosmopolitan society of Konya, imbued with refined Persian culture and the mystical thought of Ibn al-'Arabî, looked upon him as a saint. Maulânâ was indebted in many things to the Persian mystic poets, Attâr (1119?–93) and Sanâî (d. 1130), and to the philosophy of Ibn al-'Arabî, but he recognized music and dance, semâ, as the most effective means to attain mystic ecstasy, the highest degree of sufi experience. He was not a man to concern himself with rites and ceremonies but in time a tarîkat was founded in his name, taking its final form in the fifteenth century. Using his memory and his great influence, his followers established the order in various towns and gave it fixed rites and ceremonies.

As in the other tarîkats, a 'Maulânâ tradition' grew up. In the

* Ibn Khaldûn (1332–1406); historian, sociologist and philosopher, born in Tunis. He is best known for al-Mukaddima, his great work on the philosophy of history.

† Ibn Taymiyya (1263–1328); a great hanbalite theologian and legist.

accounts of his life written after his death, Maulânâ was painted as the most exalted being, to be imitated in all his actions. The rites of the tarîkat were fixed in the form of symbolic movements with a mystic significance. Music and dancing, semâ, was the chief ceremony of the Mevlevîs, who became known as the 'whirling dervishes', from their whirling dances in special dress.

When the order was founded its first centre was the 'Seat of the Pîr' in Konya, a central lodge consisting of dervishes' cells built around the mausoleum containing Maulânâ's tomb. Maulânâ's successors sent representatives to other towns where they established other lodges, approaching the local governors and representatives of the ruling class in order to secure their patronage and vakîfs for the lodges. As Maulânâ himself had been, his successors were usually close to the ruling class, and from the fifteenth century the Mevlevîs established themselves in many Ottoman cities as a tarîkat appealing to the elite. In time, four-teen large and well organized tekkes were founded in the cities and seventy-six minor tekkes in small towns. All the Ottoman sultans, in particular Murâd II, Bâyezîd II, Selîm I and Murâd III, took a close interest in the Mevlevîs. Murâd II founded a large Mevlevî lodge in Edirne. The Mevlevîs thus became a tarîkat with adherents among the Ottoman ruling classes and with an increasingly sunnî character; but another branch of the order openly adopted the esoteric doctrines of the shiites and the Kîzîlbaş and in their beliefs approached the Bektaşîs and the Melâmîs.

All Mevlevî tekkes were under the rule of a çelebi who resided in Konya and who since the fourteenth century had been chosen from Maulânâ's descendants. The influence of the çelebis was great enough to cause the government occasional suspicion and alarm; the Ottoman governors in Konya could not enforce their rule without their coopera-tion. From the sixteenth century the sultans were sometimes obliged to exile an over-influential çelebi from Konya, but in time the govern-ment's control of vakîfs enabled it to force the Mevlevîs into obedience. The şeyhs in Konya chose the heads of the other tekkes but the appoint-ment was valid only after the sultan, on the petition of the şeyhülislâm, had issued a warrant. Competition among the candidates for the çelebiship made it easier for the government to control the order.

Mevlevî tekkes in the great cities acted as cultural centres and – if the term is justified – as art academies. Art was, of course, regarded as a tool of mysticism; semâ was a ritual dance, imitating the movement of celestial bodies, and Mevlevî music a divine melody, inciting mystic enthusiasm and creating ecstasy. At the same time, members of the tekkes read and interpreted Maulânâ's Persian works, particularly the *Masnavî*. Since the ulema forbade the study of Persian in the medreses, tekkes for outsiders became centres for the study of the Persian language and literature. Establishments, called Dâr al-Masnavî, attached to the tekkes, were founded with this as their sole function. The translation into Turkish and commentary on the Masnavî led to the serious study of mysticism in these places. The most famous commentaries on the *Masnavî*, particularly those of Rusûhî Ismaîl Dede of Ankara (d. 1631) and Sarï Abdullâh (d. 1660), were written in Turkey. It is worth noting that they were usually made in the light of Ibn al-'Arabî's philosophical system.

Mevlevî-ism established itself among Ottoman intellectuals, and particularly among the bureaucratic class, who were imbued with Persian literary and cultural traditions. It was a major factor in creating classical Ottoman literature, which originally drew its main inspiration from Persian. In the eighteenth century, Mevlevîs were in the first rank of Ottoman musicians and poets; but side by side with their deep influence on classical Ottoman art the Mevlevîs, like the Bektaşîs, created their own music and literature, entirely derived from Mevlevî tradition.

GENEALOGY OF THE OTTOMAN DYNASTY

Âlâeddîn Alî

Süleyman Paşa(d. 1357)   Halîl

Savcĭ   Ya 'kûb (d.1389)

Süleyman Çelebi   Mûsâ Çelebi   Mustafa, Düzm‹
(1402-11)   (1411-13)   (1421-2)

Orhan   Mustafa Küçük (1422-23)

Âlâeddîn Alî (d. 1443)   Ahmed (d. 1451)

Mustafa (d. 1474)   Cem (1481, d. 1495)

Korkud   Ahmed   Şehinşah   Alemşah
(d. 1513)   (d. 1513)   (d. 1511)   (d. 1510)

Bâyezîd(d. 1561)   Mustafa (d. 1553)

                                          .   Mustafa I (1617-18, 1622-23)

                                                     Ibrâhîm I (1640-48), Deli

                                                     Süleymân II (1687-91)

                                                     Ahmed III (1703-30)

Mustafa III (1757-74)   Abdülhamîd (1774-1789)

Selîm III (1789-1807)   Mahmûd II (1808-39), A‹

                                                     Abdülmecîd (1839-61)

Murâd V   Mehmed V Reşâd   Abdülhamîd II
(1876)   (1909-18)   (1876-1909)

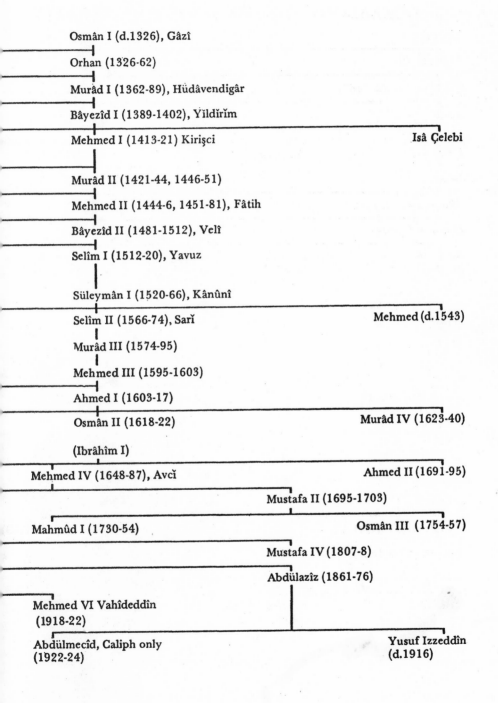

Osmân I (d.1326), Gâzî

Orhan (1326-62)

Murâd I (1362-89), Hüdâvendigâr

Bâyezîd I (1389-1402), Yïldïrïm

Mehmed I (1413-21) Kirişci   Isâ Çelebi

Murâd II (1421-44, 1446-51)

Mehmed II (1444-6, 1451-81), Fâtih

Bâyezîd II (1481-1512), Velî

Selîm I (1512-20), Yavuz

Süleymân I (1520-66), Kânûnî

Selîm II (1566-74), Sarï   Mehmed (d.1543)

Murâd III (1574-95)

Mehmed III (1595-1603)

Ahmed I (1603-17)

Osmân II (1618-22)   Murâd IV (1623-40)

(Ibrâhîm I)

Mehmed IV (1648-87), Avcï   Ahmed II (1691-95)

                    Mustafa II (1695-1703)

Mahmûd I (1730-54)   Osmân III (1754-57)

                    Mustafa IV (1807-8)

                    Abdülazîz (1861-76)

Mehmed VI Vahîdeddîn
  (1918-22)

Abdülmecîd, Caliph only   Yusuf Izzeddîn
  (1922-24)   (d.1916)

A CHRONOLOGY OF OTTOMAN HISTORY

1261–1310	The foundation of the gâzî principalities of Menteşe, Aydĭn, Saruhan, Karesi and Osmanlĭ (Ottoman) in western Anatolia.
1269	The Turks of Menteşe invade the Byzantine ports in Caria.
1301	Osmân Gâzî's victory at Baphaeon.
1304	The Catalans in the service of Byzantium against the Turks; the Turks of Menteşe conquer Ephesus.
1308	The Aydĭn Turks conquer Pyrgion (Birgi); death of Mesûd II, the last Seljuk sultan.
1313	The Saruhan Turks conquer Magnesia (Manisa); outbreak of civil war in Byzantium.
1326	The Ottoman conquest of Bursa (6 April); death of Osmân Gâzî and the accession of Orhan.
1327	The first Ottoman silver coin (akçe) minted in Bursa.
1331	The Ottoman conquest of Nicaea (Iznik).
1332	The Bey of Izmir, Umur's first Balkan expedition.
1333	Orhan's victory over Andronicus III at Pelekanon.
1335	The fall of the Mongol Empire in Iran.
1337	The Ottoman conquest of Nicomedia (Izmit).
1341–7	Civil war in Byzantium.
1344	The Crusaders capture the fort of Izmir.
1345	The Ottomans annex the principality of Karesi; Umur Bey's last expedition to the Balkans.
1346	Orhan's marriage with Theodora, daughter of John VI Cantacuzenus.
1352	Orhan grants capitalutions to the Genoese; Orhan's son, Süleymân, in Adrianople; Süleymân occupies Tzympe; beginning of the Ottoman conquests in Thrace.
1353–6	War between the Genoese and Venetians.
1354	Ottoman occupation of Ankara and Gallipoli (2 March); John V Palaeologus in Constantinople; abdication of John Cantacuzenus.

1355	Death of Stephen Dušan (20 December); dismemberment of the Serbian Empire.
1357	Death of Süleymân; Ottoman-Byzantine peace.
1359	Prince Murâd renews the Ottoman onslaught in Thrace; conquest of Tsouroullos (Çorlu) and Didymoteichos (Dimetoka).
1361	Murâd conquers Adrianople (Edirne).
1362	Death of Orhan; accession of Murâd I; uprising against the Ottomans in Anatolia.
1363–5	Ottoman conquests in southern Bulgaria and Thrace; conquest of Philippopolis.
1364	War between Byzantium and Bulgaria.
1366	John V in Buda; the Pope announces a crusade against the Ottomans; Amadeo VI of Savoy captures Gallipoli (August).
1369	John V in Rome.
1371	Ottoman victory over the Serbian princes Vukašin and Uglješa at Chermanon (26 September).
1373	Joint rebellion of Adronicus and the Ottoman Prince, Savcĭ, against their fathers (spring) and their defeat (September).
1376	Adronicus IV in Constantinople with Ottoman and Genoese support; Adronicus cedes Gallipoli to the Ottomans.
1375–80	The Ottomans annex parts of the principalities of Germiyan and Hamidili.
1379	John V Palaeologus, with Ottoman support, again occupies the Byzantine throne.
1380–81	War between the Genoese and the Venetians.
1383	The Ottomans in Serres (19 September).
1385	Ottoman conquest of Sofia.
1386	The Ottomans in Nish; Ottoman intervention in the Amasya region of northern Anatolia.
1387	Ottoman conquest of Salonica; victory over the Karamanids.
1388	A coalition of the Serbs, Bosnians and Bulgars; defeat of the Ottomans at Ploshnik (27 August); Ottoman occupation of northern Bulgaria (Autumn).
1389	Battle of Kossovo (15 June); accession of Bâyezîd I.
1389–90	Bâyezĭd's conquests in western Anatolia and of the principalities of Menteşe, Aydĭn, Saruhan, Germiyan and Hamidili.
1390	Defeat of the Karamanids, Palaeologi in Bâyezîd's army in Anatolia.
1391	The Ottomans in Adalia (Antalya) and Alâiyye (Alanya); the Ottomans capture Skopje and raid northern Albania.

1392	Ottomans in Kastamonu and Amasya; retreat before Kâdî Burhâneddîn, Sultan of Sivas.
1393	Bâyezîd returns to the Balkans and annexes Danubian Bulgaria; he calls all the vassel princes in the Balkans, including the Palaeologi, into his presence in Verria.
1394–1402	Ottoman blockade of Constantinople.
1394	Ottoman conquest of Thessaly; raids in the Morea.
1395	Bâyezîd's expedition into Hungary and Wallachia; Battle of Argesh (17 May); Wallachia becomes an Ottoman vassal state; execution of Shishman, King of Bulgaria (3 June); alliance of Venice, Hungary and Byzantium against the Ottomans.
1396	Battle of Nicopolis (25 September).
1397	Bâyezîd returns to Anatolia and annexes Karaman.
1398	Conquest of the Bulgarian principality of Vidin and of the principality of Kâdî Burhâneddîn.
1399	Conquest of the Mamlûk cities of Malatya and Elbistan in the Euphrates valley.
1400	Manuel II Palaeologus in Europe; Timur sacks Sivas (10 August).
1401	Bâyezîd in Erzincan.
1402	Battle of Ankara (28 July); Timur takes Smyrna (Izmir) from the Hospitallers (December).
1403	Bâyezîd commits suicide at Akşehir (8 March); Timur revives the Anatolian principalities; civil war between Bâyezîd's sons with Süleymân in Edirne, Îsâ in Bursa and Mehmed in Amasya; agreements between Süleymân and Christian states; Salonica returned to the Byzantines (October).
1406	War between Mehmed and Süleymân.
1410	Süleymân defeats Mûsâ in Rumelia (15 June and 11 July).
1411	Mûsâ defeats Süleymân (February) and besieges Constantinople (summer).
1412	Agreement between Mehmed and Manuel against Mûsâ (July).
1413	Mehmed defeats Mûsâ near Sofia (5 July); Mehmed I unifies Ottoman territories; the Karamanids besiege Bursa.
1414	Mehmed I besieges Konya and reconquers Hamidili.
1415	Mehmed's expedition to western Anatolia, reconquers Smyrna (Izmir) and other Ionian cities (summer); conflict with Venice.
1416	Mustafa, son of Bâyezîd I, in Rumelia; Pietro

	Lorendano destroys the Ottoman fleet at Gallipoli (29 May); the revolt of Şeyh Bedreddîn (summer) and his execution (18 December); Mirčea invades Silistra and Deliorman (autumn); Mehmed I invades Candarid territory.
1417	Mehmed I invades Karaman (autumn), and annexes Kîrşehir and Niğde.
1418	Mehmed I's expedition to Canik.
1419	Expedition against Mirčea; capture of Giurgiu.
1421	Death of Mehmed I; Murâd II in Bursa (May); Mustafa in control of Rumelia.
1422	Mustafa retreats from Ulubat and is executed in Edirne (January); Murâd besieges Constantinople (2 June–6 September); his brother Mustafa's rebellion in Anatolia.
1423	Murâd II defeats Mustafa and subdues the Candarids and Karamanids; Turahan Bey in the Morea (May).
1423–30	Salonica under Venetian rule; Ottoman-Venetian war.
1424	Peace treaty between the Ottomans and Byzantines.
1425	Ottoman annexation of Izmir and reconquest of Menteşe and Teke.
1427	Death of Stephen Lazarević of Serbia (19 July); the Hungarians in Belgrade; the Ottomans in Golubać; Sigismund takes Giurgiu; the Karamanids in Hamidili.
1428	Peace between the Ottomans and Hungarians.
1429	Shâhrukh in Azerbaijan.
1430	Ottoman conquest of Salonica (29 March) and of Ioannina.
1432–3	Rebellion in southern Albania.
1434	Ottoman-Hungarian rivalry in Wallachia, Serbia and Bosnia.
1435	Shâhrukh in Anatolia.
1437	Murâd II reconquers Hamidili; death of Sigismund.
1438	Murâd II's expedition into Transylvania.
1439	Murâd II's conquest of Semendria; the end of independent Serbia; the King of Bosnia tributary to the Ottomans.
1440	Ottoman failure at the siege of Belgrade.
1441–2	John Hunyadi defeats the Ottomans in Transylvania.
1443	Hunyadi invades the Balkans; battle of Zlatitsa (25 December); Iskender Beg's rebellion in northern Albania.
1444	Peace between Hungary and the Ottoman Empire (Edirne, 12 June); revival of Serbia;

peace between the Ottomans and the Karamanids (Yenişehir, August); abdication of Murâd II in favour of his son, Mehmed II; Battle of Varna (10 November).

1446   Murâd II's second accession to the throne.

1448   Murâd II's expedition against Iskender Beg; Battle of Kossovo (17–19 October).

1449   Expedition into Wallachia; reconquest of Giurgiu.

1450   Murâd II's second campaign against Iskender Beg.

1451   Death of Murâd II (3 February); accession of Mehmed II (18 February); Mehmed II's expedition against the Karamanids (May-June); renewal of peace with Venice (10 September) and Hungary (20 November).

1452   Erection of Rumeli Hisaﬤ, the fortress overlooking the Bosphorus (January-August); declaration of war against Byzantium.

1453   Siege of Constantinople (April 6-May 29); fall of Pera.

1454   Peace with Venice (18 April); Mehmed II's expedition to Serbia; The Ottoman fleet on the Black Sea; the Genoese colonies around the Black Sea tributary to the Ottomans.

1455   Moldavia tributary to the Ottomans (5 October); Mehmed II's second expedition to Serbia.

1456   Ottoman failure at the siege of Belgrade; the empire of Trebizond tributary to the Ottomans.

1457   Iskender Beg's victory at Albulena.

1458   Mahmûd Pasha's expedition against Serbia; Mehmed II in the Morea.

1459   Surrender of Semendria (June); conquest of Amastris (Amasra); Pius II declares a crusade.

1460   Conquest of the Morea.

1461   Conquest of the Candarid principality and the empire of Trebizond.

1462   Mehmed II invades Wallachia (summer); Mahmûd Pasha in Lesbos (September).

1463   War with Venice; Venetians in control of the Morea; Mehmed II invades Bosnia; King of Hungary in Yaitse (16 December).

1464   Ottoman reconquest of the Morea (spring); Mehmed II besieges Yaitse; death of Pius II (15 August); death of Ibrahîm the Karamanid; civil war in Karaman.

1466   Mehmed II's campaign against Iskender Beg; erection of the castle of Elbasan.

1467   Mehmed II's second campaign against Iskender

Beg; Shehsuvar of Dulkadir under Ottoman protection.

1468	Death of Iskender Beg (17 January). Mehmed II's conquest of Karaman (summer); resistance of the Turcoman tribes in the Taurus mountains.
1469–74	Pacification of Karaman.
1469	Venetian attack on Enos and New Phocaea.
1470	Mehmed II's conquest of Euboea (11 July).
1471	Uzun Hasan of Akkoyunlu, Venice, the King of Cyprus, the Knights of St John and the Emîr of Alâiyye (Alanya) form a coalition against the Ottomans.
1472	Uzun Hasan sacks Tokat; an Akkoyunlu-Karamanid army invades Karaman; the Mamlûks execute Shehsuvar.
1473	Battle of Başkent (Otluk-beli) (11 August).
1474	Ottoman raids into Transylvania; siege of Scutari in Albania.
1475	Conquest of the Genoese colonies in the Crimea; Ottoman suzerainty over the khanate of the Crimea.
1476	Matthias Corvinus takes Shabats (15 February); Mehmed II's campaign against Moldavia (summer) and his expedition against Corvinus (winter).
1477	Beylerbeyi Süleymân besieges Lepanto; Ottoman raiders before Venice.
1478	Death of Uzun Hasan (6 January); Mehmed II besieges Scutari in Albania; surrender of Croia in Albania (6 June); Ottoman raid into Friuli.
1479	Peace with Venice (25 January); Ottoman raids into Transylvania and Hungary; conquest of Anapa, Kopa and Tamatarkhan.
1480	Mesîh Pasha's siege of Rhodes; Ahmed Pasha in Otranto.
1481	Death of Mehmed II (3 May); accession of Bâyezîd II (20 May); Battle of Yenişehir between Bâyezîd and Cem (20 June); surrender of the Ottoman forces in Otranto (11 September).
1482	Cem and Kâsim the Karamanid in Anatolia; Cem's flight to Rhodes (26 July); agreement on Cem between the Knights of St John and Bâyezîd II (September); execution of Gedik Ahmed Pasha (November).
1484	Bâyezîd II's campaign against Moldavia; annexation of Kilia and Akkerman.
1484–91	War with the Mamlûks of Egypt.
1495	Death of Cem (25 February).
1496	The Ottomans in Montenegro; Albert of Poland's

	invasions of Moldavia; Polish-Hungarian alliance.
1497–9	War with Poland.
1499–1503	War with Venice.
1499	Ottoman naval victory at Navarino (12 August); conquest of Lepanto.
1500	Hungary declares war on the Ottomans; Shah Ismaîl in power in Iran; revolt of the Karamanid tribes in the Taurus mountains.
1503	Peace treaty with Venice (10 August).
1504	Shah Ismaîl in Baghdad.
1507	Ismaîl's march through Ottoman territory against Dulkadir.
1511	Insurrection in Teke of the shiite partisans of Shah Ismaîl (March); civil war in the Ottoman Empire.
1512	Selîm I forces his father to abdicate (24 April); insurrection in north-east Anatolia; death of Bâyezîd II (26 May).
1512–13	Selîm I defeats and executes his brothers and suppresses the partisans of Shah Ismaîl in Anatolia.
1514	Selîm defeats Shah Ismaîl at Çaldïran (23 August).
1515	Mutiny of the Janissaries (February); capture of Kemah (19 May); conquest of the principality of Dulkadir (June).
1516	Conquest of Diyarbekir (April); submission of eastern Anatolia to the Ottomans; Selîm defeats the Mamlûks at Marj Dâbik (24 August); Selîm in Aleppo.
1517	Battle of Reydaniyya (22 January); Tuman Bay's resistance in Cairo; submission of the Sherif of Mecca (17 July).
1520	Death of Selîm I (21 September); accession of Süleymân I (30 September).
1521	Conquest of Belgrade (29 August); defeat and execution of Janbardî Ghazâlî in Syria (February).
1522	End of the Dulkadir dynasty; conquest of Rhodes (January 21).
1523	Ibrahîm becomes grand vizier.
1524	Revolt of Ahmed Pasha in Egypt (January).
1525	Ibrahîm in Egypt (24 March–14 June).
1526	Battle of Mohács (29 August); Süleymân I in Buda (10 September); John Zapolya becomes King of Hungary (10 November).
1527	Ferdinand of Austria in Buda.
1529	Süleymân I captures Buda (8 September); Zapolya crowned in Buda (14 September); Süleymân I besieges Vienna (26 September – 16 October).

1531	The Austrians besiege Buda (December).
1532	Süleymân I's campaign against Austria; capture of Güns (28 August); Andrea Doria captures Coron (8 August).
1533	Peace with Ferdinand (22 June); Hayreddîn Barbarossa becomes grand admiral; Barbarossa's conquest of Tunis (August); reconquest of Coron (12 September); war with Iran (August).
1534	Conquest of Tabriz (13 July); allegiance of the Sultan of Gilan; Süleymân I in Baghdad.
1535	Süleymân I returns to Tabriz (spring); Charles V in Tunis (21 July).
1536	Süleymân I returns to Istanbul (8 January); execution of Ibrahîm (5 March).
1537	War with Venice; Süleymân I in Albania; Ottoman raid into Apulia (July); siege of Corfu (25 August); Süleymân I returns to Istanbul (1 October).
1538	Süleymân I in Moldavia (summer); annexation of southern Moldavia (4 October); Süleymân Pasha of Egypt before Diu (4 September); naval Battle of Préveza (29 September).
1539	Conquest of Castelnuovo (10 August).
1540	Peace with Venice (2 October); surrender of Monemvasia and Napoli di Romagna; death of Zapolya; the Austrians beseige Buda.
1541	Süleymân I's campaign against Ferdinand; Süleymân I in Buda (2 September); annexation of Hungary; Charles V before Algiers (20 October).
1543	The Franco-Ottoman fleet takes Nice (20 August); Süleymân I in Hungary; conquest of Valpovo, Pécs, Siklós, and Gran.
1544	Conquest of Vishegrad.
1545	Armistice between Süleymân I and Ferdinand.
1547	Peace treaty between the Ottomans and the Habsburgs, including the Pope, Venice and the King of France (1 August).
1548	Süleymân I's campaign against Iran; conquest of Van (25 August).
1549	Conquests in Georgia; Süleymân I returns to Istanbul (12 December).
1551	The Ottomans in Transylvania; conquest of Becskerek, Varad, Csanád and Lippa; Turgud reîs (Dragut) captures Tripoli (14 August).
1552	Conquest of Temesvar (July) and other cities in Banat; Ottoman failure against the Portuguese at Hormuz; Russian occupation of Kazan; Ottoman failure at Erlau (October).

1553	War with Iran; Süleymân I in Eregli (Karaman); execution of his son, Mustafa.
1554	Süleymân I's campaign in Iran; conquest of Nakhchevan and Erivan (summer); Russian occupation of Astrakhan.
1555	Peace with Iran at Amasya (29 May).
1556	Inauguration of the Süleymâniye mosque (16 August).
1556–9	Continued warfare against the Austrians in Hungary.
1559	Civil war between Süleymân I's sons, Selîm and Bâyezîd (May); Bâyezîd takes refuge in Iran (November).
1560	The Spaniards on Djerba; the grand admiral, Piyâle Pasha, captures Djerba (31 July).
1561	Execution of Prince Bâyezîd (25 September); the Cossacks attack Azov.
1562	Peace with the Emperor Ferdinand (1 July).
1565	Siege of Malta (20 May–11 September).
1566	Siege of Szigetvár (5 August–7 September); Süleymân I's death before Szigetvár (6 September); accession of Selîm II (24 September); occupation of Chios.
1567	Revolt of the Zaidite, Mutahhar, in Yemen.
1568	Peace with the emperor (17 February).
1569	Ottoman expedition against the Russians; Don-Volga canal project and the siege of Astrakhan (September).
1570	Peace negotiations with the tsar; Uluç Alî captures Tunis (January); expedition to Cyprus; conquest of Nicosia.
1571	Formation of Holy League against the Ottomans (20 May); Ottoman conquest of Famagusta (1 August); Battle of Lepanto (7 October).
1572	Devlet Giray invades Muscovy; the Ottomans support Henry of Valois' accession to the Polish throne; Don John of Austria captures Tunis (October).
1573	Peace treaty with Venice (7 March); renewal of peace with the emperor (3 October).
1574	Sinân Pasha reconquers Tunis (24 August); death of Selîm II (12 December).
1577	Renewal of peace with the emperor (1 January).
1578	Assassination of the grand vizier, Sokollu Mehmed; war with Iran (spring); Lâlâ Mustafa's victory at Çïldïr (10 August); annexation of Georgia; Shirvan and Darband (Derbent); Battle of Alcazar in Morocco (4 August).

1579	Persian counterattack.
1582	Ottoman defeat on the Kur river.
1583	Osmân Pasha's victory at Besh-Tepe (6 June).
1585	Osmân Pasha captures Tabriz (September).
1587	Abbâs the Great declared Shah of Iran.
1588	Ottoman conquest of Karabagh.
1589	Janissary revolt in Istanbul (3 April).
1590	Peace with Iran (21 March); renewal of peace with the emperor (29 November).
1591–2	Further Janissary uprisings and changes in the government.
1593	Rebellion of the sipâhîs in Istanbul (27 January); Sinân Pasha becomes grand vizier; Ottoman defeat at Sisak (20 June); war with Austria (autumn); Sinân in Hungary; capture of Veszprém (13 October).
1594	Sinân captures Raab; rebellion of Michael, voivoda of Wallachia.
1595	Anti-Ottoman alliance between the Habsburgs, Wallachia, Moldavia and the Prince of Transylvania (January); death of Murâd III (16 January); accession of Mehmed III (27 January); Sinân in Wallachia (August); Sinân retreats (October); Austrians in Stuhlweissenburg and Vishegrad (8 September); Michael of Wallachia in the Dobrudja.
1596	Mehmed III's campaign in Hungary; capture of Erlau (23 September); Battle of Mezökeresztes (26 October); celâlî disorders in Anatolia.
1598	Austrians recapture Raab (29 March) and Veszprém and besiege Buda; Michael attacks Nicopolis.
1599	Peace negotiations with Austria; Karayazǐcǐ besieged in Urfa (July); Michael in Transylvania.
1600	Ottoman conquest of Kanisza (September).
1601	Death of Michael (19 August); Archduke Ferdinand defeated before Kanisza (18 November).
1602	Archduke Matthias besieges Buda (autumn).
1603	Revolt of the sipâhîs (January); Shah Abbâs reconquers Tabriz (21 October); death of Mehmed III (22 December); accession of Ahmed I (23 December).
1604	Shah Abbâs conquers Erivan, Shirvan and Kars; Archduke Matthias besieges Buda.
1605	The Ottomans declare Bocskai King of Hungary; Ottoman conquest of Gran.
1606	Peace treaty between the Ottomans and Austrians at Zsitva-Torok.

GLOSSARY

Abdal:	(1) a name sometimes given to itinerant dervishes.
	(2) a rank in some dervish orders.
Acemî:	'novice'
	(1) acemî oğlan: a novice in the page-school of the Palace; a conscript later to join the Janissary corps (q.v.)
	(2) a female slave, new to the Palace harem (q.v.)
Adâletnâme:	a sultanic rescript, redressing the malpractices of a provincial authority.
Ağa:	chief; master; head servant of a household.
Ağa of the Janissaries (Turkish: 'Yeniçeri ağasï'):	the chief officer of the Janissary corps (q.v.)
Ahî:	leader of a semi-religious fraternity of late Seljuk and early Ottoman times.
Ak ağa:	a white eunuch of the Palace.
Akçe:	a silver coin, the chief unit of account in the Ottoman Empire.
Akritai:	the Byzantine frontier troops.
Altmïşlï medrese:	'a medrese of sixty'. A grade of medrese (q.v.), above the dâhil medreses (q.v.), with a müderris (q.v.) earning sixty akçes (q.v.) daily.
Âşik:	'lover', candidate for membership of the Bektaşî (q.v.), Order.
Avâriz:	extra-ordinary taxes levied on the reâyâ (q.v.) in times of emergency.
Baba:	'father'
	(1) a name sometimes given to the elders of various dervish groups.
	(2) The head of a Bektaşî (q.v.) lodge.
Babaî:	(1) a dervish follower of Baba Ishâk, who led the revolt in Anatolia in 1241.
	(2) A name sometimes given to itinerant melâmî (q.v.) dervishes.

217

Bailo: a Venetian ambassador to Constantinople.

Baş kadïn: 'head woman', the first woman of the Palace harem (*q.v.*) to bear the sultan a son.

Bâtinite:
(1) one who seeks hidden, esoteric meanings in the Koran.
(2) one who holds that the Koran, besides its obvious meaning, has an esoteric meaning, to be learned only from the shiite (*q.v.*) imam.

Bayramî Order: a dervish order founded by Hacci Bayram (d. 1430).

Bedestan: a covered market for the sale of valuable goods.

Bedreddînlü: a follower of the sect of Şeyh Bedreddîn (d. 1416); known also as *simavnî*.

Bektaşî Order: a dervish order founded by Hacci Bektaş Velî (*fl.* second half of the thirteenth century).

Bey:
(1) prince, ruler of an independent principality.
(2) governor of a district (see Sanjak, Sanjak beyi).

Beylerbeyi: 'bey of the beys', governor of a beylerbeyilik (*q.v.*), the highest rank in the provincial government of the Ottoman Empire.

Beylerbeyilik:
(1) a province, the largest administrative unit in the Ottoman Empire, and governed by a beylerbeyi (*q.v.*).
(2) The office of beylerbeyi.

Beylik: any district or principality governed by a bey (*q.v.*)

Bazirgân: 'merchants', term used for large traders handling the overseas and caravan trade; known also as *tüccâr*.

Bîat: the oath of allegiance to a new sultan, sworn by a group representing the Islamic community.

Bîrûn: the outer section of the sultan's Palace.

Çakïrcï başï: 'head-falconer', the chief of the sultan's falconers.

Câriye: 'slave girl', the lowest degree in the hierarchy of the Palace harem (*q.v.*).

Çaşnigîr başï: 'head-taster', the chief of the sultan's tasters.

Çavuş: an official of the Palace, often sent to the provinces to convey and execute orders.

Çavuş başï: 'head-çavuş', the head of the çavuşes of the Palace.

Cebeci başï: 'head-armourer'; the chief of the sultan's armourers.

Cebelü: an armed retainer, brought to war by a timar-holding sipâhî (*q.v.*).

Celâlî: a rebel against the government in sixteenth-century Anatolia.

Çelebi:	(1) a title of respect, given to men of the upper classes.
	(2) title of the leader of a religious order, especially of the Mevlevîs (*q.v.*).
Çeribaşï:	'head of troops', an officer in the provinces commanding a detachment of timar-holding sipâhîs (*q.v.*).
Çift:	a unit of agricultural land, varying in size from 60 to 150 dönüms (*q.v.*).
Çift bozan akçesi:	'farm breaker's tax', a tax paid by a peasant to a timar-holding sipâhî (*q.v.*) in compensation for having left the sipâhî's land.
Çift resmi:	'farm tax', a farm tax paid in cash by Muslim reâyâ (*q.v.*) possessing one çift (*q.v.*) of land.
Çïkma:	the graduation of the içoğlans (*q.v.*) to military or further Palace service.
Cizye:	the poll-tax paid by non-Muslims in Islamic states.
Çuhadâr:	the custodian of the sultan's outer garments.
Dâhil medrese:	'interior medrese', a higher medrese (*q.v.*) giving instruction in the religious sciences.
Dânişmend:	a specialist student in a higher medrese (*q.v.*).
Dârülhadîs:	one of the medreses (*q.v.*) attached to the Süleymaniye Mosque for the study of hadîth (*q.v.*).
Dârülharb:	'the Abode of War', the non-Islamic lands.
Dârülislâm:	'the Abode of Islam', the Islamic realms.
Dârüssaâde ağasï:	'ağa of the Abode of Felicity', the chief black eunuch of the Palace; known also as the *harem ağasï*.
Dede:	'grandfather', title given to the heads of various dervish communities, especially to the head of the Bektaşî Order (*q.v.*).
Defter Kethüdâsï:	'kethüdâ of the registers', a provincial official controlling the timar (*q.v.*) registers.
Defterdâr:	a head of the Treasury.
Derbendci:	the guardian of a pass, bridge or ford.
Dergâh-i âlî:	'the Sublime Porte', the Ottoman government.
Devşirme:	(1) the levy of Christian children to be trained for posts in the Palace, the administration or the kapïkulu (*q.v.*) military corps.
	(2) A youth so levied.
Dîvân-i hümâyûn:	'imperial council', the grand vizier's (*q.v.*) council and the central organ of the Ottoman government.
Dönüm:	a unit of land measurement; 940 square metres.
Dülbend oğlanï:	the keeper of the sultan's linen.
Ehl-i hibre:	'person of knowledge', an expert of a craft guild,

	controlling the quality of goods and helping fix prices.
Emlâk:	property, real estate.
Enderûn:	the inner section of the sultan's Palace.
Esnâf:	term used to describe small traders, artisans and shopkeepers.
Eyâlet:	a province; from the late sixteenth century the term used for a beylerbeyilik (*q.v.*).
Fakï:	from *fakîh*, jurist, a conservative preacher upholding the opinions of Mehmed of Birgi (1522–73).
Fen:	a practical art or science.
Fermân:	an edict of the sultan.
Fetvâ:	a written answer to a legal question, issued by the şeyhülislâm (*q.v.*) or other müftî (*q.v.*).
Futuwwa:	(1) a semi-religious fraternity of mediaeval Anatolia. (2) the ethics of such a fraternity.
Gazâ:	Holy War on behalf of Islam.
Gâzî:	a warrior fighting on behalf of Islam.
Gedikli:	(1) a degree in a craft guild or the bureaucracy, above apprentice and below master. (2) a degree in the hierarchy of the Palace harem (*q.v.*), below usta (*q.v.*).
Grand Vizier ('Turkish: 'vezîr-i azam'):	the chief vizier (*q.v.*) and deputy of the sultan.
Gurbet tâifesi:	'homeless men', the groups of landless and unemployed youths in sixteenth-century Anatolia.
Hâcegân:	the departmental heads in the bureaucracy.
Hadîth:	(1) a recorded tradition of the sayings and actions of the Prophet Muhammad. (2) The study of these traditions.
Halîfe:	(1) caliph; appointed successor. (2) a rank in the Bektaşî Order (*q.v.*) of dervishes.
Halvetî Order:	an Order of dervishes.
Hamzavî:	a follower of the sect of the dervish Hamza Bâlî of Bosnia (d. 1561).
Hanafite school:	one of the four legal schools of sunnî (*q.v.*) Islam, named after its nominal founder, Abû Hanîfa (d. 767).
Hanbalite school:	one of the four legal schools of sunnî (*q.v.*) Islam, named after its founder, Ahmad b. Hanbal (d. 855).
Haraç:	a poll-tax paid by non-Muslims in Islamic states.
Hareket-i altmışlï:	the higher grade of altmışlï medrese (*q.v.*).
Hareket-i hâriç:	the higher grade of hâriç medrese (*q.v.*).

Harem:	the women's apartments in a Muslim household.
Harem ağası:	'ağa of the harem', the chief black eunuch of the Palace, known also as the *dârüssaâde ağası*.
Hâriç medrese:	'exterior medrese', a medrese (*q.v.*) giving preparatory courses of instruction.
Hâs:	a domain of the sultan, prince of the blood, beylerbeyi (*q.v.*) or sanjak beyi (*q.v.*), yielding an annual revenue of more than one hundred thousand akçes (*q.v.*).
Hâseki:	a woman in the Palace receiving the sultan's special favours; known also as *hâs odalık*.
Hâs oda:	the sultan's Privy Chamber.
Hâs oda başı:	the chief of the sultan's Privy Chamber.
Hâs odalık:	'imperial concubine', a woman in the Palace receiving the sultan's special favours.
Haydarî:	a name sometimes given to itinerant melâmî (*q.v.*) dervishes.
Hazîne:	the Treasury.
Hazîne defterdârı:	'defterdâr of the Treasury', a provincial official administering the sources of revenue belonging to the Treasury.
Hisba:	the laws relating to public morals and, especially, commercial transactions; known also as *ihtisâb*.
Hükûmet sanjak:	'government sanjak', an autonomous, hereditary sanjak (*q.v.*) in eastern Anatolia, governed by a tribal chief.
Hurûfî sect:	an esoteric religious sect, founded by Fadlullâh (d. 1394).
Hutbe:	the sermon following the Friday prayer in which the sultan's or caliph's name was mentioned.
İbtidâ-yi altmışlı:	'beginning of the medrese of sixty'; the lower grade of altmışlı medrese (*q.v.*).
İbtidâ-yi dâhil:	'beginning of the interior', the lower grade of dâhil medrese (*q.v.*).
İbtidâ-yi hâriç:	'beginning of the exterior', the lower grade of hâriç medrese (*q.v.*).
İcmâ:	the consensus of opinion as the basis for the formulation of a legal principle.
İçoğlanı:	a devşirme (*q.v.*) boy, selected as a page and receiving an education in the Palace.
İhtisâb:	the laws relating to public morals and, especially, commercial transactions; known also as *hisba*.
İl yazıcısı:	'clerk of the district', the registrar of a province who made the detailed register showing all the sources of revenue in the area.
İmâret:	a complex of public buildings and institutions supported by a vakıf (*q.v.*).

İspence: the name of the çift resmi (*q.v.*) as paid by Christians.

Janissary (Turkish: 'Yeniçeri') corps: the sultan's standing infantry corps, recruited from the devşirme (*q.v.*) and paid from the Treasury.

Kadĭn: 'woman', title given to the four specially privileged hâs odalĭks (*q.v.*).

Kâdî: a judge administering both şerîat (*q.v.*) and kânûn (*q.v.*) and chief administrator of a kâdîlik (*q.v.*).

Kâdîasker: the highest judicial authority of the empire after the şeyhülislâm (*q.v.*). There were two kâdîaskers, one for Rumelia and one for Anatolia.

Kâdîlik: (1) a kâdî's (*q.v.*) administrative and judicial district; sub-division of a sanjak (*q.v.*).
(2) the office of kâdî.

Kafes: an apartment in the Palace in which a royal prince was secluded.

Kâhya bey: the grand vizier's (*q.v.*) agent in military and political matters.

Kâhya kadĭn: a female superintendent of the novices in the Palace harem (*q.v.*).

Kalenderî: a name sometimes given to itinerant melâmî (*q.v.*) dervishes.

Kalfa: (1) a senior clerk in the bureaucracy.
(2) a master in a craft guild, acting as a salaried foreman.

Kantâr: a measure of weight; 56·449 kg.

Kânûn: a secular law or laws issued by the sultan, as distinct from the şerîat (*q.v.*).

Kânûn-i osmânî: the legal code of the Ottoman sultans.

Kânûnnâme: a code of laws; a collection of sultanic laws, as distinct from the şerîat (*q.v.*).

Kapĭ: 'Gate, Porte'. The Ottoman government.

Kapĭ ağasĭ: 'the ağa of the Porte', the chief white eunuch of the Palace.

Kapĭcĭ başĭ: 'Head-gatekeeper'
(1) the chief gatekeeper of the Palace.
(2) a commander of a unit of Palace gatekeepers.

Kapĭcĭlar kethüdâsĭ: 'the lieutenant of the gatekeepers', the second-in-command of the Palace gatekeepers.

Kapĭkulu: 'slave of the Porte', a devşirme (*q.v.*) or slave employed in military, administrative or Palace service.

Kapudan-i deryâ: 'the admiral of the sea', the grand admiral of the Ottoman fleet.

Kethüdâ:	'steward, agent, representative of an organization to the government' (1) the deputy of a beylerbeyi (*q.v.*) or other provincial governor. (2) the representative to the government of a city quarter. (3) a senior officer of a craft guild, representing the guild to the government.
Kïzïlbaş:	'red-head', member of the semi-political, shiite (*q.v.*) sects in Anatolia.
Kiler:	'larder', the office of the Palace larder.
Kul:	'slave', a slave of the sultan, educated in the Palace and in the service of the state.
Kutb:	'pole', the spiritual head of a mystic religious order.
Levend:	(1) a landless and unemployed person. (2) a brigand on land or sea.
Medrese:	a higher institute of Muslim education.
Melâmetî or melâmî:	a sect of dervishes who ignored the outward forms of religion.
Mevlevî Order:	the order of dervishes following the teachings of Maulânâ Jalâl al-Dîn Rûmî (1207–73).
Mîrahûr:	the master of the sultan's horse.
Mîr-alem:	the keeper of the sultan's standards, tents and military music.
Mîrî:	(1) the possessions and revenues of the government. (2) Belonging to the government.
Molla:	title given to senior members of the ulema (*q.v.*).
Mudâraba:	a commercial undertaking where an investor places his money in another person's trading venture (*commenda*).
Muhib:	'friend', an initiated member of the Bektaşî Order (*q.v.*) of dervishes.
Muhtesib:	an inspector of markets and public morals enforcing the ihtisâb (*q.v.*) regulations.
Mûsile-yi sahn:	the eight preparatory medreses (*q.v.*) established by Mehmed II.
Müderris:	the chief teacher and administrator of a medrese (*q.v.*).
Müftî:	an officially appointed interpreter of the şerîat (*q.v.*)
Mülâzim:	a candidate for a post in a government office.
Mülk:	freehold property.
Mürîd:	a novice in a dervish order.
Mürşid:	a spiritual guide in a dervish order.

Müsellem:	one of a corps performing military and other services in return for exemption from certain taxes.
Müteferrika:	one of an elite group in the Palace formed from the sons of pashas and vassal lords.
Mütevellî:	the chief trustee of a vakîf (*q.v.*).
Nakşbendî Order:	an order of dervishes founded by Muḥammad Nakshband (1317–89).
Nâzir:	a superintendent, particularly of a vakîf (*q.v.*).
Nevrûz:	the Persian New Year's Day, falling on the vernal equinox, 22 March.
Nişancĭ:	the secretary of the imperial council who controlled the tuğra (*q.v.*) to be attached to official orders and letters.
Osmanlĭ:	Ottoman.
Pîr:	the spiritual head of a dervish order.
Pronoia:	a military fief in the Byzantine Empire and its successor states.
Reâyâ:	the tax-paying subjects of the Ottoman Empire, as distinct from the ruling military class.
Reîsülküttâb:	'chief of the clerks' (1) the head of the offices attached to the grand vizierate. (2) From the eighteenth century, minister of foreign affairs.
Rikâbdâr:	the sultan's stirrup-holder.
Sahn-i semân:	'the court of eight', the eight medreses (*q.v.*) established by Mehmed II around his mosque; known also as the *semâniyye*.
Sâlyâne:	a sum annually remitted to the capital by the governors of certain provinces where the timar (*q.v.*) system was not in force.
Sanjak:	the chief administrative unit of the Ottoman Empire, governed by a sanjak beyi (*q.v.*); subdivision of a beylerbeyilik (*q.v.*).
Sanjak beyi:	the governor of a sanjak (*q.v.*).
Sarĭca:	a provincial militia equipped with firearms.
Seferli oda:	the sultan's Campaign Chamber.
Sekban:	a provincial militia equipped with firearms.
Semâ:	the music and the whirling dance performed during a mevlevî (*q.v.*) service.
Semâniyye:	the eight medreses established by Mehmed II around his mosque; known also as the *sahn-i semân*.

Shiite:	belongings to the shîa, a Muslim sect regarding Alî, the fourth caliph, as the first true imam after Muhammad.
Sïr kâtibi:	'clerk of secrets', the sultan's or a vizier's (*q.v.*) confidential secretary.
Silahdâr:	a custodian of the sultan's weapons.
Simavnî:	a follower of the sect of Şeyh Bedreddîn (d. 1416); known also as *Bedreddînlü*.
Sipâhî:	'cavalryman'
	(1) a cavalryman holding a timar (*q.v.*) in the provinces in return for military service.
	(2) sipâhî of the Porte: a member of the sultan's standing cavalry corps.
Sipâhî bölükleri ağalari:	'the ağas of the cavalry divisions', the commanders of the kapïkulu (*q.v.*) cavalry divisions.
Subaşï:	the holder of a zeâmet (*q.v.*), commanding a detachment of timar-holding sipâhîs (*q.v.*) in the army and responsible for the maintenance of order in his district.
Subaşïlïk:	a subdivision of a sanjak (*q.v.*), administered by a subaşï (*q.v.*).
Sunnî:	orthodox (of Islam); an orthodox Muslim.
Şâgird:	(1) an apprentice in a craft guild or the bureaucracy.
	(2) a degree in the hierarchy of the Palace harem (*q.v.*), above câriye (*q.v.*) and below gedikli (*q.v.*).
Şerîat:	the sacred law of Islam.
Şeyh:	'sheikh, chief, head'
	(1) a popular religious leader.
	(2) a tribal chief.
	(3) the sultan's spiritual mentor.
	(4) the religious head of a craft guild.
Şeyhülislâm:	the head of the hierarchy of ulema (*q.v.*).
Tahtacï:	'Woodman', name of a Turcoman tribe previously engaged in felling timber in the Taurus mountains.
Tarîkat:	mystic religious order, order of dervishes.
Tekke:	a lodge of a dervish order.
Temlîk:	the grant of property rights by the sultan.
Tetimme:	a school preparing students for a higher medrese (*q.v.*) education.
Tezkere:	a memorandum from a beylerbeyi (*q.v.*) to the central government making a recommendation for a timar (*q.v.*).

Tezkereci:	(1)) a secretary of the imperial council, writing official decrees, letters and memoranda.
	(2) a secretary of a beylerbeyi's (*q.v.*) council.
Timar:	a fief with an annual value of less than twenty thousand akçes (*q.v.*), whose revenues were held in return for military service.
Timar defterdârĭ:	'defterdâr of timars', a provincial official, regulating matters concerning timars (*q.v.*).
Topçu başĭ:	'head-gunner', the chief of the sultan's gunners.
Törü:	a code of laws in ancient Turkish or Mongol tradition.
Tuğra:	the sultan's official monogram, attached to state documents to confirm their legality.
Tüccâr:	'merchants', term used for large traders handling the caravan and overseas trade; known also as *bazirgân*.
Ulema:	the doctors of Muslim canon law, tradition and theology.
Usta:	(1) a master in a craft guild or the bureaucracy.
	(2) a degree in the hierarchy of the Palace harem (*q.v.*).
Vakfiye:	the deed of endowment of a vakĭf (*q.v.*).
Vakĭf (wakf):	a grant of land or other source of revenue given in mortmain for pious or charitable purposes.
Vâlide sultan:	the mother of the reigning sultan.
Vizier (Turkish: 'vezîr'):	a minister of the sultan and member of the imperial council.
Voynik:	a Slav warrior in Ottoman service.
Yamak:	'assistant', an assistant guild working for a larger guild in a specialised aspect of a craft.
Yasa:	a code of laws in ancient Turkish or Mongol tradition.
Yasak:	a code of sultanic laws.
Yaya:	'foot-soldier'
	(1) a Turkish farmer serving with the army.
	(2) By the sixteenth century, one of a corps holding land and exempted from certain taxes in return for services to the government.
Yiğitbaşĭ:	a senior officer of a guild, directing its internal affairs.
Yürük:	a Turkish nomad in Anatolia or the Balkans.
Zâviye:	a dervish hospice, accommodating travellers.
Zeâmet:	a military fief, with an annual value of twenty to one hundred thousand akçes (*q.v.*).

NOTES

PART I: AN OUTLINE OF OTTOMAN HISTORY, 1300–1600

1. The Origins of the Ottoman State

1 H.A.Gibbons, *The Foundation of the Ottoman Empire*, Oxford, 1916, chapter 1; N.Iorga, 'L'interpénétration de l'Orient et de l'Occident au Moyen-Age', *Bulletin de la Section historique de l'Académie Roumaine*, vol. XIII, Bucarest, 1927. Against their theory of the Byzantine origin of the Ottoman state, see M.F.Köprülü, *Les origines de l'empire Ottoman*, Paris, 1935; and P.Wittek, *The Rise of the Ottoman Empire*, London, 1938.
2 H.A.R.Gibb (trans.), *The Travels of Ibn Baṭṭuṭa*, London, 1958, vol. I, p. 42.

2. From Frontier Principality to Empire, 1354–1402

1 G.G.Arnakis, 'Gregory Palamas Among the Turks and Documents of his Captivity as Historical Sources', *Speculum*, vol. XXVI (1951), pp. 104–118.
2 C.Jiraček, *Geschichte der Bulgaren*, p. 309.
3 H.İnalcik, 'L'empire Ottoman', *Rapports, The First International Congress of South-East European Srudies*, Sofia, 1969, pp. 80–85.
4 G.Ostrogorskij, *Pour l'histoire de la féodalité byzantine* (trans. H.Grégoire and P.Lemerle), Brussels, 1954; G.Ostrogorskij, *Quelques problèmes d'histoire de la paysannerie byzantine*, Brussels, 1956; P.Charanis, 'On the Social and Economic Organization of the Byzantine Empire in the Thirteenth Century and Later', *Byzantinoslavica*, vol. XII (1959), pp. 94–153; D.Angelov, 'Certains aspects de la conquête des peuples balkaniques par les Turcs', *Byzantinoslavica*, vol. XVII (1959), pp. 220–75; D.Angelov, 'Zur Frage des Feudalismus auf dem Balkan im XIII bis zum XIV Jhr.', *Études Historiques à l'Occasion du XIᵉ Congrès International des Sciences Historiques, Stockholm, 1960*, Sofia, 1960, p. 107 ff.
5 H.İnalcik,' Osmanlılarda Raiyyet Rüsûmu', *Belleten*, vol. XXIII (1959), pp. 575–610 (in Turkish); H.İnalcik, "čift-resmi" in *Encyclopaedia of Islam* (2nd ed.).
6 See H.İnalcik, 'Ottoman Methods of Conquest', *Studia Islamica*, vol. II (1954), pp. 103–29.
7 See "Bāyezīd I" in *Encyclopaedia of Islam*.

3. The Interregnum and Recovery

1 N.Iorga, *Notes et extraits pour servir à l'histoire des croisades au XVe siècle*, Paris, 1899, pp. 486–8.
2 On Murad II, see *Islâm Ansiklopedisi*, vol. VII, pp. 598–615 (in Turkish).

4. The Definitive Establishment of the Ottoman Empire, 1453–1526

1 For the siege of Constantinople, see S.Runciman, *The Fall of Constantinople*, Cambridge, 1965.
2 Franz Babinger, *Mehmed der Eroberer und seine Zeit*, Munich, 1953, pp. 212–13.
3 Zorzi Dolfin, *Assiedo e presa di Constantinopli nell'anno 1453*, Munich, 1868, chapter 20.
4 For Mehmed II, see Babinger, *Mehmed der Eroberer und seine Zeit*, and the review of it: H.İnalcik, 'Mehmed the Conqueror (1432–1481), and His Time', *Speculum*, vol. XXXV-3 (July 1960), pp. 408–27.
5 On Bâyezîd's foreign policy, see S.N.Fisher, *The Foreign Relations of Turkey, 1481–1512*, Urbana, 1948; H.Sohrweide, 'Der Sieg der Safeviden in Persien und seine Rückwirkungen auf die Schiiten Anatoliens im 16. Jahrhundert', *Der Islam*, vol. 41 (1965).

5. The Ottoman State as a World Power, 1526–96

1 Selîm I confirmed the capitulations given by the Mamlûk sultans to the consul of the Catalans and French in Egypt in 1517. Süleymân I renewed them at his accession to the throne. The capitulations which were negotiated between Ibrahîm Pasha, grand vizier, and J. de la Forest, Francis I's envoy to the sultan in 1536, were never confirmed by him; so there are no capitulations of 1536. The first Ottoman capitulations granted to the French were concluded only in 1569. See "Imtiyāzāt" in *Encyclopaedia of Islam*.
2 E.Benz, *Wittenberg und Byzanz*, Marburg, 1949; S.A.Fisher-Galati, *Ottoman Imperialism and German Protestantism, 1521–1555*, Cambridge, Mass., 1959; K.M.Setton, 'Lutheranism and the Turkish Peril', *Balkan Studies*, vol. III-1 (1962), pp. 136–65.

6. The Decline of the Ottoman Empire

1 M.Guboglu, *Paleografia si diplomatica Turco-Osmana*, Bucarest, 1958, p. 167, facsimile no. 7.
2 H.Wood, *A History of the Levant Company*, London, 1935, p. 37.
3 A.B.Hinds (ed.), *Calendar of State Papers, Venice*, London, 1909, vol. XV, documents no. 194, 299, 352, 587, 903.
4 Ö.L.Barkan, 'Essai sur les données statistiques des registres de recensement dans l'empire ottoman aux XVe et XVIe siècles', *Journal of Economic and Social History of the Orient*, vol. I-1, pp. 23–5.
5 P.Masson, *Histoire du commerce français dans le Levant au XVIIe siècle*, Paris, 1896, pp. xix–xxiii.
6 See C.D.Rouillard, *The Turk in French History, Thought and Literature*,

Paris, 1938; Bertrandon de la Broquière (ed. Ch. Schefer), *Voyage d'Outremer*, Paris, 1892; R.Schwoebel, *The Shadow of the Crescent*, New York 1967.

PART II: THE STATE

7. *The Rise of the Ottoman Dynasty*

1 Neṣẖrī (ed. Fr. Taeschner), *Ǧihānnümā*, Leipzig, 1951, p. 194.
2 Babinger, *Mehmed der Eroberer und seine Zeit*, p. 168.
3 *Ibid.*, p. 226.

8. *The Manner of Accession to the Throne*

1 Fïndïklïlï, Mehmed Ağa (ed. A.Refik), *Silāhdār Tarihi*, Istanbul, 1928, vol. 2, p. 297.

9. *The Ottoman Concept of State and the Class System*

1 M.H.Zotenberg (trans.), *Chronique*, Paris, 19, vol. 2, p. 340.
2 R.R.Arat (ed.), Ankara, 1959, verses 2057–9.
3 *Ibid.*, verses 5479–90.
4 *Tā'rïẖ-i Abu'l-Fath*, Istanbul, p. 13.
5 Tabarī, *Chronique*, pp. 218–32.
6 M.Minovi (ed.), *Kalīlah wa Dimnah*, Tehran, p. 319; Nizām al-Mulk (ed. H. Darke), *Siyar al Mulūk*, Tehran, 1962, pp. 178–9; for the Sassanids, see A.Christensen, *L'Iran sous les Sassanides*, Copenhagen, 1936, pp. 93–4, 362, 383.

10. *Law: Sultanic Law (kânún) and Religious Law (şerîat)*

1 M.Ārif (ed.), *Tā'rïẖ-i 'Osmānī Endjümeni Medjmū'asï*, supplement.
2 J. von Hammer, *Das osmanischen Reichs Staatsverfassung und Staatsverwaltung* (2 vols.), Vienna, 1815; O.L.Barkan, *XV ve XVI ïncï asïrlarda Osmanlï imparatorluğunda ziraï ekonominin hukukï ve malï esaslarï*, Istanbul, 1943.
3 See H.İnalcik, 'Raiyyet Rüsûmu', *Belleten*, vol. XXIII (1959), pp. 575–608.
4 H.İnalcik, 'Adâletnâmeler', Türk Tarih Belgeleri Dergisi (Turkish Historical Society, Ankara), vol. II–3/4, pp. 65–7.
5 See note 2 above.
6 On this question, see M.F.Köprülü, *Alcune osservazione intorno all'influenza delle instituzioni bizantine sulle instituzioni ottomane*, Rome, 1953.
7 For a collection of such laws, see R.Anhegger and H.İnalcik (eds), *Kānūnnāme-i sulṭānī ber müceb-i 'örf-i 'Osmānī*, Ankara, 1956.
8 See H.İnalcik, 'Osmanlïlar'da Raiyyet Rüsûmu', *Belleten*, vol. XXIII (1959), pp. 575–608.

11. *The Palace*

1 *Kavānin-i Yeniçeriyān*, ms. in Topkapï Sarayï Museum, Revan K. nos 1319, 1320.

2 B.Miller, *The Palace School of Muhammed the Conqueror*, Cambridge, Mass., 1941, pp. 99, 133.

3 A.H.Lybyer, *The Government of the Ottoman Empire in the Time of Suleiman the Magnificent*, Cambridge, Mass., 1913, p. 71.

4 Ç.Uluçay, *Osmanlı Sultanlarına Aşk Mektupları*, Istanbul, 1950, p. 31.

12. The Central Administration

1 V.Grecu (ed.), *Istoria*, Bucarest, 1950, p. 178; I. H. Uzunçarşih, *Merkez ve Bahriye Teşkilâti*, Ankara 1948, p. 1.

2 *Le voyage d'outremer* ed. Ch. Schefer, Paris, 1392, p. 140.

3 *Illustrations de B. de Vigenère Bourbonnois sur l'histoire de Chalcocondyle athénien*, in *Histoire de la décadence de l'empire grec et l'établissement de celvy des turcs*, Rouen, 1660, p. 19.

4 In *Tā'rīkh-i 'Osmānī Endjümeni Medjmu'asi*, supplement, p. 10.

5 See H.İnalcik, *Fatih Devri üzerinde Tetkikler ve Vesikalar*, Ankara, 1954, pp. 217–19.

13. The Provincial Administration and the Timar System

1 Fr. Babinger, *Die Aufzeichnungen des Genuesen Jacopo-de-Promontorio über den Osmanenstaat um 1475*, Sitzungsb. der Bayer. Akad. der Wissens. Phil.-His. Kl. 11.8, 1956.

2 See Cengiz Orhonlu, *Osmanlı Imparatorluğunda Göçebeleri iskân teşebbüsleri*, Istanbul, 1960.

3 Ö.L.Barkan, 'Les formes de l'organisation du travail agricole dans l'empire ottoman aux XVe et XVIe siècles', *Revue de la Faculté des Sciences Économiques de l'Université d'Istanbul*, vol. 1-1 (1939), pp. 29–74, vol. 1-4 (1940), pp. 397–447, 297–321, vol. 11 (1940). pp. 198–245, 165–180.

4 *A Voyage into the Levant*, in *A Collection of Voyages and Travels ... compiled from the curious and valuable library of the late Earl of Oxford*, London, 1745, p. 533.

5 For an example, see S.J.Shaw, *The Budget of Ottoman Egypt, 1005–1006/ 1596–1597*, Mouton, The Hague, 1969.

PART III: ECONOMIC AND SOCIAL LIFE

14. The Ottoman Empire and International Trade

1 See H.İnalcik, 'Bursa and the Commerce of the Levant', *Journal of Economic and Social History of the Orient*, vol. 111-2 (1960), pp. 131–42.

2 Gibb (ed.), *The Travels of Ibn Baṭṭuṭa*, pp. 450–52.

3 J.E.Telfer (ed.), *Travels and Bondage*, London, 1879, p. 34.

4 G.R.E.Richards, *Florentine Merchants in the Age of the Medicis*, Cambridge, Mass., 1932, p. 122.

5 See "Harīr" in *Encyclopaedia of Islam* (2nd ed.).

6 See my 'Bursa and the Commerce of the Levant', p. 137.

7 For the Ottoman-Portuguese struggle in the Indian Ocean, see L.Dames, 'The Portuguese and Turks in the Indian Ocean in the Sixteenth

Century', *Journal of the Royal Asiatic Society*, 1921, part 1; E.Denison Ross, 'The Portuguese in India and Arabia, 1517–1538, *ibid.*, 1922, part 1; R.B.Serjeant, *The Portuguese off the South Arabian Coast*, Oxford, 1963; Hajji Khalifeh, *The History of the Maritime Wars of the Turks* (trans. J.Mitchell), London, 1831; L.O.Schuman, *Political History of the Yemen at the Beginning of the Sixteenth Century*, Amsterdam, 1961.

8 F.Braudel, *La Méditerranée et le monde méditerranéen à l'époque de Philippe II*, Paris, 1949, pp. 425–33.

9 For the trade of Antalya, see my 'Bursa and the Commerce of the Levant', p. 143.

10 F.Dalsar, *Bursa'da İpekcilik*, Istanbul, 1960, pp. 166, 191–3.

11 Richards, *Florentine Merchants in the Age of the Medicis*, pp. 120–21.

12 See "Imtiyāzāt" in *Encyclopaedia of Islam* (2nd ed.).

13 See H.İnalcïk, 'Remarks on an Essay on the Economic Situation of Turkey During the Foundation and Rise of the Ottoman Empire', *Belleten*, vol. XV (1951), pp. 656–61; Ö.L.Barkan, 'XVI. Asrïn Ikinci yarïsïnda Türkiye'de Fiyat Hareketleri', *Belleten*, vol. XXXIV (1970), pp. 557–607.

15. The Ottoman Cities and Road Network, Urban Population, Guilds and Merchants

1 I.Neṣhri (ed. Fr. Taeschner), p. 182.

2 See Ö.L.Barkan and E.H.Ayverdi (eds), *Istanbul Vakïflarï Tahrir Defteri*, Istanbul, 1970. It must be pointed out that only a small part of these *vakïfs* created new religious or charitable institutions with commercial establishments to support them. Most of these vakïfs were small.

3 R.Mantran, *Istanbul dans la seconde moitié du XVIIe siècle*, Paris, 1962, pp. 44–7.

4 These figures are given by Hüseyin Hezārfen (see Barkan and Ayverdi, Introduction). Compare the much exaggerated figures given by Evliyâ Çelebi in Mantran, pp. 353–7.

5 La Boullaye-Le Gouz, *Les voyages et observations du Sieur de la Boullaye-le Gouz*, Paris, 1653, cited by Mantran (note 3 above), p. 481 (note 2).

6 For the Ottoman routes, see R.Taeschner, *Das anatolische wegenetz nach osmanischen Quellen* (2 vols), Leipzig, 1924–6; O.Zirojević, *The Constantinople Road from Beograd to Sofia*, Beograd, 1970 (in Serbian).

7 *Die Heerstrasse Belgrad nach Constantinopel und die Balkanpässe*, Prague, 1877, p. 113.

8 Ö.L.Barkan, 'Kolonizatör Türk Dervişleri', *Vakïflar Dergisi*, vol. II (1942), pp. 305–53.

9 Ibn Baṭṭuṭa, p. 419.

10 See also "*Akhi*" in *Encyclopaedia of Islam*.

11 B.Lewis, 'The Islamic Guilds', *Economic History Review*, vol. VIII, no. 1 (1937), pp. 20–37.

12 G.Baer, 'The Administrative, Economic and Social Functions of Turkish Guilds', *Intern. Journal of Middle East Studies*, vol. 1 (1970); cf. "Harīr" in *Encyclopaedia of Islam* (2nd ed.).

13 Evliyā Çelebi, *Seyahatnâme*, vol. 3, Istanbul, p. 287; cf. Naima, *Ta'rikh*, vol. 5, p. 97.

14 H.İnalcik, 'The Capital Formation in the Ottoman Empire', in *The Journal of Economic History*, vol. xxix, 97–140.

PART IV: RELIGION AND CULTURE IN THE OTTOMAN EMPIRE

18. The Triumph of Fanaticism

1 See P. Kahle, *Die verschollene Colombus-Karte von 1498 in einer türkischen Weltkarte von 1513*, Berlin, 1933.

19. Popular Culture and the Tarîkats – Mystic Orders

1 *Istoria Turco-Bizantina*, Bucarest, 1948, pp. 148–50.

2 F.Babinger, 'Von Amurath zu Amurath' in *Oriens*, III–2 (1950) p. 245.

3 See J.K.Birge, *The Bektashi Order of Dervishes*, London 1937.

SELECTED BIBLIOGRAPHY

I. GENERAL HISTORIES

J.von Hammer-Purgstall, *Geschichte des osmanischen Reiches* (10 vols), Pest, 1827–35 (reprint, Graz, 1963). Mostly a compilation of the Ottoman chronicles.

J.W.Zinkeisen, *Geschichte des osmanischen Reiches in Europa* (7 vols), Hamburg and Gotha, 1840–63, (reprint, 1962). A more systematic treatment of the subject with the use of European sources.

N.Jorga, *Geschichte des osmanischen Reiches* (5 vols), Gotha, 1908–13 (reprint 1962). More emphasis on the history of the Balkans.

I.H.Uzunçarşılı, *Osmanlı Tarihi*, *(4 vols)*, *(Ottoman History)* Ankara 1947–59 (in Turkish). A popular book.

Demetrius Cantemir, *The History of the Growth and Decay of the Ottoman Empire* (tr. N.Tindal), London, 1734.

Fr. Sansovino, *Historia universale dell'origine et imperio de Turchi*, Venice, 1582.

P.Ricaut (Rycaut) and R.Knolles, *The Turkish History from the Original of that nation to the Growth of the Ottoman Empire* (3 vols), London, 1687–1700.

R.F.Kreutel, *Vom Hirtenzelt zur Hohen Pforte*, Graz, 1959. Translation into German of Ashikpasazâde's history containing the Ottoman traditions of the fourteenth and fifteenth centuries.

Shorter histories

S.Lane-Pool, *The Story of Turkey*, London, 1888. The Ottoman history in one volume: outdated.

E.S.Creasy, *History of the Ottoman Turks*, London, 1877 (reprint, Beirut, 1961).

R.Davison, *Turkey*, Englewood Cliffs, N.J., 1968.

D.Vaughan, *Europe and the Turk, 1350–1700*, Liverpool 1954.

Cambridge History of Islam, I, Cambridge, 1970, pp. 263–393.

II. BIBLIOGRAPHIES

J.K.Birge, *A Guide to Turkish Area Studies*, Washington, 1949.

V.Michoff, *Sources bibliographiques sur l'histoire de la Turquie et de la Bulgarie* (4 vols), Sofia, 1914–34.

V.Michoff, *Bibliographie des articles de périodiques allemands, anglais et italiens sur la Turquie et la Bulgarie*, Sofia, 1938.

Historiographie Yougoslave, 1955–1965, Beograd, 1965.

Modern Greek Culture: A Selected Bibliography in English-French-German-Italian (third edition), Athens, 1970.

Bibliographie d'Etudes Balkaniques, vol. I: 1966, Sofia, 1968; vol. II: 1967, Sofia, 1969.

J.D.Pearson, *Index Islamicus, 1906–1955, A Catalogue of Articles on Islamic subjects in Periodicals and Other Collective Publications.* Cambridge, 1958; *Supplement.* 1956–1960, Cambridge, 1962; *Supplement*, 1960–1965, Cambridge 1967. Each volume has a special section on the Ottomans.

Enver Koray, *A Bibliography of the Turkish Publications on History*, 1729–1955, vol. I, Ankara, 1952 (in Turkish). Vol. 2, 1955–1968, Ank. 1971.

B.Lewis and P.M.Holt (eds)., *Historians of the Middle East*, Oxford, 1962.

Istanbul Kütüphaneleri Tarih – Coğrafya Yazmalari Katalogu I Türkçe Tarih Yazmalari (10 vols.), Istanbul, 1943–51, A Catalogue of the mss in Turkish in the libraries of Istanbul.

Franz Babinger, *Geschichtsschreiber der Osmanen und ihre Werke*, Leipzig, 1927. A bibliography of the Ottoman chronicles, published or unpublished, with the biographies of the authors.

B.Spuler and L.Forrer, *Der vordere Orient in ilsamischer Zeit*, Bern, 1955, pp. 193–215. Annotated bibliography on the Ottomans.

L.Forrer, 'Handschriften osmanischer Historiker in Istanbul,' *Der Islam*, XXVI-2, pp. 173–220.

A.S.Levend, *Gazavâtnâmeler ve Mihal-oğlu Ali Bey Gazavâtnâmesi*, Ankara, 1958 (in Turkish). A bibliography of the Ottoman literature on the military expeditions with the edition of the *Gazavâtnâme* of Ali Bey.

Fehmi E.Karatay, *Topkapı Sarayı Müzesi Kütüphanesi, Türkçe Yazmalar Katalogu* (2 vols.), Istanbul 1961. A catalogue of the Turkish mss. at the Topkapı Palace Library.

Fehmi E.Karatay, *Topkapı Sarayı Müzesi Kütüphanesi, Farsca Yazmalar Katalogu*, Istanbul, 1961. A catalogue of the Persian mss.

Carl Göllner, *Turcica, Die europäischen Turkendrucke des XVI. Jahrhunderts*, I.Band: 1501–1550, Bucarest-Berlin 1961: II. Band: 1551–1600, Bucarest-Baden 1968. An exhaustive inquiry.

H.Bowen, *British Contributions to Turkish Studies*, New York, 1945.

Berna Moran, *A Bibliography of the Publications in English Concerning the Turks, XV-XVIIIth Centuries*, Istanbul, 1964.

III. PRINCIPAL PERIODICALS, ENCYCLOPEDIAS AND DICTIONARIES CONTAINING ARTICLES ON THE OTTOMAN TURKS

a. In Turkish

Târîh-i Osmânî Encümeni Mecmuası 1911–22, Continued as *Türk Tarih Encümeni Mecmuası*, 1922–31.

Tarih Vesikaları, published by the Ministry of Pub. Educ., I-XVII (1941–58).

Belleten, published by the Turkish Historical Society, Ankara 1937 to date.

Tarih Dergisi, published by the Faculty of Letters, University of Istanbul, 1949 to date.

Türkiyat Mecmuasi, published by the Institute of Turcology, Istanbul, 1925 to date.

Tarih Araştirmalari Dergisi, published by the Faculty of Letters, University of Ankara, 1963 to date.

Belgeler, published by the Turkish Historical Society, Ankara. A periodical for publication of the Ottoman documents.

Vakiflar Dergisi. Ankara, 1938 to date. A review publishing documents and studies concerning the institutions connected with the Ottoman wakfs.

Islâm Ansiklopedisi, Istanbul, 1950 to date. Turkish translation of the first edition of the *Encyclopaedia of Islam* (*l'Encyc. de l'Islam*) with additions and the articles being expanded on Turks. Indispensable reference book on the Ottomans.

M.Z.Pakalin, *Osmanli Tarih Deyimleri ve Terimleri Sözlügü* (3 vols.) Istanbul, 1946–55. A dictionary of Ottoman historical terms and expressions (in Turkish).

M.Süreyya, *Sicill-i Osmânî* (4 vols.), Istanbul, 1890–95. (in Turkish). Ottoman biographical dictionary.

b. In western languages:

Mitteilungen zur osmanischen Geschichte, I–II, Vienna, 1921–3.

Archivum Ottomanicum, ed. T.Halasi-Kun and H.Inalcik, Leiden, (first issue to appear in 1973).

Turcica, Revue d'études turques, first issue 1969 (Paris).

A.Tietze and H. and R.Kahane, *The Lingua Franca in the Levant*, Urbana, 1958.

C.Mostras, *Dictionaire géographique de l'Empire Ottoman*, St Petersbourg, 1873.

Encyclopaedia of Islam (*l'Encyclopédie de l'Islam*), new edition Leiden-London, 1960, completed to the letter I in 1971. An indispensable reference.

IV. OTTOMAN DIPLOMATICS AND COLLECTIONS OF DOCUMENTS

a. Ottoman

F.Kraelitz-Greifenhorst, *Osmanische Urkunden in türkische Sprache aus der zweiten hälfte der 15. Jhr.*, Vienna, 1921.

L.Fekete, *Einführung in die osmanisch-türkische Diplomatik der türkischen Bottmässigkeit in Ungarn*, Budapest, 1926.

L.Fekete, *Die Siyāqat-Schrift in der türkischen Finanzverwaltung* (2 vols.), Budapest, 1955.

J.Reychman and A.Zajaczkowski. *Handbook of Ottoman-Turkish Diplomatics*, revised and expanded, tr. A.S.Ehrenkreutz, ed. T.Halasi-Kun, the Hague, Paris, 1968.

Arşiv Kilavuzu (2 vols.), Istanbul, 1938–40. A catalogue of the documents in the archives of the Topkapi Palace; incomplete.

L.Fekete, 'Ueber Archivalien und Archivwesen in der Türkei', *Acta Orientalia*, vol. III/iii (1953).

S.Shaw, 'Archival Sources for Ottoman History: The Archives of Turkey', *Journal of the American Oriental Society*, vol. 80 (1960), pp. 1–12.

Bernard Lewis, 'The Ottoman Archives, a Source for European History', *Report on Current Research*, Washington, 1956, pp. 17–25.

Bernard Lewis, 'The Ottoman Archives as a Source of History for the Arab Lands', *Journal of the Royal Asiatic Society*, 1951, pp. 139–155.

Bernard Lewis, 'Studies in the Ottoman Archives', *BSOAS*, vol. xvi-3 (1954), pp. 469–501

Bernard Lewis, *Notes and Documents from the Turkish Archives*, Jerusalem, 1952.

A.Bombaci, 'La collezione di documenti turchi dell'archivio di Venezia', *Riv. Studi Orient.*, vol. xxiv (1949).

G.Elezović, *Turski spomenići, I*, parts 1 and 2, Beograd, 1940–52.

K.Schwartz, *Osmanische Sultansurkunden des SINAI-Klosters*, Freiburg, 1970.

T.Gökbilgin, *Edirne ve Paşa Livasí*, Istanbul, 1952 (in Turkish). A collection of the wakf deeds and financial records concerning Rumeli of the fifteenth and sixteenth centuries.

Istanbul Vakíflarí Tahrir Defteri, 953 (1546), ed. Ö.L.Barkan and E.H.Ayverdi. The wakf deeds of Istanbul.

Collection of documents in western Languages

A. von Gevay (ed.), *Urkunden und aktenstücke zur Geschichte der Verhältnisse zwischen Oesterreich, Ungarn und der Pforte im xvi. und xvii. Jahrh. (3 vols.)*, Vienna, 1838–42.

E.Alberi, *Relazione degli ambasciatori Veneti al senato* (3d series), vols. I–III, Florence, 1840, 1844 and 1855.

E.Charrière, *Négociations de la France dans le Levant*, (4 vols.), Paris, 1848–60. A collection of the French documents, 1515–1589.

I. de Testa *Recueil des Traités de la Porte Ottomane avec les puissances étrangères* (10 vols.), Paris, 1864–1901.

P.Dupare, *Recueil des instructions aux ambassadeurs et ministres de France*, vol. xxix, Turquie, Paris, 1969.

V. DESCRIPTIONS OF WESTERN TRAVELLERS AND OBSERVERS

F.Babinger, *Die Aufzeichnungun des Genuesen Iacopo de Promontorio-de Campis über den Osmanenstaat um 1475*, Münich, 1957.

A. von Harff, *The Pilgrimage of Arnold von Harff* (tr. M. Letts), London, 1946.

M.Sanuto, *I Diarii* (58 vols.), Venice, 1879–1903.

Th. Spandugino, *De la Origine degli imperatori ottomani, ordini dela corte, forma del guerreggiare, loro religione, rito et costumi dela natione*, published in Sathas, *Documents inédits*, vol. ix, Paris, 1890, pp. 138–261.

G.A.Menavino, *Trattato de' costumi et vita de' Turchi*, Florence, 1548.

H.Dernschwam, *Tagebuch einer Reise nach Konstantinopel und Kleinasien* (1553–1555), ed. F.Babinger, Münich, 1923. One of the best observers on the daily life in Turkey.

J.Chesneau, *Le Voyage de Monsieur d'Aramon (1549)*, ed. Ch. Schefer, Paris, 1887.

G.Postel, *De la République des Turecs*, Poitiers, 1552.

Kaiserliche Gesandtschaften aus Goldene Horn, ed. Karl Teply, Stuttgart, 1968.

C. de Villalon, *Viaje de Turquia, 1557*, in M.Serrano y Sanz, *Autobiografias y Memorias*, Madrid, 1905.

N. de Nicolay, *Les Navigations, pérégrinations et voyages*, Antwerp, 1576.

P.Belon du Mans, *Les observations de plusieurs singularités et choses mémorables trouvées en Grèce, Asie, Judée Egypte, Arabie et autres pays*, Paris, 1588.

Reinhold Lubenau, *Beschreibung der Reisen (1573–1589)*, ed. W.Sahm, Königsberg, 1912.

Du Fresne Canaye, *Voyage du Levant (1573)*, ed. H.Hauser, Paris, 1897.

Johann Wild, *Neue Reysbeschreibung eines gefangenen Christen, 1604–10*, Nürnberg, 1613.

A.Carayon, *Relations inédites des missions de la Société de Jésus à Constantinople*, Paris, 1864.

Thomas Roe, *The Negotiations ... in his Embassy to the Ottoman Porte*, from the Year of 1621 to 1628, ed. S. Richardson, 1740.

G.Sandys, *Travels (1610)*, fifth ed., London, 1652.

T.Sherley, *Discourse of the Turks*, ed. E.Denison Ross, London, 1936.

A.Sherley, *His Relations of his Travels*, London, 1613.

H.Blount, *A Voyage into the Levant*, 2nd ed., London, 1636.

Alberto Bobovio (*Ali Bey*), *Relazione del Seraglio del Gran Signore*, published in Cornelio Magni, *Viaggie dimore per la Turchia*, Venetia, 1682.

VI. PERIODS OF OTTOMAN HISTORY (POLITICAL HISTORY)

a. Origins

Fr. Giese, 'Das Problem der Entstehung des osmanischen Reiches', *Zeitschrift für Semitistik und verwandte Gebiete*, vol. 11 (1924), pp. 246–71. The first critical study of the problem of the origins of the Ottoman state by a specialist. He emphasises the role of the *ahis*.

H.A.Gibbons, *The Foundation of the Ottoman Empire*, Oxford, 1916. (reprint 1968). A description of the Ottoman expansion from 1300 to 1402.

M.Fuad Köprülü, *Les Origines de l'Empire Ottoman*, Paris, 1935. Criticising Gibbons' theory of the Greek origins of the Ottomans and Ottoman state, Köprülü stresses the Anatolian Seljuk origins of them on the basis of the critical use of the oriental sources.

M.F.Köprülüzâde, 'Bemerkungen zur Religionsgeschichte Kleinasiens' *Mitteilungen zur osmanischen Geschichte*, vol. I, pp. 203–22.

M.Fuad Köprülü, 'Problems of the Ethnic Origins of the Ottoman Empire', *Belleten* vol. VII (Ankara, 1943), pp. 219–314 (in Turkish). A thoroughgoing study of the problem.

C.Cahen, *Pre-Ottoman Turkey*, London, 1968. A concise history of Anatolia before the Ottomans.

O.Turan, 'Anatolia in the Period of the Seljuks and the Beyliks', *The Cambridge History of Islam*, Cambridge, 1970, pp. 231–62.

P.Wittek, 'Deux chapitres de l'histoire des Turcs de Roum', *Byzantion*, vol. XI (1936), pp. 285–319.

P.Wittek, *The Rise of the Ottoman Empire*, London, *1938*. A summary of earlier studies, discussing critically the Seljuk origins of the Ottomans with the emphasis on the role of the *ghazi* tradition.

b. Beyliks (Turcoman Principalities)

P.Wittek, *Das Fürstentum Mentesche, Studie zur Geschichte Kleinasiens im 13–15. Jahrhundert*, Istanbul, 1934. Fundamental study on the formation of the Turcoman principalities in Western Anatolia.

P.Lemerle, *L'Emirat d'Aydin, Byzance et l'Occident, Recherches sur 'La geste d'Umur Pacha'*, Paris, 1957. Analysis of this important Turkish source with the use of the Byzantine sources.

B.Flemming, *Landschaftsgeschichte von Pamphylien, Pisidien und Lykien im spätmittelalter*, Wiesbaden, 1964.

I.H.Uzunçarşĭlĭ, *The Beyliks in Anatolia*, Ankara, 1937 (in Turkish). A survey; uncritical.

F.Köprülü, 'Notes on the History of the Beyliks in Anatolia', *Türkiyat Mecmuasĭ*, vol. II (1928), pp. 1–32 (in Turkish).

Fr. Taeschner, 'Beiträge zur Geschichte der Achis in Anatolien (14–15. Jahrhundert'), *Islamica* vol. IV (1931), pp. 1–47.

Fr. Taeschner, Die islamische Futwwabunde, *ZDMG*, vol. 12 (1933) pp. 6–49.

Fr. Taeschner, 'Akhi', *Encyclopaedia of Islam*, 2nd ed., vol. I.

c. From frontier principality to empire (1352–1402)

Besides the general accounts by Hammer, Zinkeisen and Jorga, see

I.Beldiceanu-Steinherr, *Recherches sur les actes des règnes des Sultans Osman, Orhan et Murad I*, Münich, 1967.

H.Inalcík, 'Ottoman Methods of Conquest', *Studia Islamica*, vol. II, pp. 103–129.

G.G.Arnakis, *The Early Ottomans*, Athens, 1947 (in Greek). Important study based on the Ottoman and Byzantine sources.

G.G.Arnakis 'Gregory Palamas among the Turks and Documents of His Captivity as Historical Sources', *Speculum*, vol. XXVI (1951), pp. 104–18.

The Travels of Ibn Battuta, tr. H.A.R.Gibb, vols I–II, London, 1956–61. Eyewitness of Orhan's principality.

P.Charanis, 'The Strife Among the Palaeologi and the Ottoman Turks, 1370–1402' *Byzantion*, vol. XVI (1942–3), pp. 286–314, vol. XVII, pp. 104–18. A study based on the Byzantine sources.

Fr. Babinger, *Beiträge zur frühgeschichte der Türkenherrschaft in Rumelien (14–15. Jahrhundert)*, Münich, 1944.

H.Inalcík, 'Edirne'nin Fethi', *Edirne'nin 600 Fetih Yıldönümü Armagan Kitabĭ*, Ankara, 1965, pp. 137–59 (in Turkish).

D.Angelov, 'Certains aspects de la conquête des peuples balkaniques par les Turcs' *Byzantinoslavica*, vol. XVII (1956), pp. 220–75.

M.Braun, *Kosovo*, Leipzig, 1937.

M.Braun, *Lebensbeschreibung des Despoten Stefan Lazarević von Konstantin dem Philosophen im auszug herausgegeben und übersetzt*, Göttingen, 1956.

H.Inalcík, 'Bāyazīd I' *Encyclopaedia of Islam*, 2nd ed. vol. I.

A.S.Atiya, *The Crusade of Nicopolis*, London, 1938.

M.Silberschmidt, *Das orientalische Problem zur Zeit der Entstehung des türkischen Reiches, 1381–1400*, Leipzig, 1923. An important study based on the Venetian documents.

M.M.Alexandrescu-Dersca, *La campagne de Timur en Anatolie, 1402*, Bucarest, 1942. For the review of it, see *Belleten*, vol. XI–42 (1947), pp. 341–5.

G.Ostrogorsky, 'La prise de Serrès par les Turcs, *Byzantion*, vol. 35 (1965), pp. 302–19.

H.H.Giesecke, *Das Werk des Azīz ibn Ardašir Astarābādī, Ein Quelle zur Geschichte des Spätmittelalters in Kleinasien*. Leipzig, 1940. An important source on the history of central Anatolia in the second half of the fourteenth century.

Ernst Werner, *Die Geburt einer Grossmacht-Die Osmanen (1300–1481), Ein Beitrag zur Genesis des türkischen Feudalismus*, Berlin, 1966. A Marxist interpretation.

d. The interregnum and recovery (1402–51)

P.Wittek, 'De la défaite d'Ankara à la prise de Constantinople', *Revue des Etudes Islamiques*, vol. 12 (1938), pp. 1–34. This essay deals with the problems of the interregnum period.

J.W.Barker, *Manuel II Palaeologus, 1391–1425*, New Brunswick, 1969.

H.J.Kissling, 'Das Menāqybnāme Scheich Bedr ed-dîns, des Sohnes des Richters von Samavna', *ZDMG*, no. 100 (1950), pp. 112–76.

H.Inalcík, 'Arnawutluk', *Encyclopaedia of Islam*, 2nd ed. vol I, pp. 653–8.

Bertrandon de la Broquière, *Le Voyage d'Outremer*, ed. Ch. Schefer, Paris, 1892. The author visited the Ottoman empire in 1432–3.

Ducas, *Istoria Turco-Bizantina (1341–1462)*, ed. Vasile Grecu, Bucarest, 1958. An important source for the reigns of Murad II and Mehmed II.

F.Thiriet, *Régestes des déliberations du Senat de Venise Concernant La Romanie*, vols I–III, Paris, 1958–61.

N.Jorga, *Notes et Extraits pour servir à l'histoire des croisades au XVe siecle*, vols I–II, Paris, 1899.

W.Miller, *Essays on the Latin Orient*, Cambridge, 1921.

A.E.Vacalopoulos, 'Les limites de l'empire byzantin', *Byzant. Zeitschrift*, vol. 55 (1962), pp. 56–65.

G.Beckmann, *Der Kampf Kaiser Sigmunds gegen die werdende Weltmacht der Osmanen, (1392–1437)*, Gotha, 1902.

O.Halecki, *The Crusade of Varna*, New York, 1943.

J.Dabrovski, 'L' année 1444', *Bulletin Inter. de l'Académie polonaise des sciences et des lettres, Classe d'his. et de phil.*, Cracovie, 1952. Dabrovski takes an opposite view to Halecki.

H.Inalcík, *Studies and Documents on the Reign of Mehmed the Conqueror*, Ankara, 1954 (in Turkish). In the first chapter (pp. 1–53) the problems concerning the crisis of 1444 are discussed in the light of a newly discovered Ottoman chronicle.

F.Babinger, 'Von Amurath zu Amurath'. Vor – und Nachspiel der Schlacht bei Varna (1444), *Oriens*, vol. III–2 (1950), pp. 233–44.

H.Inalcík, 'Murad II', *Islâm Ansiklopedisi*, vol. VIII, pp. 589–615.

F.Taeschner and P.Wittek, 'Die Vezirfamilie der Candarlyzâde (14.–15. Jah.) und ihre Denkmäler', *Der Islam*, vol. 18. (1929), pp. 60–115.

G.Ostrogorsky, 'Byzance, état tributaire de l'empire turc', *Zbornik Rodova* (1958), pp. 49–58.

e. Definitive establishment of the Ottoman Empire (1453–1526)

F.Babinger, *Mehme der Eroberer und seine Zeit*, Münich, 1953 (enlarged Italian version: Torino, 1967), Reviewed by H.Inalcík, 'Mehmed the Conqueror (1432–1481) and His Time', *Speculum*, vol. XXXV (1960), pp. 408–27.

S.Runciman, *The Fall of Constantinople*, Cambridge, 1965.

A.Mercati, 'Due lettere di Giorgio da Trebisonda a Maometto II', *Orien. Chr. Period*, vol. 9 (1943), pp. 285–322.

Kritovoulos, *History of Mehmed the Conqueror*, tr. Ch. Riggs, Princeton, 1964.

H.Inalcík, 'The Policy of Mehmed II toward the Greek Population of Istanbul and the Byzantine Buildings of the City', *Dumbarton Oaks Papers*, No. 23 (1970), pp. 213–49.

H.Inalcík, 'Mehmed II' *Islâm Ansiklopedisi* vol. VII, pp. 506–35 (in Turkish).

E.Hocks, *Pius II und der Halbmond*, Freiburg i. Br., 1941.

Fr. Babinger, 'Relazioni Visconteo-sforesche con la corte ottomana durante il sec. XV', *Atti del Convegno di Studi su la Lombardia e l'Oriente*, Milano, 1963.

A.Bombaci, 'Venezia e l' impresa turca di Otranto', *Rivista Storico Italiana* no. 66 (1954), pp. 159–203.

Fr. Babinger, 'Lorenzo il Magnifico e la Corte ottomana', *Archivio Storico Italiano* (1963).

Fr. Babinger, 'Maometto II il Conquistatore e l'Italia', *Riv. Stor. It.*, vol. 63 (1951).

S.Tansel, *Sultan II. Bayezit'in Siyasî Hayatî (A Political History of Bavezid II's Reign)*, Istanbul, 1964 (in Turkish).

N.Beldiceanu, 'La conquête des cités marchandes de Kilia et de Cetăteă Alba par Bayezid II', *Südost-Forschungen*, vol. XXIII, pp. 36–115.

S.N.Fisher, *The Foreign Relations of Turkey, 1481–1512*, Urbana, 1948.

R.S.Schwoebel, *The Shadow of the Crescent: The Renaissance Image of the Turk (1453–1517)*, New York, 1967.

H.Pfefferman, *Die Zusammenarbeit der Renaissancepäpste mit den Turken*, Wintertuhr, 1946.

Donado da Lezze, *Historia Turchesca (1300–1514)*, ed. I.Ursu, Bucharest, 1909. An important contemporary source.

H.S.Kissling, *Sultan Bayezid II's Beziehungen zu Markgraf Francesco von Gonzaga*, Münich, 1965.

L.Thusane, *Djem-Sultan*, Paris, 1892. Cf. H.Inalcík, 'Djem', *Encyclopaedia of Islam*, 2nd ed. vol. 2, pp. 529–32.

H.A. von Burski, *Kemâl Re'is: Ein Beitrag zur Geschichte der Türkischen Flotte*, Bonn, 1928.

F.Babinger, 'Vier Bauvorschläge Lionardo da Vinci's an Sultan Bayezid II (1502–1503)', *Nachr. der Academie der Wissensch. in Göttingen* (Phil.-his. Kl., 1958, no. 1).

Fr. Babinger, 'Kaiser Maximiliens I. "geheime Praktiken" mit den Osmanen (1510/11)', *Südost-Forschungen*, vol. xv (1956).

V.Minorsky, *La Perse au XVe siécle entre la Turquie et Venise*, Paris, 1933.

H.Sohrweide, 'Der Sieg der Safeviden in Persien und seine Rückwirkungen auf die Schiiten Anatoliens im 16. Jahrhundert', *Der Islam*, vol. 41 (1965), pp. 95–223.

E.Eberhard, *Osmanische Polemik gegen die Safeviden im 16. Jahr. nach arabischen Handschriften*, Freiburg, 1970.

S.Tansel, *Yavuz Sultan Selim*, Istanbul, 1969 (in Turkish). With the reproduction of many important documents from the Turkish archives.

H.Jansky, 'Die Eroberung Syriens durch Sultan Selim I', *Mitt. zur osmanischen Geschichte*, vol. II (1923), pp. 173–241.

H.Jansky, 'Die Chronik des Ibn Tūlūn als Geschichtsquelle über den Feldzug Sultan Selīms I. gegen die Mamluken', *Der Islam*, vol. XVIII (1929), pp. 24–33.

Ibn Iyas, *An account of the Ottoman Conquest of Egypt*, tr. W.H.Salmon, London, 1921.

Marie-Therese Speiser, *Das Selimnāme des Sa'dī b. 'Abd al-Mute'āl*, Zurich, 1946.

H.Massé, 'Selīm Ier en Syrie, d'après le Sélim-Nāme', *Mélanges René Dussaud*, vol. 2 (1939), pp. 779–82.

H.A.R.Gibb, 'Lutfi Paşa on the Ottoman Califate', *Oriens*, vol, 15 (1962), pp. 287–95.

H.A.R.Gibb, 'Some Considerations on the Sunni Theory of the Califate', *Studies on the Civilisation of Islam*, ed. S.J.Shaw and W.R.Polk, Boston, 1962, pp. 141–50.

C.A.Nallino, *Notes sur la nature du 'Califat' en général et sur la prétendu 'Califat Ottoman'*, Rome, 1919.

C.H.Becker, 'Barthold's Studien über Kalif und Sultan', *Der Islam*, vol. VI, pp. 386–412.

M.Hartmann, 'Das Privileg Selims I für die Venezianer von 1517', *Orientalist. Stud. F.Hommel*, vol II (1918), pp. 201–22.

Şinasi Altundag, 'Selîm I' *Islâm Anksilopedisi*, vol X, pp. 423–34 (in Turkish). Especially useful for the bibliography of the Ottoman sources.

H.Edhem, *Sultan Selim's aegyptischer Feldzug*, Weimar, 1916.

R.B.Merriman, *Suleiman the Magnificent*, Cambridge, Mass., 1944

L.Forrer, *Die osmanische Chronik des Rüstem Pascha*, Leipzig, 1923.

F.Tauer, *Histoire de la campagne du Sultan Suleyman Ier contre Belgrade en 1521*, Prague, 1924.

J.H.Mordtmann, *Zur Kapitulation von Buda im Jahre 1526*, Budapest-Constantinople, 1918.

M.Pavet de Courteille, *Histoire de la campagne de Mohacz par Kemal Pacha Zadeh*, Paris, 1859.

f. The Ottoman Empire as a world power (1526–96)

I.Ursu, *La politique orientale de François Ier*, Paris, 1908.

E.Oberhummer, *Konstantinopel unter Süleiman dem Grosses*, Münich, 1902.

M.Luther, *Vom Kriege wider die Türcken*, Wittenberg (?) 1529.

F.Tauer, 'Soliman's Wiener Feldzug' *Archiv Orientalni*, vol. 24 (1956).

W.Sturminger, *Bibliographie und Ikonographie der Türkenbelagerungen Wiens 1529 und 1683*, Graz-Köln, 1955.

K.Brandi, *Kaiser Karl V*, (2 vols.), Münich, 1937–41.

S.A.Fischer-Galati, *Ottoman Imperialism and German Protestantism. 1521–1555*, Cambridge, Mass., 1959.

H.Inalcík, 'The Origin of the Ottoman-Russian Rivalry and the Don-Volga Canal', Annales de L'Univ. d'Ankara, vol. 1, (1947), pp. 47–110.

S.Chew, *The Crescent and the Rose*, New York, 1937.

C.D.Rouillard, *The Turk in French History, Thought and Literature (1520–1660)*, Paris, 1941.

E.S.Forster, (tr.), *The Turkish Letters of Ogier Chiselin de Busbecq, Imperial Ambassador at Constantinople, 1554–1562* (reprint), Oxford, 1968.

Şerafettin Turan, *Rebellion of Prince Bayezid, Son of Sultan Süleyman*, Ankara, 1961 (in Turkish).

P.Argenti, *Chios Vincta*, Cambridge, 1941.

A.Vambery (tr. and ed.), *Travels and Adventures of the Turkish Admiral Sidi Ali Reis*, London, 1899.

R.B.Serjeant, *The Portuguese Off the South Arabian Coast*, Oxford, 1963.

L.Dames, 'The Portuguese and Turks in the Indian Ocean in the Sixteenth Century', *Journal of the Royal Asiatic Society*, part 1, 1921.

Hajji Khalifeh, *The History of the Maritime Wars of the Turks*, tr. James Mitchell, London, 1831.

E.Denison Ross, 'The Portuguese in India and Arabia, 1517–1538', *J.A.S.* part 1, 1922.

W.E.D.Allen, *Problems of Turkish Power in the Sixteenth Century*, London, 1963.

A.Bombaci, 'Le fonti turcho della battaglia delle Gerbe', *Rivista di Studi Orientali*, vol. 19 (1941), pp. 193–248.

A.C.Hess, 'The Evolution of the Ottoman Seaborne Empire in the Age of the Oceanic Discoveries, 1453–1525', *The American Hist. Rev.*, vol. LXXV–7 (1970), pp. 1892–1919.

g. Decline

M.Naima, *Annals of the Turkish Empire from 1591 to 1659*, tr. C.Fraser, 1, London, 1832.

L. von Ranke, *Die Osmanen und die spanische Monarchie*, Leipzig, 1877.

F.Braudel, *La Méditerranée et le monde méditerranéen à l'époque de Philippe II*, Paris, 1949 (2nd ed., 2 vols.) Paris, 1967.

U.Heyd, *Ottoman Documents on Palestine, 1552–1615*, Oxford, 1960.

Orhan Burian, *The Report of Lello, Third English Ambassador to the Sublime Porte*, Ankara, 1952.

S.Bono, *I corsari barbareschi*, Turin, 1964.

J.Pignon, 'La milice des Janissaires de Tunis au temps des Deys (1590–1650)', *Cahiers de Tunis*, vol. IV (1956).

R.C.Anderson, *Naval Wars in the Levant, 1559–1853*, Princeton, 1952.

G.Hill, *A History of Cyprus* (4 vols), Cambridge, 1940–52.

H.Inalcík, *Ottoman Policy and Administration in Cyprus after the Conquest*, Ankara, 1969.

C.Roth, *The House of Nasi: the Dukes of Naxos*, Philadelphia, 1949.

G.E.Rothenberg, *The Austrian Military Border in Croatia, 1522–1747*, Urbana, 1960.

James C.Davis, *Pursuit of Power, Venetian Ambassadors' Reports on Turkey, France and Spain, 1560–1600*, New York, 1970.

Suraiya Faroqhi, *Die Vorlagen (telhïs) des Grosswesirs Sinan paša an Sultan Murād III*, (dissertation), Hamburg, 1967.

Cengiz Orhonlu, *Telhisler, (1597–1607)*, Istanbul, 1970. The reports of the grand viziers to the sultan.

N.H.Biegman, *The Turco-Ragusan Relationship, 1575–1595*, The Hague, Paris, 1967.

A.H.Wratislaw (tr.), *Adventures of Baron Wenceslas Wratislaw of Mitrowiz, 1599*, London, 1862.

Le Strange (tr.) *Don Juan of Persia, 1560–1604*, London, 1926.

P.Paolo Carali, *Fakhr ad-dīn II, Principe del Libano e la Corte di Toscana, 1605–1635* (2 vols), Rome, 1936.

F.A.Behrnauer, 'Koğabeg's Abhandlung über den Verfall des osmanischen Staatsgebäudes seit Sultan Suleiman dem Grossen', *ZDMG*, vol. 15 (1861), pp. 272–332.

F.A.Behrnauer, 'Das Nasīhatnāme. Dritter Beitrag zur osmanischen Gesellschaft', *ZDMG*, vol. xviii (Leipzig, 1864), pp. 699–740.

Kātib Chelebi, *The Balance of Truth*, tr. G.L.Lewis, London, 1957.

R.Tschudi (ed. and tr.), *Das Asafnāme des Luftī Pascha*, Berlin, 1910.

B.Lewis 'Ottoman Observers of Ottoman Decline' in *Islamic Studies*, vol. 1 (Karachi, 1962), pp. 71–87.

H.Inalcík, *The Ottoman Decline and Its Effects Upon the Reaya*, Rapport to the Second International Congress of Studies on South-East Europe, Athens, 1970.

VII. OTTOMAN LAW AND FINANCES

P.Horster, *Zur Anwendung des islamischen Rechts im 16. Jh. Die juristischen Darlegungen (ma'ruzāt) des Schejch ül-Islam Ebu Su'ūd (ges. 1574)*, Stuttgart, 1935.

Ö.L.Barkan, *XV. ve XVI. asırlarda osmanlı imparatorluğunda ziraî ekonominin hunukî ve malî esasları* (The Juridical and Financial Laws Concerning the Rural Economy in the Ottoman Empire), Istanbul, 1943. A collection of documents; basic source for the Ottoman law and finances in the sixteenth century.

Ö.L.Barkan, 'The Ottoman Budgets', *Revue de la Faculté des Sciences Econ. de l'Univ. d'Istanbul*, vol. xvii, (1955–6), pp. 193–347.

H.Inalcík, 'Süleyman the Lawgiver and Ottoman Law', *Archivum Ottomanicum*, vol. 1.

H.Inalcík, 'Land Problems in Turkish History', *Muslim World*, vol. 45 (1955).

R.R.Arat, 'Un yarlík de Mehmed ii le Conquerant', *Annali*, nuova serie, vol. 1 (Rome, 1940), pp. 25–68.

N.Beldiceanu, *Les actes des premiers sultans*, Paris La Haye, 1960. For the review of this book, see H.Inalcik, 'Notes', *Der Islam*, Bd. 43 (1967), pp. 139–57.

R.Mantran, *Réglements fiscaux ottomans, la police des marchés de Stamboul au début du XVI siècle, in Cahiers de Tunisie*, vol. IV (1956), pp. 213–41.

R.Mantran–J.Sauvaget, *Réglements fiscaux ottomans*, Beirut, 1951.

W.Hinz, 'Das Steuerwesen Ostanatoliens im 15. und 16. Jh.', *ZDMG*, vol. XXV (1950), pp. 177–201.

A.Galanté, *Turcs et Juifs, Etude historique et politique*, Istanbul, 1932.

M.Crusius, *Turco-Graeciae*, libro octo, Basle, 1584.

F.Scheel, *Die staatrechtliche Stellung der ökumenischen Kirchenfürsten in den alten Türkei*, Berlin, 1943.

N.Zernov, *Eastern Christendom*, London, 1961.

S.Runciman, *The Great Church in Captivity*, Cambridge, 1968.

L.Hadrovics, *Le peuple serbe et son église sous la domination turque*, Paris, 1947.

G.Stadtmüller, 'Osmanische Reichsgeschichte und balkanische Volksgeschichte', *Leipziger Viertelsj. für Südost-Europa*, no. 3 (1939), pp. 1–24.

M.Mladonovic, 'Die Herrschaft der Osmanen in Serbien im lichte der Sprache', *Südost-Forschungen*, vol. XX (1961), pp. 159–203.

R.M.Dawkins, 'The Crypto-Christians of Turkey', *Byzantion*, vol. VIII (1933), pp. 247–77.

L.Fekete and Gy. Kaldy-Nagy, *Rechnungsbücher türkischer Finanzstellen in Buda (Offen), 1550–1580, türkischer text*, Budapest, 1962.

S.J.Shaw, *The Budget of Ottoman Egypt*, The Hague–Paris, 1968.

S.J.Shaw, *Organization and Development of Ottoman Egypt, 1517–1789*, Princeton N.J., 1962.

R.Anhegger, *Beiträge zur Geschichte des Bergbaus im osmanischen Reich*, (3 vols), Istanbul, 1943–5.

VIII. THE OTTOMAN PALACE AND GOVERNMENT

J. von Hammer, *Das osmanischen Reichs Staatsverfassung und Staatsverwaltung* (2 vols.), Vienna, 1815.

Mouradgea d'Ohsson, *Tableau général de l'empire ottoman* (7 vols.), Paris, 1788–1824.

P.Rycaut, *Present State of the Ottoman Empire*, London, 1670.

I.H.Uzunçarşílí *Kapíkulu Ocaklarí* (2 vols), Ankara, 1943–4 (in Turkish). The Janissary corps and other military organizations at the Porte.

I.H.Uzunçarşílí, *Osmanlí Devletinin Merkez ve Bahriye Teşkilâtí*, Ankara, 1948 (in Turkish). Central government and imperial navy in the Ottoman Empire.

I.H.Uzunçarşílí, *Osmanlí devletinin Saray teşkilâtí*, Ankara, 1945, (in Turkish). The Ottoman Palace.

I.H.Uzunçarşílí, *Ilmiye Teşkilâtí* Ankara, 1963 (in Turkish).

H.A.R.Gibb and H.Bowen, *Islamic Society and the West*, vol. I in 2 parts, London, 1950–57.

V.L.Ménage, 'Notes and Communications. Sidelights on the *Dewshirme* from Idrīs and Sa'duddīn', *BSOAS*, vol. 18 (1956), pp. 181–3.

B.D.Papoulia, *Ursprung und Wesen der 'Knabenlese' im osmanischen Reich*, Münich, 1963.

N.M.Penzer, *The Harem*, London–Bombay–Sydney, 1936.

J.A.B.Palmer, 'The Origins of the Janissaries', *Bulletin of the John Rylands Library*, vol. xxxv (1953), pp. 448–81.

U.Heyd, 'Moses Hamon, Chief Jewish Physician to Sultan Suleyman The Magnificient', *Oriens*, vol. 16 (1963), pp. 153–70.

M.Baudier, *Histoire générale du serrail et de la cour du Grand Seigneur*, Paris, 1623.

B.Miller, *The Palace School of Muhammed the Conqueror*, Cambridge, 1941.

B.Miller, *Beyond the Sublime Porte: The Grand Seraglio of Stambul*, New Haven, 1931. Based on A.Bobovio's *Relazione*.

W.L.Wright, *Ottoman Statecraft: The Book of Counsel for Viziers and Governors of Sari Mehmed Pasha*, Princeton, 1935.

Also see part v: Descriptions of Western Travellers and Observers.

IX. POPULATION, CITIES AND ROUTES

Ömer L.Barkan, 'Les déportations comme méthode de peuplement et de colonisation dans l'empire ottoman', *Revue de la Faculté des Sciences Economiques de l'Université d'Istanbul*, vol, xi (1946–50), pp. 524–569, vol. xɪɪɪ, pp. 56–79, vol. xv, pp. 209–329.

Ömer L.Barkan. 'Essai sur les données statistiques des registres de recensement dans l'empire ottoman au XVᵉ et XVIᵉ siècles', *Journal of Eco. and Soc. History of the Orient*, vol. 1 (1957).

Ömer L.Barkan 'Les formes de l'organisation du travail agricole dans l'empire Ottoman aux XVᵉ siècles', *Revue de la Faculté des Sciences Economiques de l'Univ. d' Istanbul*, vol. I–II (1939) pp. 29–74. Résumé, in French 14–44, vol. II (1940), pp. 198–245, Résumé in French, pp. 165–180.

Ömer L.Barkan, 'Quelques observations sur l'organization économique et sociale des villes ottomanes, des XVIᵉ et XVIIᵉ siècles', *Recueil Société Jean Bodin*, vol. VII (1955), pp. 289–311.

N.Todorov, 'La situation démographique de la péninsule balkanique au cours des XVᵉ et XVIᵉ siècles', *Annuaire de L'Univ. de Sofia*, vol. LIII-2, 1959.

Franz Taeschner, *Das anatolische wegenetz nach osmanischen Quellen* (2 vols), Leipzig, 1924–6.

N.Todorov (ed), *La ville balkanique, XVᵉ–XIXᵉ Siècles*, Académie bulgare des sciences, Sofia, 1970.

G.Baer, *The Administrative, Economic and Social Functions of Turkish Guilds*, in *International Journal of Middle East Studies*, vol. 1 (1970), pp. 28–50.

M.Alexandrescu-Dersca, 'Contribution à l'étude de l'approvisionnement en blé de Constantinople au XVIIIᵉ siècle', *Studia et Acta Orientalia*, vol. 1, 1957, pp. 13–37.

W.Behrnauer, 'Mémoire sur les institutions de police chez les Arabes, les Persans et les Turcs', *Journal Asiatique*, Vᵉ serie, t. XV (1861), pp. 347–92.

F.Taeschner, *Alt-Stambuler Hof und Volksleben*, Hanover, 1925.

A.Refik, *Istanbul Hayati* (2 vols.), Istanbul, 1930–31 (in Turkish). *Documents on the Economic and Social History of Istanbul in the Sixteenth and Seventeenth Centuries*.

Evliyā Chelebi, *Travels*, (10 vols.), editors N.Asím, Kilisli Rifat and H.N. Orkun, Istanbul, 1896–1938 (in Turkish). A mine of information on the social history of the Ottoman Empire in the seventeenth century. In-complete English translation: *Narrative of Travels in Europe, Asia and Africa*, (2 vols), trans. J. von Hammer, London, 1834.

A.A.Pallis, *In the Days of the Janissaries*, London, 1951. Selections from Evliyā Chelebi.

B.Lewis, *Istanbul and the Civilisation of the Ottoman Empire*, Oklahoma, 1963.

R.Mantran, *Istanbul dans la seconde moitié du XVIIᵉ siècle*, Paris, 1962.

M.Hadzijahić, 'Die privilegierten Städte zur zeit des osmanischen Feuda-lismus', *Südost–Forschungen*, vol. XX (1961), pp. 130–58.

X. COMMERCE

W.Heyd, *Histoire du Commerce du Levant* (2 vols.), Leipzig, 1936.

H.Inalcík, 'Harīr', *Encyclopaedia of Islam*, second ed., vol. III.

H.Inalcík, 'Bursa and the Commerce of the Levant', *Journal of Econ. and Social Hist. of the Orient*, vol. III/2 (1960), pp. 131–47.

G.R.B.Richards, *Florentine Merchants in the Age of Medicis*, Cambridge, Mass., 1932.

A.C.Wood, History of the Levant Company, London, 1935.

P.Masson, *Histoire du commerce français dans le Levant au XVIIᵉ siècle*, Paris, 1896.

U.Dorini-T.Bertele, *Il libro dei conti di Giacomo Badoer, Constantinopoli, 1436–1440*, Rome, 1956.

F.Thiriet, 'Les lettres commerciales des Bembo et le commerce vénitien dans l'empire ottoman à la fin du XVᵉ siècle' *Studi in onore di Armando Sapori*, Milan, 1957, pp. 911–33.

H.Inalcík, 'Capital Formation in the Ottoman Empire', *The Journal of Economic History*, vol. XXIX (1969), pp. 97–140.

J.Tadić, 'Le commerce en Dalmatie et à Raguse et la décadence économique de Venise au XVIIᵉ siècle' *Civiltá Veneziana studi 9*, Venezia-Roma pp. 237–74.

H.Inalcík, 'Imtiyāzāt: Ottoman', *Encyclopaedia of Islam*, 2nd ed., vol. IV. A study of the capitulations.

M.Berza, 'La colonia fiorentina di Constantinopoli nei secoli XV.-XVI.', *Revue hist. du Sud-Est Européen*, vol. XXI (1944), pp. 137–54.

XI. CULTURE

A.Bombaci, *Storia della letteratura turca dall'antico imperio di Mongolia all'odierna Turchia*, Milan, 1956.

A.A.Adívar, *Osmanlí Türklerinde Ilim*, Istanbul, 1943 (in Turkish), first appeared in French.

E.J.W.Gibb, *History of Ottoman Poetry* (6 vols), London, 1900–9.

R.Ettinghausen (preface), M.S.Ipşiroğlu and S.Eyüboğlu (intro.), *Turkey, Ancient Miniatures*, UNESCO World Series, Paris, 1961.

E.Esin, *Turkish Miniature Painting*, Vermont–Tokyo, 1960.

G.M.Meredith-Owens, *Turkish Miniatures*, The British Museum, London, 1963.

I.Stchoukine, *La peinture turque d'après les manuscrits illustrés, Iᵉʳᵉ partie de Süleyman I à Osmān II, 1520–1622*, Paris, 1966.

F.Öğütmen, *Miniature Art from the XIIth to the XVIIth Century*, Istanbul, 1966.

C.E.Arseven, *L'art turc depuis son origine jusqu'à nos jours*, Istanbul, 1939.

K.Erdmann, *Orientteppiche aus vier Jahrhunderten*, Hamburg, 1950.

K.Erdmann, *Das anatolische Karavansaray* (2 vols.), Berlin, 1961.

M.K.Özergin, 'Anadolu'da Selçuk Kervanseraylarí', *Tarih Dergisi*, no. 20, pp. 141–70.

A.Gabriel, 'Les mosquées de Constantinople', *Syria*, vol. VII (1926), pp. 359–419.

A.Gabriel, *Une capitale turque: Brousse* (2 vols.), Paris, 1958.

C.Gurlitt, *Die Baukunst Konstantinopels*, Berlin, 1912.

J.Karabacek, *Abendlaendische Künstler zur Konstantinopel im 15. und 16. Jhdt.*, Vienna, 1917.

Tahsin Öz, *Turkish Textiles and Velvets*, Ankara, 1950.

E.Diez and O.Aslanapa, *Turkish Art*, Istanbul, 1955 (in Turkish).

E.Diez, 'The Architect Sinan and his Works', *Atlantis*, April 1953.

R.M.Meriç, *Sinan, the Architect, His Life and Art*, vol. I, *Texts concerning his life and works*, Ankara, 1965 (in Turkish).

H.Glück, *Die Kunst der Osmanen*, Leipzig, 1922.

K.Erdmann, *Zur türkischen Baukunst seldschukischer und osmanischer Zeit*, Istanbul, 1958.

E.Akurgal, C.Mango and R.Ettinghausen, *Treasures of Turkey*, SKIRA, 1966.

U.Vogt-Göknil, *Les mosquées turques*, Zurich, 1953.

U.Vogt-Göknil, *Living Architecture: Ottoman*, Oldbourne London, 1966.

Aptullah Kuran, *The Mosque in Early Ottoman Architecture*, Chicago, London, n.d.

H.Glück, *Die Bäder Constantinopels*, Vienna, 1921.

C.Gurlitt, 'Die Bauten Adrianopels', *Orientalische Archiv.* (Leipzig), vol. I (1910–11).

A.Gabriel, *Châteaux turcs du Bosphore*, Paris, 1943.

A.Gabriel, *Monuments turcs d'Anatolie* (2 vols.), Paris, 1931–45.

K.Otto-Dorn, *Das islamische Iznik*, Berlin, 1941.

E.Egli, *Sinan, der Baumeister osmanischer Glanzzeit*, Zurich, 1954.

Metin And, *A History of Theatre and Popular Entertainment in Turkey*, Ankara, 1963–4.

Metin And, *Dances of Anatolian Turkey*, New York, 1959.

H.Ritter, *Karagöz, türkische Schattenspiele* (3 vols): I, Hanover 1924, II, Istanbul, 1941, III, Wiesbaden, 1953.

Semavi Eyice, 'Sultaniye – Karapínar'a Dair', *Tarih Dergisi*, no. 20 (1965), pp. 117–40 (in Turkish). A study of a complex of buildings on the caravan route Konya-Eregli by Sinan.

N.Göyünç, 'Eski Malatya'da Silâhdar Mustafa Paşa Hani', *Tarih Enstitüsü Dergisi*, Faculty of Letters, Univ. of Istanbul, vol. I (1970), pp. 63–92. A study of the caravanseray of Mustafa Pasha (1637).

Taşköprîzâde, *Eš-Šaqāiq en-no'manijje, enthaltend die Biographen der türkischen und im osmanischen Reiche wirkenen Gelehrten, Derwisch-Scheikh's und Ärtzte ...* tr. O.Rescher, Constantinople–Galata, 1927.

J.K.Birge, *The Bektashi Order of Dervishes*, London, 1937.

SELECTED BIBLIOGRAPHY

I.Beldiceanu-Steinherr, *Scheich Üftāde, der Begründer des Gelvetijje Ordens*, Munich, 1961.

H.J.Kissling, 'Aus der Geschichte des Chalwetijje-Ordens', *ZDMG*, vol. 103-2 (1953), pp. 233-89.

H.J.Kissling, 'The Role of the Dervish Orders in the Ottoman Empire', *Studies in Islamic Cultural History*, ed. G.E. von Grunebaum, *American Anthropologist*, Memoire no. 76 (1954).

F.W.Hasluck, *Christianity and Islam under the Sultans* (2 vols), Oxford, 1929.

P.Kahle, *Pīrī Re'ī's Bahrīye, Das türkische Segelhandbuch für das Mittelländische Meer vom Jahre 1521*, Berlin–Leipzig, 1926.

Piri Reîs, *Kitāb-i Bahrīye*, Istanbul, 1935.

INDEX

253